Lingnan Food Culture

By Zhou Songfang

Translated by Deng Chengdan

CHICAGO ACADEMIC PRESS

Lingnan Food Culture
By Zhou Songfang
Translated by Deng Chengdan
Language: English
Word Count (for space of all pages): 216 Thousand words
Publisher: Chicago Academic Press
Number of Pages: 310
ISBN: 979-8-901-86014-4

Publishing	Chicago Academic Press
	5923 N Artesian Ave
	Chicago IL 60659
Email	contact@chicagoacademicpress.com
Website	http://chicagoacademicpress.com/
Book Size	6X9 inches
First Edition	December, 2025

Translator Profile

Dr. Deng Chengdan, based in Maoming, Guangdong Province, China, is a dedicated lecturer in the School of Foreign Languages at Guangdong University of Petrochemical Technology. In her teaching role, Dr. Deng primarily delivers courses such as College English Reading and Writing, College English Listening and Speaking, and Business English. Her innovative pedagogical approaches emphasize practical language skills, cultural integration, and real-world application, fostering students' communicative competence in diverse contexts. Her research interests span cultural translation, pedagogical studies, and cultural tourism studies, reflecting a passion for bridging linguistic and cultural divides. To date, she has published over 10 academic papers in reputable journals, contributing valuable insights to language education and cross-cultural studies.

Preface

Looking around the world, the food and its culture in various regions are all based on local ingredients, but they can keep pace with the times, be inclusive, and develop iteratively. The outstanding ones can thus become a major cuisine of a country, and the place can then be among the world's famous food capitals. Cantonese cuisine is just like this. The early Lingnan region was "vast and sparsely populated, with rice as its staple food and fish as its primary dish, using primitive farming methods such as fire cultivation (slash-and-burn agriculture) and water-weeding; there were various vegetable food and animal food, such as fruits and clams, which were sufficient without being sold; the terrain was rich in food, and there was no worry of famine." Although food was easy to obtain in ancient Lingnan, due to the low and humid terrain, food was not easy to preserve. After obtaining ingredients of food, people were accustomed to eating them on the spot and in a timely manner, thus leaving behind the food gene of seeking freshness and not avoiding raw and fishy foods. However, if we draw on the "stimulus-response theory" in world history, the development of food and its culture around the world depends not only on the development and progress of the economic society, including food cultivation, animal husbandry, and cooking utensils, but also on the stimulation of external ingredients of food, cooking utensils, and cooking methods. The unearthed relics of the Nanyue King's Tomb in Guangzhou displayed the style of the Nanyue King's banquet, which not only shows the characteristics of the ancient Lingnan people using local ingredients in their diet, but also reflects that, during the Qin and Han dynasties, Lingnan cooking utensils were obviously influenced by the Central Plains of China and overseas regions.

On the eve of Cantonese cuisine becoming famous across the country, Qu Dajun in the early Qing Dynasty said that the beauty of Lingnan food was due to "almost all the food products in the world being available in Guangdong." However, during the Xianfeng and Tongzhi periods, the food industry in Guangzhou was still controlled by the Suzhou Restaurant Association. In the late Qing Dynasty and the early Republic of China, the eight major "Dayao restaurants" mainly served official and political figures and provided on-site banquet services. Juxin, Guanzhen, Pin Rongsheng, Nanyang Tang, Yulaochun, Yuansheng, Bazhen, and Xinrui, were all organized by the Suzhou Restaurant Association. Mr. Feng Han, an old timer, further stated that during the heyday of Cantonese cuisine in the 1920s and 1930s, there were still more than 100 "Dayao restaurants" in the whole city, which shows the influence and lingering charm of the Suzhou Restaurant Association and fully reflects the role and significance of foreign food culture in the formation of Cantonese cuisine.

In fact, the era when Guangzhou became the ideal place for gourmets, which is called "Eating in Guangzhou", was not as early as we usually think, and the place where it became popular was not in Guangzhou, but in Shanghai. Modern Shanghai was a real big market and the grand stage for major cuisines to compete. During the competition, the status of "Eating in

Guangzhou" was established due to the reason that Cantonese cuisine could be inclusive, strive to innovate, and finally succeed with the help of the advocacy of the media center. In fact, the features of almost all the "Eight Major Cuisines in China" were formed after they spread outside of their hometowns, developing integratively across different regions and markets, adapting to the tastes of the public, thus being recognized as a famous cuisine nationwide. Furthermore, Cantonese cuisine took the lead in going abroad, conquering the appetite of Westerners, and representing Chinese food to win a great reputation, which also helped Guangzhou become "the ideal place for gourmets." At the same time, the reputation of "Eating in Guangzhou" could largely be attributed to the introduction of Western food and Western-style business. Many owners and managers of famous Cantonese restaurants being overseas returnees from Guangdong, Western food (foreign food) always took the front-line role when Cantonese cuisine went out of Guangdong, whether in Beijing or Shanghai.

So, while sorting out the development process and characteristics of Cantonese cuisine, this book also discusses the situation and influence of Cantonese cuisine going out of Guangdong and abroad, and writes about the development process and influence of other cuisine restaurants in Guangdong. In addition, the appendix of this book includes two articles that I co-authored with Professor Qi Wene of South China Agricultural University: *Weng Tonghe's Lingnan Food Serendipity and Tan Yankai's Love for Guangdong Lychees* and *Carrying Lychee Wine across the South of the Yangtze River*, which supplement and explain the influence of Lingnan food and its cultural transmission from two special perspectives. Weng Tonghe was a "student of the Son of Heaven" (the top scholar in the Xianfeng period) and a "teacher of the Son of Heaven" (the teacher of the Tongzhi and Guangxu emperors). He successively held the positions of Minister of the Ministry of Punishment, Minister of the Ministry of Works, Minister of the Ministry of Revenue, Minister of the General Administration of Foreign Affairs, Minister of the Military Affairs Office, etc. He interacted with Beijing officials born in Guangdong, such as Li Wenti, Xu Yingjun, Zhang Yinhuan, Ding Richang, etc. They appreciated and admired each other and had extremely frequent food banquets and outings. Cantonese cuisine, especially fresh sashimi, left a deep impression on Weng Tonghe and won his extreme praise. He even invited the chefs of Li Wenti and Zhang Yinhuan to help host his family banquets from time to time. It can be seen that the status of "Eating in Guangzhou" was already well established among official chefs. As the founder of Hunan cuisine and a generation of "Gourmet God", Tan Yankai had a deep origin with Guangdong. This book only gives a brief glimpse of such a connection by selecting his serendipity with lychees, the most representative Guangdong-produced fruit. As for the article *Carrying Lychee Wine across the South of the Yangtze River*, it writes about the glorious history of wine, which is an important aspect of Lingnan food, by introducing the lychee wine that was popular in the South of the Yangtze River during the Ming and Qing dynasties, thereby enhancing the interest and readability of this book.

Contents

Chapter 1 Rice and Fish: The Early Development of Lingnan Cuisine

Sima Qian said in *Records of the Grand Historian • Biographies of Merchants and Producers*, "The land of Chu and Yue was vast and sparsely populated, with rice as its staple food and fish as its primary dish, using primitive farming methods such as slash-and-burn farming and water-weeding; there were various vegetable food and animal food, such as fruits and clams, which were sufficient without being sold; the terrain was rich in food, and there was no worry about famine. Therefore, people lived a lazy and carefree life, with no accumulation and mostly poor, which was the major reason why no people were suffering from cold and hunger, nor were there any wealthy families in the south of the Yangtze River and Huaihe River." This can be said to be one of the earliest documents on Lingnan cuisine. Although being merely included in the document, Lingnan has become an important inheritance of the Lingnan food gene with the development of the economic society. Moreover, the food characteristics of Lingnan have been highlighted more because of the degradation of the natural conditions described in this history book in the mainland. For this reason, we must first make a correct interpretation of a piece of historical data.

According to *Annotations to the Records of the Grand Historian* of Zhang Shoujie in the Tang Dynasty, the ancient land of Chu and Yue, which is now the vast area south of the Yangtze River and Huaihe River, was vast and sparsely populated. People lived on rice as the staple food and fish as the main dish. Whether it was fire cultivation or water weeding (to eliminate weeds and shrubs through burning or soaking) for planting rice, it only required simple labor. There were enough snails, fish, and turtles, which can be collected, wrapped, and cooked at will without buying from others. The advantage of the land made it easy for people to obtain abundant food, leaving no worry about famine. Therefore, people lived a carefree life, with little surplus at home, and mostly showing poverty. Also for this reason, no people suffered from cold and hunger, nor were there any wealthy families in the south of the Yangtze River and Huaihe River. Moreover, when the mainland gradually withdrew from this living state with the development of the economic society and population growth, the Lingnan area could still continue such living state for a relatively long period. Therefore, this food gene is more clearly reflected in the later Lingnan cuisine.

Well, since it was possible to easily obtain food locally, there was no shortage of coarse food, though poor, and also no pursuit of fine food for not being rich, thus being short of cooking methods. From the historical development of cooking, we know that the attention to cooking methods was roughly based on two major reasons: on the one hand, because of the scarcity of food and the shortage in seasons, it was necessary to store food for famine, and various food processing methods such as pickling, drying in the sun, and drying with fire appeared to facilitate storage; on the other hand, wealthy families were never tired of fine food and fine dishes. They spent thousands of gold on food every day but found it tasteless to eat, thus trying to find the solution by using different types of cooking methods. In the long history of China, the peaceful and prosperous times were very short, and wars and famines continued on and off. The flavor foods of the poor in various places were passed down from generation to generation, while the foods of the rich were mostly recorded in documents, and it was difficult to have stable inheritance. Therefore, from the unearthed cultural relics of the Nanyue King, we can not only find out some regional cooking characteristics of obtaining ingredients locally, but also find the huge difference between court food and folk food, obtaining ingredients locally being the only thing that can be inherited together.

1.1 The Terrain and Products of Lingnan

Due to the barrier of towering mountains, backward transportation conditions, and the fear of "miasma" formed by the hot and humid climate, early Lingnan was like an isolated land beyond the mountains, giving people a sense of being in a foreign land. However, as Professor Zeng Zhaoxuan, who has long been engaged in historical geography research, especially Lingnan historical geography, said, "Different geographical environments breed different cultures." Mr. Su Bingqi, a famous contemporary Chinese archaeologist, praised this place as the "true South" and a "key" to exploring the relationship between ancient China and the Indochinese Peninsula, even the South Pacific region. The arguments of these experts are based on archaeological excavations, and new discoveries continue to confirm previous theories. Since the founding of the People's Republic of China, 81 Paleolithic sites of ancient humans have been discovered in South China, most of which are found in the Pearl River Basin. In Guangdong, there are mainly Dongzhong Rock in Fengkai, Shizi Rock in Maba, Qujiang, Fanzeng Mountain in Luoding, Dushizai in Yangchun, etc. These ancient human sites have left the footprints of the ancestors in Lingnan. Among them, the Maba Man discovered in 1958, estimated to be 129,000 years old, and the Dongzhong Rock Man in Fengkai discovered in 1978, estimated to be 148,000 years old, are among the earliest ancestors of humans in Lingnan. The relationship between time and space also further confirms the view of the famous paleoanthropologist Academician Jia Lanpo that "the Guangdong-Guangxi region is the only way for ancient humans to move eastward."

The unearthed pottery jars and pots in the Guangzhou area

In the early days, Lingnan had its own independent system in culture, and the same was true in diet. The unearthed cultural relics from the Neolithic Age have demonstrated the unique pursuit of Lingnan food culture. For example, the food utensils unearthed from the Shixia Culture Site in Qujiang, which dates back to 3,500-5,500 years, vividly reflect the early food style of the Lingnan mountainous area. Cooking utensils mainly include sand-tempered pottery cauldrons, steamers, plate-shaped tripods, basin-shaped tripods, cauldron-shaped tripods, small-mouthed cauldrons, etc. Tableware includes three-legged plates, ring-footed plates, Tao Dou (a shallow pottery dish with a raised foot, mainly used for serving side dishes), bowls, ring-footed pots, cups, jars, urns, etc. The common use of sand-tempered pottery cauldrons can be regarded as the origin of the cookware for Cantonese Clay Pot Rice (a Cantonese dish where rice and ingredients are cooked together in a small clay pot, creating a crispy bottom) that is still popular today. The use of steamers indicates that people at that time knew how to use steam to cook food. Flat-bottomed plate-shaped tripods were used for frying, basin-shaped tripods for boiling, and cauldron-shaped tripods for Peng (a cooking technique where heat-treated ingredients are doused with hot sauce; high heat then vaporizes much of the sauce, driving it into the ingredients and rapidly drying them). It can be seen that cooking techniques such as braising, frying, and boiling were all been available in that distant era, which can be called the historical gene of "Eating in Guangzhou". Different from the emphasis on sacrificial rituals in the Central Plains and the North, most of the bronze ritual vessels unearthed from large tombs in Lingnan during the Bronze Age are tripods for holding meat and food, as well as water basins and other utensils, and their shapes and functions are very similar to the local pottery. This can be regarded as the inheritance and development of the Lingnan food culture gene of "food comes first" in the Stone Age.

The production tools such as axes, adzes, chisels, arrowheads, and shovels unearthed from the Shixia Culture Site, especially the stone hoe, which is long-bodied and bow-backed with a wide and a narrow edge at both ends, up to 31 centimeters long, are sharp tools suitable for deep plowing in southern red soil. Artificially cultivated rice varieties were also unearthed, marking that the Lingnan food culture had stepped onto a new stage. The most important cornerstone of Chinese food culture lies in the emergence and development of agricultural civilization. However, as stated in *Records of the Grand Historian*: *Biographies of Merchants and Producers*, good natural conditions, in a sense, restricted the development of agriculture and the progress of food culture. Therefore, although unearthed cultural relics prove that Lingnan people cultivated rice very early, the legend of the Five Goats that is said to have occurred during the Zhou Yiwang period seems to indicate that the Lingnan rice civilization or high-yield rice civilization was still relatively backward. The legend goes that five immortals, wearing colorful clothes, riding five-colored goats, and holding excellent grain seeds with one stem and six ears, arrived at "Chuting" (the earliest name for Guangzhou), gave the ears of grain to the local people, and blessed the city with no more famine. After saying that, the five immortals went into the sky, and the five goats turned into stones. In memory of the five immortals who spread excellent grain seeds, the local people built a Five Immortals Temple, which is said to be the location of "Chuting". Thus, Guangzhou is also known as

"City of Goats" or "City of Sui", where "Sui" signifies grain ears."

In summary, in the early days, the ancient people of Lingnan not only had the conditions for an exquisite diet and successful attempts, but also had the conditions for not needing to be exquisite, that is, food was easy to obtain. Therefore, the real new chapter of Lingnan food culture started from the metropolitan era and the royal court era. From the perspective of cultural inheritance, what can really be inherited is basically the food regulations of the upper class and the food customs of the city. Only these can be written in books and records, and used by later generations, thus becoming the origin of food culture.

The Five Goats Statue on Yuexiu Mountain

1.2 Openness and Inclusiveness: Royal Court Style and Folk Inheritance

The Qin's conquest of Nanyue and establishment of prefectures not only brought Lingnan into the era of written records but also gradually ushered it into the metropolitan age. Lingnan food culture began to be documented in historical records, and Lingnan food civilization opened a new chapter in history.

In 122 BC, Zhao Mo (also known as Zhao Hu), the second king of the Nanyue Kingdom, was buried in Xianggang, Panyu (now Guangzhou) after his death. This is the Western Han Nanyue King's Tomb excavated in 1983. Among the various unearthed cultural relics, there are more than 1,500 food utensils and a large amount of buried food. Among them, there are more than 200 bones of reed buntings. The broken condition of the bones shows that the reed buntings were plucked, decapitated, and clawed when buried, exactly the same as the processing methods of Cantonese chefs today, reflecting the long history of Lingnan cuisine. A copper roasting stove was also unearthed from the tomb, leading people to imagine that the chefs of the Nanyue royal court might have used this stove to roast food for the Nanyue King.

Blood clams are one of the most abundant marine products with Lingnan characteristics unearthed from the Nanyue King's Tomb, produced in the sand or crevices of rocks under the sea. More than 2,000 blood clams were unearthed from the tomb, the largest number among all kinds of unearthed food, reflecting Zhao Mo's preference for blood clams during his lifetime. According to statistics, these blood clams are mainly found in the unearthed bronze tripods, mou (cooking vessels), cylindrical containers, pots, and jian (similar to later refrigerators).

The unearthed copper roasting stove from the Nanyue King's Tomb

Tripods and mou are cooking utensils using water as a heat transfer medium, cylindrical containers and pots are wine vessels, and jian is similar to a refrigerator. Therefore, it is inferred that the chefs of the Nanyue royal court mainly used tripods and mou to prepare blood clams as food and wine for Zhao Mo. Blood clams have tender and fat meat, which can be eaten after slightly heating, suitable for making soup and hot pot. In addition to blood clams, the unearthed bronze tripods often contain pig bones, fish bones, etc., indicating that the tripod was used to make soup dishes like blanched blood clams, and the mixed pig bones were likely used for making soup.

More than 1,500 goose barnacles (named "turtle feet" in Chinese) were unearthed from the Nanyue King's Tomb, second only to blood clams in the number of buried food, reflecting Zhao Mo's preference for these two seafoods during his lifetime. The goose barnacles unearthed from the tomb are not the feet of turtles but a marine hermaphroditic stalked cirripede, scientifically named Pollicipes, commonly known as "turtle feet" in Chinese because they resemble turtle feet. After shelling and cleaning, goose barnacles have fresh and tender meat, so they can be eaten after being slightly boiled in boiling water. From the shape of the bronze mou, it is an ideal cooking utensil for blanching and hot pot, which explains why the unearthed goose barnacles are mainly distributed in the bronze mou.

The grand scene of the upper-class society in Lingnan (mainly the royal food culture) seen from the unearthed cultural relics of the Nanyue King's Tomb is inseparable from the influence of the administrative center, especially the political establishment, and correspondingly, from the economic aggregation and foreign trade expansion formed thereby. Therefore, Sima Qian wrote in *Records of the Grand Historian: Biographies of Merchants and Producers* that among the nine major metropolises in the country, "Panyu is also one of the metropolises, a gathering place for pearls, rhinoceros horns, tortoiseshells, fruits, and fabrics." At that time, Panyu, later Guangzhou, was unique as a metropolis mainly engaged in the distribution of overseas treasures. Later, *the Book of Han* also inherited this statement and stated its influence on the interior, "Located near the sea, rich in rhinoceros, elephants, tortoiseshells, pearls, silver, copper, fruits, and fabrics, many merchants from the Central Plains went there to get rich. Panyu is one of the metropolises." This is the Han Dynasty version of the saying "North, south, east, west; Guangdong gathers wealth best", which was popular in the 1980s.

Economic prosperity brought about the rise of food culture, and food customs were passed down from the royal court to the folk, thus being frequently recorded in folk books. The earliest is *Strange Things of the Southern Border* by Yang Fu, a senior councilor in the Eastern Han Dynasty (some abbreviated as *Strange Things*). In the East Jin and West Jin Dynasties, there were more, such as *Records of Jiaozhou* by Liu Xinqi, *Records of Southern Plants* by Ji Han, and *Records of Guangzhou* by Pei Yuan, etc. The most recorded are Lingnan fruits and vegetables. For example, Ji Han's *Records of Southern Plants* says that Alpinia oxyphylla was once a precious tribute, "Alpinia oxyphylla is like a writing brush, seven to eight fen long. It flowers in February, with lotus-like color, and bears fruit, which ripens in May and June. It is pungent, fragrant when mixed with five flavors, and can also be salted and sun-dried. It is produced in Jiaozhi and Hepu. In the eighth year of Jian'an, Zhang Jin, the governor of Jiaozhou, once presented Alpinia oxyphylla rice dumplings to Emperor Wu of Wei." The record of Averrhoa carambola is also very interesting: "Averrhoa carambola is as big as a papaya, yellow, with crisp and soft flesh, extremely sour. It has five ridges, as if carved out. Southerners call a ridge 'lian', hence the name. When soaked in honey, it is sweet and sour and delicious. It is produced in the South Sea." Averrhoa carambola is the star fruit, also the "Sanlian" in Yang Fu's *Strange Things* of the Eastern Han Dynasty. Star fruit is often called "yangtao" (foreign peach), giving people a sense of being imported. In fact, like lemon, which also gives people a sense of being imported, both are native to Lingnan.

Starfruit

At that time, some vegetables that were very cheap in Lingnan were regarded as table treasures in the interior. For example, the "water spinach" recorded in Ji Han's *Records of Southern Plants* was then called "a strange vegetable of the South," and it was said that Cao Cao "could eat a lot of wild arrowroot after eating this vegetable first."

1.3 Pursuit of Freshness and Live Seafood

Guangdong is located at the southernmost tip of the Chinese mainland, with mountains on one side and the sea on the other. The Nanling Mountains serve as a natural climatic barrier, and the Tropic of Cancer passes through Conghua in the north of Guangzhou. The climate is hot and humid, with rivers crossing the territory. The Pearl River system is the second largest and third longest water system in the country. In addition, it has a mainland coastline of more than 4,000 kilometers, the longest in the country. It produces extremely rich land animals, fish, and shellfish in rivers, lakes, and seas, as well as fruits, vegetables, and other plants, many of which are not found in the interior and are treasured by the world. Like a gratitude for the gifts of nature, Lingnan cuisine has been characterized by a preference for natural food and a tolerance for raw and fishy flavors since the beginning, and this has continued to the present day. In early documents, there is no better description of raw and fishy food, especially live seafood, than Han Yu's *First Taste of Southern Cuisine: Presented to Yuan Shiba, Assistant Law Officer*:

> Like horseshoe crabs, their shells a polished sheen,
>
> Their bony eyes in tandem march, unseen.
>
> Oysters cling, a mountain to behold,
>
> A hundred buds, in clustered stories told.
>
> The reedy fish, with serpentine tail so long,
>
> Its mouth and eyes ignore where they belong.
>
> The clam, a toad, in form it may appear,
>
> Same substance held, though names are varied here.
>
> The clam-shrimp struts, with armored, plated might,

Displaying strangeness, wondrous to the sight.
And dozens more, of kinds I cannot name,
All cause for awe, a captivating game.
I come to feast, to banish spectral fright,
And savor tastes of southern, pure delight.
With salt and sour, the flavors I shall blend,
And spice with pepper, orange, to transcend.
The pungent scent, the essence starts to rise,
I chew and swallow, sweat upon my eyes.
Yet of the snake, though known to me of old,
Its gaping jaws, a terror to behold.
I let it go, from the cage it takes its flight,
Though coiled and vexed, it harbors inward spite.
To sell you forth, is not my guilty deed,
To spare your life, a compassionate creed.
I seek no boon, no magic pearl's reward,
But hope no grudges shall my heart afford.

So let me sing, this feast to bear in mind,

And share this tale, with those of kindred kind.

Although this poem is often claimed by Chaoshan food culture, it actually has little to do with Chaozhou. It was written by Han Yu on his way to being demoted to Chaozhou and has nothing to do with Chaoshan cuisine. It should be a record and feeling of Han Yu's first taste of seafood, frogs, snakes, and other Lingnan foods after entering the Pearl River Delta and before arriving in Guangzhou. Mr. Qian Zhonglian, a master of Chinese studies, said, "The Wei edition quotes Fan Rulin as saying, 'It was written after arriving in Chaozhou in the fourteenth year of Yuanhe.' Supplementary explanation: In the previous Poem of *Farewell to Yuan Shiba*, following its narrative, it was probably a farewell on the way, so this poem should not have been written after arriving in Chaozhou." Yuan Shiba, named Jixu, styled Keji, a former Assistant Law Officer, was then in the service of Pei Xingli, the Observing Envoy of Guiguan. According to *Six Poems of Farewell to Yuan Shiba, Assistant Law Officer* and Qian Zhonglian's explanation, Yuan Shiba was ordered by his master Pei Xingli to welcome Han Yu on his demoted journey, presenting books and medicine. When passing through Longcheng (Liuzhou), he also brought the concern and greetings of Liu Zongyuan, who wrote *Preface to Sending Yuan Shiba, a Reclusive Scholar on his Southern Journey*. From the sixth poem, it can be seen that they left Qingyuan's Beixia Mountain together, then bid farewell to the mountain journey, entered the Pearl River Delta, and went southeast to Chaozhou via Guangzhou, arriving at Fuxu, southeast of Guangzhou, the area around Nanhai Temple of today. They traveled together and finally parted here. It can be seen that the "First Taste of Southern Cuisine" must not have been after "farewell", but after leaving Xiashan.

Roasted oyster

In any case, it has nothing to do with Chaozhou cuisine. However, although Han Yu's "First Taste of Southern Cuisine" should no longer be claimed by Chaoshan people, it is worthy of being repeatedly claimed by Cantonese people. Before this, no poem had described Guangdong seafood as vividly and wildly as Han Yu did.

China's coastline stretches for thousands of miles from north to south, but no region is as oceanic as Lingnan, and no region's food culture has such distinct oceanic characteristics. When it comes to seafood, no one fails to think of Lingnan; almost everyone who comes to Lingnan does so for its seafood, despite the countless delicacies in Lingnan.

Lingnan seafood is famous in the world first due to its natural quality, which is determined by the natural environment. The South China Sea is much cleaner and deeper than other seas around China. Lingnan seafood is pure and of superior quality. For one thing, it is less affected by river sediments; for another, it has a vast ocean landscape. Therefore, it is said that, "The sea becomes different in the south, with particularly large and numerous strange fish, not only absent in the central plains but also unseen in the East Sea and North Sea." In fact, Cantonese people also use the word "seafood" in a general sense, including river fresh. This is reasonable. The Pearl River's water is remarkably clean and abundant in China, which is why its river fresh is comparable to seafood. Furthermore, Lingnan has a unique feature of coexisting river and sea seafood. Zhang Qu, a Qing Dynasty scholar, mentioned in *Records of What I Saw and Heard in Guangdong*, "As the saying goes: 'Fish produced in saltwater do not enter rivers, and those produced in freshwater do not enter the sea.' Only Guangdong fish are not entirely like this." The most prominent example is the pufferfish at the mouth of the Pearl River, which tastes much better than the pure freshwater pufferfish in the Jiangnan region. These natural qualities make Lingnan people extremely fond of seafood, so much so that, being close to the source, it is also expensive. There are many records in documents about the high price of Lingnan seafood, and folk songs also sing, “If you want to eat seafood, don’t spare your money.” People in western Lingnan even regard seafood as vegetarian food to break the taboo of not eating meat during funerals.

Bai’e Tan in Guangzhou

Although this is the case, it later became increasingly difficult for Guangzhou people to eat seafood. As the Pearl River Delta gradually silted up to form land, the coastline continued to recede. Coupled with the risk costs of offshore fishing and the relatively backward transportation and preservation conditions at that time, the sales of seafood were indeed a major problem. For example, Zapo of Hailing Island in Yangjiang City, now a famous tourist destination and fishing port in Guangdong, was still a designated poverty alleviation target of a provincial unit until the late 1990s. Therefore, even for Guangzhou people, eating fresh seafood was not an easy task; they mostly relied on dried seafood. The so-called four precious seafood products—abalone, sea cucumber, shark fin, and fish maw—were all dried goods. Han Yu was able to eat live seafood because the river near Guangzhou was as vast as the ocean at that time. That's why Guangzhou people used to call crossing the Pearl River "crossing the sea." The Qixinggang in today's Haizhu District retains a famous ancient coastal site. In the Song Dynasty, the Pearl River water flowing through the city was still salty, and so was the well water. Therefore, when Su Dongpo was demoted to Huizhou and passed through Guangzhou, after visiting Baiyun Mountain, he suggested to the then Guangzhou Prefect that large bamboos abundant in Guangzhou be used to divert mountain spring water from Baiyun Mountain into Guangzhou, which can be called the world's earliest large-scale "tap water" project. By the mid-late Ming Dynasty, when Tang Xianzu was demoted to Xuwen and passed through Guangzhou, he already felt that the water was not salty and wrote the famous poem *Two Poems on Guangcheng (the First One)*, "By the river, thousands of wells hustle; on the land, a thousand ships surge. With such a majestic aura, it has always been Guangzhou."

Guangzhou Shuzhu Bridge

Especially in areas like Etan, where the waterway forks before and after entering the city, it is a nearby sea (river) fishing area. Since seafood is prioritized for its freshness, it is naturally best consumed near the production area. As the saying goes, "Hurry to sell fresh fish in the market, a small boat rides the waves. The west wind reports the beauty of white shrimp, and crabs with roe are even better." In the Qing Dynasty, near Bai'e Tan, at the intersection of Shuzhu Creek and the Pearl River, where fishermen of Haizhu Island gathered, restaurants and food boats specializing in live seafood emerged. Jin Wuxiang's *Suxiang Random Notes* records that when Wang Yuyang, a great poet of the Qing Dynasty, came here, he was greatly astonished and inspired to write a poem, "Wine cups urge people to enjoy life, and restaurants by Shuzhu Bridge open. When the seafood market arrives, every moment is contested, for fear of being the second to taste the new." In Cen Zheng's *Liang Luofang Invites to Dine at Shuzhu Bridge Restaurant states*, "Ethereal tall buildings stand by the water, and Shuzhu Bridge Market has long been renowned. Many masts anchor food boats, and even after candles are extinguished, the sound of wine betting can still be heard." He Renjing's *Spring Rhyme on the West City* says, "Every family teaches the little red flute, competing to row painted oars on the misty waves. Exquisite white shrimp and extremely fresh crabs, at sunset, all anchor at Shuzhu Bridge." The above two poems mention both restaurants and food boats. Perhaps more importantly, by Shuzhu Bridge, in addition to food, there were also cultural customs. As Huang Fuyi's *Records of Guangzhou City Squares* states, "Restaurants by the river beside the bridge, with red windows shining in all directions, flower boats moored nearby, a variety of delicacies presented, fresh dishes served together. People carry wine there every day... Taking a small melon rind-shaped boat with two or three close friends, returning slightly drunk, even the Qinhuai water pavilions cannot claim exclusive beauty." It is a pity that after continuing to the mid-Republican period, with the construction of Nanhua Road and the demolition of Shuzhu Bridge, these food cultures and customs vanished. The poem *Pearl River Spring Night* of Pan Feisheng praising Shuzhu Bridge is like a historical prophecy, saying "Last night, the rainbow boat approached the beautiful cottage, and the singing was too short for the pitiful night." It is the case for Guangzhou, the central provincial capital. It goes without saying for other coastal seafood production areas.

1.4 Delicious charr, Fresh fish sashimi

In earlier times, live seafood was not readily available; dried seafood was the norm. Yet Cantonese people's love of freshness runs deep. When seafood was hard to obtain, freshwater fish were persistently sought after, and good fish were often found; there are many excellent species because the Pearl River system has abundant water and high-quality water. For example, in recent years, the West River (Xijiang), which has been extensively canal-fed to supply Guangzhou, is renowned for its superior water quality. Among West River produce, such as the "Han Fish" (scientific name: hemibagrus guttatus), the flesh is delicate, the taste fresh, and the nutritional value high, earning it the title of "the king of freshwater." The most celebrated "Jia Fish" (charr) is a supreme delicacy that has captivated poets and scholars throughout history; among its most representative figures is Qu Dajun.

The name "Jia Fish" was first seen in *The Book of Songs*. Zhou Qufei of the Song Dynasty wrote in *Answers from Beyond the Lingnan*, "Jia Fish comes from the south of the Cangwu River, where there is a mountain called Huoshan. Below it is the Bing Cave, from which Jia Fish emerges. This is what the poet referred to as 'There are fine fish in the south.' Jia Fish resembles a large shad, with abundant fat on its belly. The locals fry it, and it tastes delicious." It also records the cooking method: "When frying, place the fish in a dry wok. Shortly, the fat melts and naturally fries the fish without using additional oil, called 'self-basting'." Liu Xun of the Tang Dynasty recorded another cooking method in *Records of the Lingnan Wonders*, speaking even more highly of it, "Jia Fish is shaped like a trout, emerging from the water outlet of Rongcheng County, Wuzhou. It is extremely plump and delicious, incomparable to other fish. It is best made into 'ting' (a type of fish sauce). When grilling, use a banana leaf to separate it from the fire, lest the fat drips extinguish the flame." However, Liu Xun's record is inaccurate; Jia Fish mainly originates from Guangdong rather than Guangxi (or perhaps Liu Xun followed ancient sayings, as the ancient prefecture of Wuzhou was located in present-day Fengkai, Guangdong). Qu Dajun's *New Words on Guangdong* details its origin and why it is extremely delicious: "It first appears in late autumn during heavy fog, necessarily among rapid streams and high gorges. It has a pure nature and does not enter turbid currents, often inhabiting stone caves, feeding on moss and drinking spring water to nourish itself. When the river is clear and cold with no tides, it emerges from the cave to inhale snow water. In Guangdong's Daxia and Xiaoxia Xiang Gorges (located in the current Qingyuan region), it emerges from the cave in October and enters in March. If the West River has not risen, it may not enter until April or May." Wu Zhenfang's later *Miscellaneous Records of Lingnan* confirms this: "Jia Fish is the finest among fish. Guangdong fish lack flavor, but this fish comes from stone caves, feeding on spring water, hence its plumpness and deliciousness." As the saying goes, different waters raise different fish. So, good water naturally produces good fish. A folk song by "Lianchuan Nüshi" in the late Qing Dynasty and early

Republic of China not only reflects that Jia Fish was still abundant at the time but also confirms the best season for catching it: "Conch is less crisp than oyster fresh; the best Jia Fish is in February. Winter solstice brings fish sashimi; summer solstice brings stew. How many fine flavors grace the banquet in a year?"

Qu Dajun depicted and praised Lingnan scenery and products abundantly, with Jia Fish being his greatest focus. His *Ode to Jia Fish with Preface* was written for Wu Xingzuo, the Governor of Guangdong and Guangxi in the early Qing Dynasty. His praise of Jia Fish was clearly not just personal preference. Besides the ode, there is also *Congratulations to the Governor of Liangyue*, "The vice premier brings might to the Five Ridges; the southeastern pillar is Songtai. Peace brings natural longevity like Kang Gong, who matches Jifu's talent in civil and military affairs? Last year, Lingyang Gorge had cold snow; this year, Yuanwu has many warm plums. Jia Fish again awaits Zhang Zhong; the solstice scenery fills jade cups. (In November of Guihai year, Lingyang Gorge was covered in snow, Jia Fish emerged from Xiaoxiang Gorge, sold in Songtai market in winter)." The preciousness of Jia Fish at dignitaries' banquets was like that of Guilv lychee among lychees. For example, Qu Dajun's poem *Wang Guancha Invites to Taste Jia Fish, Composed for Farewell*, "Poets sing of grand banquets, prizing Jia Fish above all. Joy abounds in fishing nets; even sturgeon and shark cannot compare. Who expects the water of Jinkang to resemble fishing in Miannan? Emerging from the cave only in winter, shared with you from the imperial feast." "Who knows you in the south? Come on, follow the Da Xiang and Xiao Xiang (rivers) here. Golden plates often serve it; jade chopsticks hold its fragrance. Banquets are hard to repeat, parting sorrows linger. When shall we visit Bing Cave to taste it again with you, sir? (Mr. Wang is going to serve in Mid-Shu)" "At this Jia Fish gathering, tears well up as I raise the cup. Trout and bream cannot stay; upon what can I rely? When missing you deeply in the future, do not fail to send letters. A pair by Brocade River stay, drinking from spring's milky spray." Therefore, He Mengyao, a renowned scholar of the Xijiang in the Qing Dynasty, sighed in a poem on his sixtieth birthday, "My family drinks Xijiang water daily, yet at sixty, I've never known Jia Fish's beauty." Just as few Cantonese have tasted Guilv lychee, which was a tribute. Even during the Republic of China era, Qu Duizhi, a famous scholar and master of anecdotes (son of Qu Hongji, a late Qing Grand Councilor), visited Guangdong twice. When feasted at the famous Nanyuan Restaurant in Guangzhou, he expressed the most representative contemporary view, "The host ushered me to the table; the pure shark fin was indeed rich and delicious, yet still inferior to Jia Fish. Jia Fish comes from the Xijiang, thin with many fine bones, its flavor clear and mellow." (*Ten Letters from Guangdong Trip* by Zhu'an, *Travel Magazine*, Vol. 10, No. 5, 1936) Thus, the beauty of Jia Fish is truly like Guilv among lyches. On February 21, 1923, Tan Yankai, the "Gourmet God" of the Republic of China era, followed Sun Yat-sen from Shanghai to Guangzhou. On May 9, at a banquet hosted by Sun Ke (son of Sun Yat-sen) and others, he tasted the rare Jia Fish and naturally ranked it first: "Attending the invitation of Xu Guqing, Sun Ke, Wu Gong'an, Cai Chang, etc., we ate four types of fish, with Jia Fish being the best."

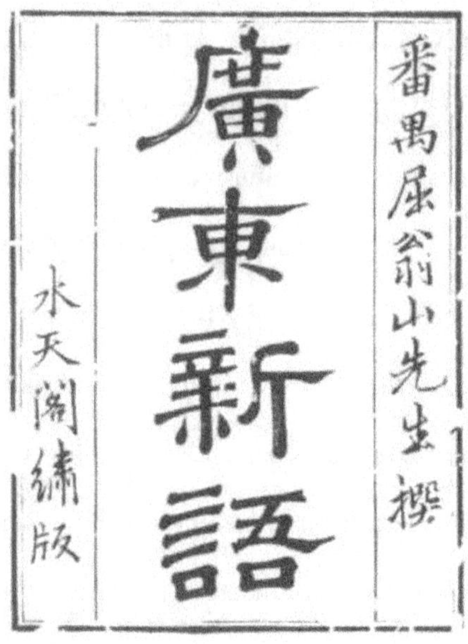
番禺屈翁山先生撰
廣東新語
水天閣繡版

Photocopy of *New Words on Guangdong*

In addition, Qu Dajun wrote more than ten poems eulogizing Jia Fish, which cannot all be listed here. It should be particularly noted that in his poems, Qu Dajun mentioned the cooking method of Jia Fish, "frequent serving of fish sashimi on golden plates", that is, eating "fish sashimi". In another poem, Jia Fish, he also said, "How can the fragrance of perch compare to you? Minced and served on golden plates. Meat reflects the tenderness of moss flowers; fat contains the coldness of stone milk. Laughing as I buy from the girls, sad to dine alone. How can a letter be sent? Scales struggle to exit the gorge." This also describes the method of making "fish sashimi". "Kuai" (fish sashimi), that is, eating fish sashimi, is undoubtedly the highest realm of pursuing fresh and live food. Of course, only fine fish are worthy of being made into kuai. In *Rowing under Haimu Mountain to Catch Shad for Kuai*, Qu Dajun used the renowned shad of southern China to make fish sashimi, "The rain departs, the boundless sea reveals its gaze; the retiring tide is met by the approaching tide. Abundant shad, with cherry-like cheeks, arrive daily for us to prepare as fish sashimi. (Shad with cherry-red cheeks are top-grade; yellow cheeks and iron cheeks come second; rotten scales and pink cheeks are lowest. When catching shad, the call of the 'scraping wok bird' is the signal. The 'scraping wok' is a bird's name.)" According to "Haimu Mountain" in *General Gazetteer of the Qing Dynasty: Guangzhou Prefecture*, "Located 140 li (0.5 km) southwest of Nanhai County in the Jiujiang Sea, with both banks standing parallel like eyes, the foot of the mountain is full of strange rocks." At that time, the Jiujiang section of the Xijiang was still as broad as the sea, with mountains rising in the midst of rivers and seas. As the lower reaches of the Xijiang flow here, it is the confluence of saltwater and freshwater, where various aquatic products taste most delicious, not to mention shad. Thus, Qu Dajun also said, "Jia Fish at Lingyang Gorge is delicious, but not as fresh as shad at Haimu. Yellow-cheeked slices are as white as snow, green wine pours like a spring." "When the 'scraping wok bird' calls and spring snow melts, shad compete to ride the Jiujiang tide. With my own slicing gear, I visit the fisherfolk afloat; No call is needed as twin oars fly like wings on the boat. (Near Haimu is Jiujiang Village.)"

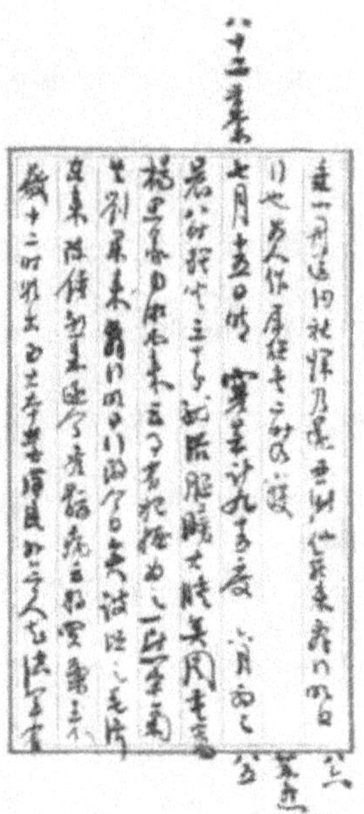

Tan Yankai's Dairy

Fish flavor values freshness, and fish sashimi is the freshest. Thus, Qu Dajun dedicated a special entry, "Fish Sashimi", in *New Words on Guangdong*. Fish sashimi can be regarded as one of the most important traditions of Cantonese cuisine.

Later, due to the influence of Japanese cuisine in China, many once believed fish sashimi was a Japanese import. Hence, the famous writer Gao Yang stated in *Ancient and Modern Food Affairs*, "When it comes to fish sashimi, it's not unique to Japanese cuisine. Cantonese fish sashimi is even more exquisite. Generally, any tender, boneless freshwater fish can be used;

Cantonese fish sashimi also adds many condiments, mainly extremely dry shredded radish (naturally neither spicy nor bitter), followed by crispy items like thin crackers, fried dough twists, or fried pasta, crushed and mixed in; seasonings include salt, sesame oil, pepper, shredded red chili, coriander, and finely shredded orange leaves, with soy sauce uniquely being omitted. When eating, a large plate is placed in the center, into which ingredients and seasonings are poured, and everyone mixes them together. Snow-white fish slices and shredded radish are mixed with bright red chili shreds, green coriander, and orange leaves, presenting a fresh color that enhances appetite."

Qu Dajun's *New Words on Guangdong* records that Cantonese people love fish sashimi not only for its exquisite preparation and delicious taste but also for its ceremonial propriety, reflecting the deep tradition of eating fish sashimi in Guangdong. "At banquets, it is essential to serve fish sashimi as a gesture of respect. It is best eaten on an empty stomach at dawn. Every time the fish is sliced; honey wine is poured; and ginger and betel are added; everyone beams with joy, eating and laughing." Chen Huiyan of the Qing Dynasty explained why Lingnan people ate fish sashimi from another angle in *Travel Notes of Nanyue*, "Lingnan people like to take live grass carp, butcher it into shreds, and mix them with melon seeds, peanuts, radish, fungus, lettuce, fried noodles, vermicelli, and dried tofu to eat together, calling it 'fish sashimi'. It is consumed with boiling soup or hot wine to counteract the coldness." Eating fish sashimi requires drinking wine, which dispels both cold and disinfects. Thus, this custom remained popular in the

Republic of China era, "Fish sashimi is universal on the Winter solstice, fresh fish sliced like jade. A cup of hot wine dispels the cold, continuing the fish-eating tradition of the former dynasty" (*Bamboo Branch Poems of Yangcheng* by Wang Zhaoquan). Therefore, currently advocating for a ban on fish sashimi due to the risk of parasitic diseases ignores the actual climate and natural environment of Lingnan. Furthermore, instead of banning, we should focus on establishing standards to ensure hygiene, while also considering the health needs dictated by climate and geography, not just pursuing taste and appearance, but emphasizing "weisheng" (hygiene, literally "protecting life") and reviving the "ancient way" of fish sashimi. In fact, this aligns with China's tradition of innovation through revival, embodying another form of fashion. It should be noted that the traditional Lingnan fish sashimi mentioned above mostly refers to freshwater fish, mainly because seafood was relatively expensive and unaffordable for ordinary people. Due to the superior quality of seafood itself, less emphasis was placed on ingredients, hence sparse records. But this does not mean Lingnan people disliked seafood sashimi.

Fish sashimi has always been a top delicacy in Guangdong. Although some textual researches claim that "kuai" in "Stewed Soft-Shelled Turtle and Sliced Carp" from *June* in *Minor Odes*, *The Book of Songs*, refers to fish sashimi, and "kuai" in "Jin Ji Yu Kuai" (a favorite "southeast delicacy" of Emperor Yang of the Sui Dynasty) is also fish sashimi, which is not necessarily true. Confucius said, "Never tired of having the rice finely cleaned, nor of having the minced meat cut quite small." Slicing fish and meat thinly, whether stir-frying or hot-potting them instead of eating raw, ensures easy cooking, freshness, and better taste. It was not until the Ming Dynasty that documents confirmed "kuai" could refer to fish sashimi. Liu Bowen's *Handbook of Many Skills* in the late Yuan and early Ming dynasties states in the "Fish Kuai" section, "Fish, regardless of size, should be fresh and live. Remove head, tail, and belly, slice thinly, spread on white paper to air-dry for a while, then mince into threads. Finely chop radish, twist in a cloth to extract juice, mix fish with ginger threads onto a plate, and dress with lettuce, coriander, mustard, and vinegar." Li Shizhen's warning in Compendium of Materia Medica proves fish kuai is raw from the opposite perspective: "Eating fish sashimi is extremely harmful to people."

Shunde fish sashimi

However, amid the warnings of medical masters, while eating fish sashimi elsewhere became documented legend, the custom of eating fish sashimi in Lingnan, as seen in documents, gradually reached its peak. First, Qu Dajun's extensive documentation in *New Words on Guangdong* during the late Ming and early Qing dynasties. Other note materials, whenever writing about Guangdong scenery, often mention fish sashimi. For example, the poem proverb compiled in Ling Yangzao's *Poems of Lingnan* in the Qing Dynasty says, "One is not a Lingnan person if not eating fish sashimi." Zhang Xintai's *Brief Notes on Travels in Guangdong* states, "Cantonese like to serve fish sashimi to guests with dozens of different side dishes, called 'eating fish sashimi.' After eating, the remaining fish sashimi is used to make congee, called 'fish sashimi congee.' The proverb 'winter solstice fish sashimi' reflects this." Li Tiaoyuan's *Sixteen Bamboo Branch Poems of Nanhai* says, "After each Jiujiang tide ebbs, southerners eat fish sashimi every meal." In the late Qing Dynasty, *Current Affairs Pictorial* published a vivid Eating Fish Sashimi illustration with an attached text, "Fish sashimi rivals the taste of Songjiang perch. Cantonese are particularly fond of it. Sliced fish and shredded radish—when autumn wind blows, assorted fish sashimi is ready to enjoy, no need to wait for the winter solstice." Comparing it to the famous Songjiang perch in Jiangnan, it was regarded as a major feature of Lingnan. A contemporary bamboo branch poem echoed, "Autumn swells the ocean's bounty where tides roll. Banqueting with comrades nourishes the soul. Why crave homeland herbs with fish thinly laid? When here, blade-kissed slicings of fat spawn gourmet's crusade?"

This custom intensified in the Republic of China era. The most vivid and detailed account of Guangdong fish sashimi during the Republic of China era comes from Yoshida Satoshi of Japan (where sashimi is traditional). He first clarified, "Most Chinese think sashimi exists only in Japan, but Guangdong, Fuzhou, and other regions have always loved fish sashimi." He also believed ancient China had a tradition of eating fish sashimi: "The saying 'Fear hot soup and blow on minced food' means burning the throat on soup makes one cautious with minced food, proving ancient China ate fish sashimi." He then described the grand occasion of Guangdong fish sashimi in the Republic of China era from personal experience: "Walking through streets in Jiangmen and Shunde, Guangdong, in autumn, fish sashimi is everywhere, especially in Jiangmen, where there are restaurants specializing in it." He finally sighed, "Truly, only those who have eaten fish sashimi know its deliciousness." (*Fish and Chinese Cuisine* by Yoshida Satoshi (Japan), *Dazhong* Magazine, Issue 16, 1944)

1.5 Dace Surpasses Perch

Jia Fish is nearly a legend, rare at Chinese banquets, while Shunde dace remains one of the symbols of "Cuisine from Fengcheng (Shunde)"—not to mention the must-order Shunde fish cakes at banquets, even Ganzhu-brand dace canned food remains popular today. It is not only famous locally but also in Shanghai during the Republic of China era. Tracing its historical origin is like unfolding a chapter of Lingnan cultural history.

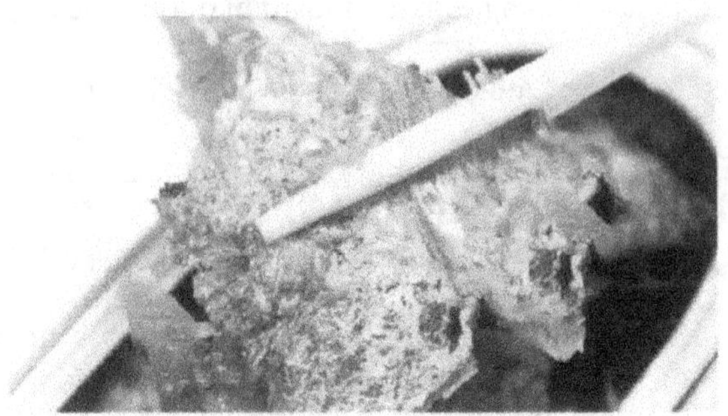

Canned dace

In his early years, Huang Jie, a renowned professor from Peking University and a native of Shunde, affectionately chanted about this hometown delicacy, "Guest chefs have their own fresh cooking methods, but none match hometown-style fermented soybean dace!" Ms. Wu Huizhen of Guangzhou serialized *Cantonese Cuisine Cooking Methods* in Shanghai's *Home* magazine from 1943 to 1944, highly recommending dace dishes. She said, "Local dace produced in Shunde, Guangdong, is the most plump and delicious, known for its smooth meat and fresh taste. Any cooking method brings out its excellent flavor, a unique treat for Cantonese." Dace can be made into various dishes, and Wu Huizhen introduced several specialties, such as steamed local dace, "Fortune and Wish" (dried hair seaweed fish balls, adding a little salted Caobai fish when mincing for extra flavor), fragrant wine dace, pickled fried dace, savory sauce dace, crab fin meatballs, etc., rarely seen today.

Golden Sister's Fish Rings, a famous Foshan dish popular in Guangdong and Hong Kong, is also a dace delicacy. Golden Sister was a renowned female chef of the Republic of China era, serving on purple cave boats around Zhongshan Bridge and Civil Affairs Bridge in Foshan.

A dish called "Jade Sunflower Treasure Fan" from Shanghai Xiuse Grand Restaurant, tasted by Tang Lusun, is the most legendary local dace dish, hiding a poignant and beautiful story. It is said that a young noble, Mr. Luo, had a family-heirloom fan capable of bringing the dead back to life. Coincidentally, one day, Mr. Luo's fiancée fell into the river and died while washing clothes by the stream. Mr. Luo waved the treasure fan personally for a whole day and night, finally rescuing her. Shunde people prefer to have steamed fish with rice. When fresh local dace is steamed together with top-grade salted Caobai fish, the blend of fresh and salty flavors is like Mr. Luo reviving his fiancée in the story, hence the name "Jade Sunflower Treasure Fan". The steamed fish features red muscles and white texture, whetting the appetite and living up to its beautiful name. Liu Yusheng, who once held a puppet government position and later became a renowned sinologist in Australia under the name Liu Cunren, also said, "Local dace tastes extremely delicious." (Liu Yusheng, *Ode to Eating in Guangzhou*, *Ancient and Modern Monthly*, Issue 7, 1942) Therefore, Ye Xinfo's *Lingnan Foods: Dace and Crab Seeds* vividly expresses his deep affection for dace, which is very touching. "I am a Cantonese, having lived in Shanghai for more than ten years. Among Guangdong local products, I love to eat dace and crab seeds best. For more than ten years, I have been unable to eat fresh ones, often lamenting my lack of good fortune. Only when relatives and friends know my preference do they pickle and send them to me, which is a comfort, better than nothing. In ancient times, people remembered water shield and perch when the autumn wind rose. Now, in the bright spring, dace and crab seeds have long been on the market. Thinking of them but unable to get them, I write this article, unable to stop my mouth from watering." (*Shenbao*, June 11, 1926)

Back in Guangzhou, there is also a dish of superior soup dace noodles, a favorite of Sun Ke, uniquely created by Luo Chang, the "Fish King" of Guangzhou Beiyuan Restaurant. The method is to first beat fresh dace into fish gelatin, mix it with egg white, steam it until firm, then cut it into noodle-like strips and braise in superior soup, which is smooth, refreshing, and sweet. Li He, a Shunde-born head chef of Beiyuan Restaurant later, also adapted a classic dish using dace: he replaced the tofu in Beiyuan's traditional home-cooked dish "Suburban Fish Head" with dace tofu, which suddenly increased in value and became one of Beiyuan's top ten famous dishes. This dace tofu is a traditional Shunde dish, and "Lecong Fish Tofu" remains a gold medal dish in Shunde today.

In addition to these dishes, during the Republic of China era, Weilan Porridge Shop at the intersection of Jianglan Road in Xiguan made a chrysanthemum dace ball congee. The authentic and sweet taste of local dace, combined with chrysanthemum petals blooming in autumn, was a masterpiece in color, aroma, and taste, sensationalizing the food industry and enduring for a long time.

With so many ways to cook dace, it is evident how delicious it is and how deeply Shunde people love it. The delicious taste of dace made Jiangnan people envious, and Shunde people comforted them by saying, "Canned products have recently been available and can be sold everywhere." This was during the late Qing Dynasty and the Republic of China era. The earliest record of dace cans is an advertisement in the *Shenbao* on April 4, 1897, *Notice from Tongxiecheng on Hongkou Road*, "Our shop has newly arrived Guangdong canned dace, fresh and tender bamboo shoots, white snow clear noodles..." This is also a known record of the industrialization of Guangdong food, and can be regarded as a symbol of the prosperity of "Eating in Guangzhou". Today, various dace cans, especially Ganzhu-brand dace cans, are still popular at home and abroad, demonstrating their eternal charm.

Brewed dace

Today, Shunde chefs continue to innovate and pursue excellence in cooking skills. A representative new dace dish is Eight Treasures Stuffed Dace, which would have made food connoisseurs in the Republic of China era eager to try: the method is quite difficult - first remove the bones and meat of the dace while keeping the skin intact; mix the removed fish meat with various fine ingredients to make fish paste, then stuff it back into the fish skin to form a complete "dace". When fried or steamed, it is affectionately called "Eight Immortals Dace". In terms of styles, it is now more complex and diverse than in the Republic of China era. Mr. Luo Funan, President of Shunde Chefs Association, said they can make more than 130 dishes with dace, which is a super-standard hundred-fish banquet. Wu Wangqun, a famous Shunde female chef known as the "Grandma Group", once participated in making a dace banquet that was broadcast on CCTV. The surviving menu shows: Splendid Platter (Clam Sauce Dace Cake, Scallion Egg Fried Dace Intestines with Qiaoshe Signature Chicken), Fortune Dace Soup, Green Fried Dace Balls, Hometown Stuffed Fish (i.e., Stuffed Dace), Emerald Fried Fish Rolls, Welcome to Fish and Rice Township (Dace Roe), Dace (Bone) Superior Soup Seasonal Vegetables, etc.

Chapter 2 Single Port Trade: Lingnan Cuisine Rises to Prominence

Diet is a reflection of both economy and culture. With the southward shift of China's economic center starting from the late Tang Dynasty, the development of Lingnan accelerated further in the Song Dynasty. From the Song to the Ming Dynasty, it was an important era for the leapfrog development of Lingnan's economy and culture. As Qu Dajun said in *New Words on Guangdong*, "It was a barbarian land before the Qin and Han dynasties, but became a divine land after the Tang and Song dynasties." If the Song Dynasty was the transition of Lingnan from a barbarian land to a divine land, by the Mi itself ng Dynasty, Lingnan could already pride in the divine land. This was not only caused by the general trend of China's economic southward shift but also by the unique advantage of Guangzhou's long-term single-port trade in the Ming Dynasty, which emphasized agriculture and suppressed commerce while banning sea trade to prevent Japanese pirates, thus forming a situation similar to the saying "North, south, east, west; Guangdong gathers wealth best" that emerged in the 1980s, which was the connotation of "going to Guangdong" in the Ming Dynasty. In such a prosperous scene, as Ye Quan said in *Travel Notes of Lingnan*, "Lingnan was once known as a miasma region, where only exiles and banished officials would go. Now, looking at the mountains in Lingnan, they are not as low as those in Wu and Yue. Below, green pines line the road, open and spacious.

From Nan'an to Nanxiong, it is said to be 120 li (60 km), but can be reached in half a day by starting early. Officials are happy to serve there, and merchants are willing to travel through it." We can also say, "Food lovers are eager to taste its flavor."

2.1 Single-port Trade and the "Going to Guangdong" Effect

Today, when people talk about "Eating in Guangzhou", they all quote Qu Dajun's words in *New Words on Guangdong*, "Almost all food products in the world can be found in Guangdong; while food products in Guangdong may not be found everywhere in the world" as evidence. Chen Mengyin even directly called "Eating in Guangzhou" in *Origins of Cantonese Cuisine*, but this only refers to the richness of ingredients. Furthermore, when the public regards "Grand Historian Cuisine" and "Tan Family Cuisine" as symbols of Guangzhou, "they often say that Cantonese cuisine has absorbed and integrated some advantages of Huaiyang cuisine. Why is this so? All this can be traced back to "going to Guangdong."

Guangzhou Shisan Hang in the Qing Dynasty

Since its establishment over 2,000 years ago, Guangzhou has almost always been open to the outside world. Although the early Ming Dynasty stipulated that "not a single plank shall go to sea," Guangzhou was hardly banned. Especially after the Zhejiang and Fujian Maritime Trade Departments were abolished in the first year of Jiajing, Guangzhou obtained the status of single-port trade. Even when three ports coexisted, "Ningbo traded with Japan, Quanzhou with Ryukyu, and Guangzhou with Champa, Siam, and Western countries," the other two were far less splendid than Guangzhou. The Maritime Silk Road, which is highly praised today, was often dominated by Guangzhou. Therefore, after the mid-Ming Dynasty, Shunde, close to Guangzhou, became the most typical area of mulberry fish ponds in the Pearl River Delta, and 18 trades emerged from the raw silk industry: silk satin trade, variegated satin trade, yuanqing satin trade, huaju satin trade, ramie satin trade, niulangsha trade, silk trade, maoling trade, hualing trade, jincai trade, bianjin trade, duibian trade, railing trade, jisha trade, dousha trade, yanglingchou trade, etc. But this still could not meet the needs of Guangzhou's silk export trade. A large amount of raw silk from the Suzhou-Hangzhou region of the Yangtze River Delta was purchased for processing. The woven "Guangdong satin is dense and uniform in texture, bright and splendid in color, shiny and smooth, "inferior to none in Jinling, Suzhou, and Hangzhou, and "was valued by the East and the West," supplying "most of Europe's needs," winning world reputation, and being beyond the reach of contemporary European products. Europeans had to lament, "There is no country in the world whose craftsmanship is so exquisite."

Against this background, merchants from Jiangsu and Zhejiang would "secretly buy silk, mercury, raw copper, medicinal materials, and all other goods for overseas trade, sell them in Guangdong, and then buy Guangdong goods back to Zhejiang. Originally called transportation, they cleverly named it 'going to Guangdong'" (Hu Zongxian's *Map Compilation for Coastal Defense*). Not only Jiangsu and Zhejiang, but also other provinces were "going to Guangdong" one after another. *Jiang Xingge Reunites with the Pearl Shirt* in the famous Ming Dynasty novel *Wonders of the Present and the Past* says that Jiang Shize followed his father-in-law, Mr. Luo, to Guangdong to do business. Because of the substantial profits, even though his wife had died and his son was young, he could not give it up. The Luo family had been doing this for three generations. It was precisely because of "going to Guangdong" that Qu Dajun could say, "Almost all food products in the world can be found in Guangdong." Thus, "Eating in Guangzhou" was, to a certain extent, shaped by "going to Guangdong."

Bird's nest soup

If "going to Guangdong" in the Ming Dynasty was a choice, in the Qing Dynasty, it became a necessity. The Qing court reopened the sea ban, and Guangzhou was the only port for trade, leaving no other way, so there was no need to mention "going to Guangdong." At this time, the West had entered the great age of navigation. Driven by both, Guangzhou truly ushered in an unprecedented prosperous scene, and the pattern of "Eating in Guangzhou" gradually took shape. In the works of many famous writers, although "Eating in Guangzhou" was not labeled, the reality of "Eating in Guangzhou" was already described.

In 1770, Zhao Yi, a great historian and writer from Yanghu (now Changzhou), was transferred to serve as the Prefect of Guangzhou. He was astonished by the luxurious diet in Guangzhou. Not to mention the restaurants and brothels, even in the prefectural yamen, as an upright and diligent official who "had no free time and never enjoyed luxury, and "each meal only consisted of three dishes of fish and a bowl of soup," the institutional supplies were incomparable to the much-criticized "Official Government Consumption (referring to spending on vehicles, overseas trips, and entertainment)" today. "The yamen consumed two dan (about 100 kg) of rice daily, had seven kitchen rooms, and three large iron woks. Boiling hundreds of hu (about 50 liters) of water for bathing was still insufficient. Six water carriers were specially assigned to carry tea water from Longquan Mountain, often complaining of calluses on their feet. Banquets with opera performances were held several times a month, with piles of wax tears and shoes. The so-called 'dining with bells ringing and tripods steaming' in ancient times could hardly compare." What kind of pomp would a pleasure-seeking prefect have? Therefore, he said, "Throughout my life as an official, only the year in Guangzhou enjoyed such prosperity." In Zhao Yi's view, there was no other place in the country where food and drink were as prosperous as in Guangzhou; Guangzhou finally became the "master"!

Decades later, from the newly published *The Lost Chinese History in the West*, we can specifically see the luxury of official banquets from the records by Westerners. On June 24, 1843, Qi Ying, the imperial commissioner of the Qing government, hosted a banquet for the British Hong Kong authorities: in front of the plates on the table were mountains of cold dishes such as pickles, sauerkraut, and dried radishes. When bird's nest soup was served, the banquet officially began. And which were venison, duck, shark's fin (which could not be praised enough), chestnut soup, spare ribs, vegetable meat pies fried in a pan with gravy and lard, venison tenderloin soup, shark soup (second only to shark's fin), peanut mixed stew, a gelatinous substance made from softened and boiled ox bone marrow, mushroom chestnut soup, stewed ham with sugar or syrup, braised bamboo shoots, fish maw, and numerous hot soups and dishes difficult to describe in words. In the center of the table were roasted peacock, pheasant, and ham.

Restaurants, especially those in foreign trade houses, were even more luxurious. Ivan, a Frenchman, recorded in *Inside Guangzhou City* that Pan

Shicheng, a famous merchant, once boasted to him, "Our chefs are renowned throughout the empire. Where else but here can such exquisite dishes as brainless duck and hollow five-spice minced meatballs be created?" Most Guangzhou people today have never heard of these two dishes. Some were so luxurious that they seemed like wanton waste, to the extent that during the Xiguan fire in the second year of the Daoguang reign (1822), "more than seventy streets, ten lanes, and over ten thousand houses were destroyed, spanning one li in width and seven li in length. Dozens of people were burned to death, and twenty-seven people were trampled to death at Daguan Bridge. Centenarians sighed that such a disaster had never been seen before." Some even believed it was divine punishment. "At that time, foreign ships were gradually opening trade in Guangdong, and foreign merchants were just becoming prosperous. Pearl-inlaid goods crowded Xiguan. There were seas of wine and forests of meat, luxurious clothes, and precious food. Even butchers became rich and indulged in unprecedented extravagance. Heaven was probably angry with their debauchery, so it turned the mirage into ashes with a single fire, delivering a severe warning." (Chen Kangqi, *First Notes of Langqian*). A hundred years later, Qu Duiyi, a famous scholar and son of Qu Hongji, a late Qing Grand Councilor, still agreed, "Mr. Chen's words are deeply poignant. Seeing the fall of civilization, we know it serves as a warning for a hundred years." (Qu Duiyi, *Compendium of Characters, Customs, and Systems*). However, two years after the fire, Zhao Guang from Kunming saw during his tour of Guangdong that the prosperous scene had not only recovered but exceeded the past. "At that time, Guangdong was the richest province in the country, with abundant capital among ocean salt merchants, tea merchants, and silk merchants. There were more than ten foreign trade ports and thirteen foreign trade houses. Foreign buildings and ships gathered outside the city. From Qingbo Gate to Shiba Pu, the streets were ten times more prosperous than Suzhou and Hangzhou."

At this point, no one should object to the saying "Guangzhou is the ideal place for gourmets"; some even changed the proverb to "Born in Guangzhou, die in Liuzhou" to show their infinite fascination with Guangzhou's food.

2.2 Shunde Chefs and Foshan Bosses

"Eating in Guangzhou, Cooking from Fengcheng"—Fengcheng is Daliang, the county seat of Shunde. Among the counties under Guangzhou, Shunde had the largest number of excellent chefs, with Daliang being the best. Many believe Shunde is the birthplace of Cantonese cuisine. After all, "even a clever woman can't cook without rice"—with good ingredients but no good chefs, nothing can be achieved. Liang Jiexiang of the Qing Dynasty wrote in *Record of a Dream Tour in Fengcheng*, "Shunde is a land of milk and honey; in terms of food, Guangzhou is inferior in exquisiteness." Without Shunde chefs, "Eating in Guangzhou" could hardly be sustained. A brief review of the "glorious history" of Shunde chefs and the reasons for their "glory" will convince you, among the vast Guangfu region and its numerous excellent chefs, only Shunde can be regarded as the representative.

The single-port trade quickly turned Shunde into the "Silk Capital of the South." "Thousands of loads of golden grain, nightly feasts in houses with wok-shaped eaves"—this depicts the food customs of prosperous and affluent Shunde, the Silk Capital. In fact, this only represents the grand banquets of wealthy families. The wok aroma of "Fengcheng stir-fries" generated by the bustling restaurants in the silk trading center is the hallmark of "Cooking from Fengcheng." Later, some grand restaurants in Hong Kong, such as Yingjing in Wan Chai, displayed wall advertisements for "Fengcheng Wok Aroma" and "Guangzhou Superior Soup," showing that one county could rival the whole country.

Bosses and young masters could enjoy nightly feasts, while mulberry farmers and silkworm households could visit teahouses and restaurants every day. In the slang of the time, "Just three mulberry leaves were enough to settle the bill." This prosperity continued until the mid-Republican period. According to statistics, in the 1920s-1930s, the town of Rongqi alone had dozens of restaurants mainly serving silkworm farmers, including high-end and fashionable grand restaurants like "Haijing," "Changle, "Hengji, "Zhanji," "Da Shanyuan," and "Qiongzhen," and even some Western restaurants. In the view of Mr. Liao Xixiang, a senior research expert on Shunde food culture, the Shunde stir-fries generated by prosperous commercial trade not only brought a revolution in cooking methods but also in business operations. From then on, Shunde chefs, carrying "Fengcheng delicacies," conquered cities and further strengthened the legend of "Cooking from Fengcheng."

Later generations believe that the flavor of the Silk Capital directly influenced "Eating in Guangzhou." Before the founding of the People's Republic of China, an article about Guangzhou Flavor published in *Shanghai's Travel Magazine* said, "Guangzhou's food culture is indescribable. The hundreds of years of luxurious food culture are said to have two sources: Shunde County, famous for its silk industry and banking industry, was extremely wealthy, and its descendants, accustomed to a pampered life, daily focused on exquisite dining and constant innovation. The so-called 'Fengcheng food' was highly praised by Guangzhou people. The second source is Xiaguan in Guangzhou, also a gathering place for the rich, so the food culture in Xiaguan was particularly prosperous, producing many famous chefs." The silk trade was one of the key factors contributing to the wealth of Xiaguan. In short, the flavor of the Silk Capital played a huge role.

In this process, the iron smelting and casting industry promoted by the single-port trade also greatly assisted the formation of "Fengcheng stir-fries." Foshan, which was still a "Foshan Ferry" in the Yuan Dynasty and became a village in the early Ming Dynasty, developed into one of the "Four Great Towns of the World" by the mid-Ming Dynasty. Shunde was known for silk, and Foshan for iron, each excelling in its field. Foshan invented "red mold casting" technology and craftsmanship, making the quality and craftsmanship of cast iron the best in the country. Zhang Xintai of the Qing

Dynasty wrote in *Brief Notes on Travels in Guangdong*, "The best iron production area in the world is Guangdong, and the best iron smelting craftsmen are in Foshan." Especially the high-quality, thin, light, and smooth "Guangdong woks" became a major commodity in domestic and foreign trade. It was the excellent woks cast in Foshan that enabled large-scale stir-frying and selling of stir-fries, making them famous worldwide.

The "Silk Capital of the South" led to "abandoning rice for mulberry." By the Guangxu period, the annual grain harvest was insufficient to meet the needs of the county's people for half a month, which created a Chencun Grain Wharf. Chencun in Shunde, located at the transportation hub of Guangzhou, Nanhai, Shunde, Panyu, and Foshan, is one of the "Four Famous Towns of Guangdong" alongside Guangzhou, Foshan, and Shilong in Dongguan, becoming the grain trading center for the entire Pearl River Delta. Grain from Guangxi, Hunan, Jiangxi, and other provinces basically gathered here first, making it the "grain wharf" of Guangzhou's grain wharves. Romance always thrives with grain wharves, and this was true for both Guangzhou and Chencun. Grain wharf feasts became the unique flavor of the Silk Capital. The grain wharf romance in Chencun was no less than that in Guangzhou. Guangzhou's grain wharf romance contributed to "Eating in Guangzhou," and Chencun's grain wharf romance also made corresponding contributions to "Cooking from Fengcheng." Mr. Luo Funan said that the Hong Kong Chef Champion in the 1980s came from Chencun's "Flower Feast Hall." The famous Zidong Ting cuisine, comparable to Suzhou boat cuisine, was actually mostly from Chencun Grain Wharf in Shunde, as described by the senior Chen Jinghong.

Shunde people are good at eating, and chefs are good at cooking, passed down from generation to generation, thus producing national chefs. After the liberation of Shanghai in 1951, the state established “New China’s first state guesthouse”—Jinjiang Hotel. The first executive chef, Xiao Liangchu (1906-1985), was from Shunde. It is said that in order to protect his interests in Shanghai at that time, he formed a brotherhood with nine other Shunde-born chefs to support each other.

Xiao Liangchu

He was the eldest, and he also had a master named Guo Dakai, who was also a renowned chef of a generation, of course, also from Shunde. It is said that in 1961, the monthly salary of the Secretary of Shunde Daliang

Commune was 70 yuan, while the salary of a first-class university professor, such as Mr. Chen Yinke from Sun Yat-sen University, was only 381 yuan (commonly known as the "381 highland"), and Xiao Liangchu's monthly salary at Jinjiang Hotel was 540 yuan. This shows how high his worth was, essentially doing socialist work but receiving capitalist wages. Without special skills, one could not enjoy such special treatment. The ancient saying goes, "A gentleman stays away from the kitchen." This time, however, the chefs have overwhelmed the "gentleman." Haha! Coincidentally, Liang Di, a local dim sum master from Shunde, also received a first-class salary of 125 yuan at that time - this was the deepest political and economic foundation for "Cooking from Fengcheng!"

At Jinjiang Hotel, Xiao Liangchu has personally cooked or arranged dishes for heads of state, presidents, prime ministers, and other dignitaries from more than 100 countries. Among his works, the "three masterpieces" are worthy of being recorded in culinary history. The first was in 1952, when he, as the first chef representative sent by New China, participated in the Leipzig International Exposition. Not only did he win the gold medal in the cooking show with a "Lotus Leaf Salt-Baked Chicken," but he also "conquered" President Pieck of the German Democratic Republic, who presented him with a gold pen and a personally signed photo, which can be regarded as a diplomatic anecdote. The second was in 1954, when the comedy master Charlie Chaplin visited Shanghai. After tasting Xiao Liangchu's "Jinjiang Crispy Duck," he lamented it as the "most unforgettable delicacy in his life" and even proposed to Premier Zhou to pack two ducks to take back to the United States to share with his family. The third was in 1982, when Mrs. Thatcher visited Shanghai. Bao Yugang, the Hong Kong shipping magnate, hosted a banquet for her at Jinjiang. At the age of seventy-six, Xiao Liangchu came out of retirement to take charge of the kitchen, which immediately ignited the excitement of the Hong Kong media. Reports almost stole the spotlight, "Shipping Magnate's Luncheon for British Prime Minister, Shunde Chef at the Stove," "Head Chef is seventy-eight (actually seventy-six) - year-old Xiao Liangchu, a native of Shunde Daliang"... In fact, the pinnacle of Chef Xiao Liangchu's legendary career should be at the 1961 UN Geneva Conference. In 1954, New China first participated in a UN conference discussing major international issues as one of the five major powers and achieved a series of important results. To maintain this achievement, the UN reconvened the Geneva Conference in 1961. The old saying "dealing with diplomatic issues over dinner", that is, resolving major issues during banquets and toasts, was one of Premier and Foreign Minister Zhou Enlai's best skills. The performance of the chef was crucial to the effectiveness of such diplomatic banquets. At this juncture, Foreign Minister Chen Yi personally appointed Xiao Liangchu as the chef. In return, Xiao Liangchu created the Eight Treasures Salt-Baked Chicken, which was highly praised by guests from various countries. This famous dish was based on the Guangdong Hakka dish "Dongjiang Salt-Baked Chicken." Ingredients such as chicken liver, duck liver, cured meat, cured sausage, cured duck liver, cured duck intestines, cured tendon, and marinated phoenix goose granules were added to the chicken cavity, wrapped in lotus leaves and tin foil, and baked in sea salt. The freshness of the chicken, the richness of the saltiness, the lightness of the lotus fragrance, and the full-bodied flavor of the cured meat were magically integrated.

After the expansion of the Beijing Hotel in 1955, the State Council sent a special person to Shanghai and entrusted Jinjiang Hotel to help select chefs. Xiao Liangchu recommended Kang Hui, a 31-year-old fellow townsman from Shunde, without avoiding relatives. Kang Hui quickly stood out and was entrusted with an important task in 1961: going to Zhongnanhai to be Mao Zedong's chef, becoming a veritable "imperial chef." In addition, he also served as the "imperial chef" for Ho Chi Minh for a period of time. He invented "Crispy Chicken" became Ho's favorite. In return, Ho Chi Minh would invite Kang Hui to "accompany" him every time he visited China. During meals, Ho would even personally serve him food, treating him as an honored guest, which made Kang Hui feel extremely flattered. Soong Ching Ling, the Honorary President of the People's Republic of China, had a special love for her hometown's Cantonese cuisine. Every time she entertained relatives, friends, and foreign guests at home, she would invite Kang Hui to be the head chef, which can be called "appointing the imperial chef." His "Wine-Baked Flounder" became Soong's favorite. When recalling later, Mr. Kang said lightly, "After the flounder is baked, pour a little salad oil, and it can be served on the table." "The method is very simple and doesn't take much time." In fact, what he called "not taking much time" actually took 5 hours from start to finish!

Kang Hui's most cherished experience was cooking the New Year's Eve dinner for Chairman Mao in 1962, the first year after the three-year difficult period. Kang Hui was only allowed to make a few dishes of Hunan-style chili peppers, bitter gourd, fermented black beans, and other side dishes for the Chairman, paired with rice and steamed buns. The only grand thing was the wine, because the Chairman also invited Pu Yi, Zhang Shizhao, and three other celebrities. The scale of this New Year's Eve dinner was unimaginable to outsiders, and it was impossible for Kang Hui not to remember it deeply.

Kang Hui

Later, Kang Hui served as the executive chef of Beijing Hotel and was responsible for the construction of the Diaoyutai State Guesthouse and the restaurant of the Great Hall of the People, forming a tripartite structure of Beijing's state banquets. Till now, the two major state guesthouses in the north and south have all been under the control of Shunde chefs. In a sense,

Shunde cuisine became the “national cuisine” of the new era, and Kang Hui became a national treasure among Chinese chefs: from 1982 to 1984, he was invited to France three times to exchange and share cooking skills, becoming famous in France. He was invited to be a member of the French Famous Chefs Association and awarded the title of “Culinary Master”; in 1985, he won the title of Beijing Model Worker; in 1987, he was elected as an executive director of the Chinese Culinary Association; in 1988, he served as a judge in the second International Culinary Competition held in Japan; in 2002, he was awarded the title of “National Treasure Culinary Master”, only sixteen people in the country received this honor.

When Kang Hui and Xiao Liangchu were serving as “imperial chefs” and hosting state banquets in Beijing and Shanghai, Li He (born in 1916), also from Shunde, was becoming the authentic “Cantonese Cuisine Champion” in Guangzhou. He created two signature dishes for Beiyuan Restaurant: Clay Pot Huadiao Chicken and Suburban Fish Head. Suburban Fish Head was originally a traditional home-cooked famous dish. Li He replaced the tofu with Shunde specialty food fish curd and made slight adjustments in cooking, immediately elevating it to a high-end level. These two signature dishes are just representatives of the nearly 3,000 dishes created by Li He; and 3,000 dishes are a concentrated reflection of “Shunde Stir-Fries.” Li He joined the “Top Ten Famous Chefs in Guangzhou” in the 1950s and participated in the national culinary competition as the chief chef of Guangdong, winning the title of “National Excellent Chef”.

While Li He was the "Champion" in Guangzhou, another Shunde-born chef, Liang Jing (born in 1913), was competing for the "Champion" in Hong Kong. Liang Jing was born in Chencun Zhongxing Flower Feast Hall and was best at high-end "skilled dishes" such as abalone, sea cucumber, and shark fin. When he went to Jinling Restaurant in Hong Kong, he quickly earned the nickname "Jin Shui Jing". His creation "Almond Juice Stewed White Lung" was praised by Ouyang Yingji in Hong Kong Flavor as "a first-class best in stewed soup", which can be called "jade liquid and fine wine"! By the 1980s, he was respected as the head of the "Top Ten Famous Chefs in Hong Kong", a veritable "Champion".

Huadiao chicken

If Shunde strongly supported "Eating in Guangzhou" with its chefs, Foshan "contributed" with its bosses. With the northward shift of the trade center due to the establishment of five ports (Guangzhou, Fuzhou, Xiamen, Ningbo, and Shanghai), Foshan and Shunde were more impacted than

Guangzhou, the central city. Guangzhou, as the central city, instead produced a certain siphon effect, not only attracting some chefs from Shunde but also absorbing some capital from Foshan. The old master Feng Mingquan said that during the Xianfeng and Tongzhi periods, although Cantonese people attached great importance to drinking tea, commercial high-end teahouses were rare, and most were small teahouses with brick-wood structures. Therefore, they were not called "buildings" but "residences." It was not until Foshan's commercial status declined and commercial capital poured into Guangzhou in large numbers, with a considerable part invested in the food industry they were familiar with, that a number of three-story spacious teahouses were built, and Guangzhou truly entered the era of teahouses. "The rich go upstairs, and the poor squat downstairs" also became a popular saying at that time.

The Foshan Gang has made great contributions to the development of Guangzhou's food culture, and most of the main old teahouse brands inherited till now were also founded by them. Two main figures, Tan Xinyi and Tan Qingbo, were veritable two generations of teahouse kings. The signs of Foshan Gang teahouses liked to use the character "Ru" because of its good meaning. At most, there were more than ten, such as Dongru, Xiru, Nanru, Tairu, Huiru, Duoru, Sanru, Wuru, Jiuru, Tianru, Ruiru, Furu, Baoru, etc. Among them, Xiru, Dongru, Nanru, Wuru, Sanru, Tairu, and Huiru were all founded or participated in by Tan Xinyi. In addition, he also owned Mingzhen, Hexin, Jinjiang (Chengjiang), and Lianxianglou, which was truly a teahouse king. In 1908, Tan Xinyi, who already owned several teahouses such as Xiru Teahouse, Huiru Tower, and Tairu Tower, in order to seek greater development, together with Tan Qingbo and others, raised 12,420 taels at once, and purchased Lianxiang Tea and Fruit Shop, which mainly operated sacrificial and wedding return gift foods such as sponge cake, fried dough balls, Dafa, red envelopes, and xiangtang. He also purchased more than 350 square meters of adjacent real estate, all of which were demolished and rebuilt into Lianxianglou. “Lotus flavor is fresh and fragrant, and it is not hot all day when evaluating tea; the fragrant wind is sent far, and whose cooking cake is round under the moon.” The sign of Lianxianglou still stands today.

2.3 Grand Historian’s Food Style and “Eating in Guangzhou”

The formation of a cuisine is akin to the creation of a mountain: it requires top restaurants and their representative figures as the peak, as well as a solid and broad foundation to sustain its grandeur. If the economic development of Guangdong in the Ming and Qing dynasties and Shunde chefs are regarded as representatives of the foundation, then Tan Family Cuisine in Beijing, Grand Historian Cuisine in Guangdong, and the later Four Great Restaurants can be seen as the mountain and its summit. In fact, in Guangzhou during the late Qing and early Republic of China, there were two “Grand Historians” renowned for both poetry and cuisine: Liang Dingfen (Jie’an) earlier, and Jiang Kongyin later. Although Jiang Kongyin enjoys a more prominent reputation in culinary history, Liang Dingfen was no less accomplished—only his fame for integrity and loyalty overshadowed his culinary legacy. Jiang Kongyin's Grand Historian Snake Soup and other dishes have been widely discussed, so the focus here is on the Liang Grand Historian's culinary style.

In the summer of 1911, at the age of 53, Liang Dingfen gathered with colleagues for a banquet at Yanhulou in Kongyuan. He later left a manuscript titled *The Essence of Dining and Revelry at Nengxiu Jinglu*, documented in Mr. Wu Tianren's *Chronology of Liang Dingfen*, detailing ingredients and the principles of seasonal tableware:

Liang Dingfen

Four Fresh Fruits

All should be firm, large, fragrant, and clean, not sliced, served on fine porcelain plates.

Two Seasonal Staples

Like lychees at this time—carefully selected for uniformity in size and roundness. While available to all, ours must excel—this should be the standard for all matters.

Two kinds of New Produce

Such as peaches (original note: pointed beak) and lotus roots (original note: pure white).

This is the primary principle for a grand feast; the host should pay close attention.

Eight Surrounding Dishes

In summer: six vegetarian dishes, two meat dishes; in winter: six meat dishes, two vegetarian dishes; spring and autumn: three meat dishes and three vegetarian dishes. This is a general guideline, not restricted by specific dishes (original note: it is borrowed from *Han Shu*).

In thirty years of banqueting, the surrounding dishes at Miao Xiaoshan's were unrivaled. Their excellence lay in artistic charm, scholarly ambiance, rustic appeal, and floral fragrance—hence their perfection.

Ham Prohibited

If Mr. Li Liuan is present, use it for his preference. However, ham is a mundane ingredient; if used, select the finest from Xuanwei and Jinhua, stew in good Shaoxing wine until tender but not mushy, and cut into slices equal to the number of guests. Consuming it promptly demonstrates the host's prestige.

Use fine porcelain for surrounding dishes; if the host lacks it, borrow or pool funds to purchase.

Shark's Fin

In summer: clear stew, served in red-green bowls; in winter: braised, served in plain bowls. Braising is easier than clear stewing—hosts should gauge their ability. If unsure, use braising in summer for reliability. Select ingredients a day in advance, requiring both quantity and quality. The saying "quality over quantity" does not apply here—mediocre ingredients are acceptable, but quality without quantity is not. Why? Mediocre food can be ignored, but quality in short supply halts the feast abruptly, like a beauty departing too soon or a garden's fragrance fading—deeply disappointing. Sufficient shark's fin inspires guests like a phoenix or unicorn, inspiring mythical beasts (original note: Kongyuan's shark's fin is fine but insufficient).

Use large bowls

Different styles and colors are ideal; funds can be pooled to store them in Kongyuan. Medium bowls prohibited: for over six guests, medium bowls leave no soup after two servings—Kongyuan's past practice resembled "clear ripples revealing the bottom." Small bowls are even worse.

Dishes are too many to list; here are a few:

Mountain Soft-Shell Turtle and River Fish (original note: exquisite)

Prepare clear or braised based on shark's fin—contrasting styles like rigidity and flexibility in affairs, or richness and subtlety in poetry. Omit if the host does not eat it.

Fish Lips (original note: exquisite)

Prepared like shark's fin—choose one in summer, both in winter.

Fish Maw (original note: exquisite)

Suitable for all seasons; a top dish in our hometown.

Crab Soup with Fresh Lotus Seeds or Shrimp with Fresh Lotus (original note: marketable)

No issue with repeated use or large portions.

Fresh Water Chestnuts, Premium Winter Mushrooms, Fresh Bamboo

All excel in summer; use selectively or altogether.

Duck Feet (original note: goose throat and "ladder")

Ordinary, but a favorite of the elderly—serve as with ham for Mr. Li Liuan. Never tire of them, like Du Fu's love for the yellow croaker. Rare in Hubei, only four or five servings if available.

Vegetables

Cook with excellent chicken soup, absorbing all flavor without excess juice—a signature dish of the Minister. Serve on large fine porcelain plates, widely applicable.

Balance emptiness with substance (original note: braised dishes). The host, like a painter, needs no advice on arrangement.

Roast Suckling Pig Prohibited

Rare at Hubei banquets, and subpar when available—Kongyuan's exception was excellent. This dish reeks of officialdom and is costly; avoided unless in mid-winter.

Wine

The host should prepare and taste it a day in advance—it is the banquet's lifeblood. Use elegant and varied wine vessels. Serve personal collections or borrow from wine connoisseurs—buying from markets is a last resort. If subpar, the host first drinks ten cups of inferior wine as punishment, with repeat offenders forfeiting hosting duties.

Tea

Everyone knows the importance of wine, but few realize that tea is equally crucial. Prepare it as wine, and use similar utensils. Place a teapot on the table with several fine porcelain cups for drunk guests to pour themselves.

Also, set a covered cup for each person: lifting the lid reveals clear, dust-free water with tiny tea buds floating—such a sight elevates mood and ensures a joyful day. Kongyuan's Longjing tea is excellent.

By the window, casually place one or two vases of flowers and several types of melons and fruits. Outside the railing, set basins of well water for washing hands.

Dim Sum

Like the keyword in a poem or the core of an essay, never overlook dim sum for its size.

Salty: Too many to list; flour-wrapped ones are top-grade. Lu Family's are exquisite, comparable to Kong Family's. The two times I ate at Yanhulou are unforgettable.

Sweet: Too many to list; watermelon cake is top-grade. Cantonese red melon is inferior, but its fresh color makes elegant cakes when served on a white porcelain plate—what Lu Shiheng called "refined beauty".

Soups: Small bowls are prohibited for both types.

Steamed rice and dishes: Tofu soup, served in large bowls, add sliced meat, straw mushrooms, and shrimp.

Four dishes: use 7-inch plates, not 5-inch. Include greens, salted fish, and scrambled eggs. One such dish is flexible.

Two more vegetarian soups: choose one from melon, lotus root, bamboo shoots, or dried vegetables.

Four final dishes prohibited: Said to be like provisional officials, the most obnoxious. Public opinion agrees. No one defends them. As Lu You wrote, "No thing lasts like public opinion"—truer than true!

Rice: White and soft.

Congee: Clear and fragrant, served in bowls larger than rice bowls. Add mung beans in summer, served separately.

This special menu reveals the high standards of late Qing Lingnan cuisine, so memorable that Jiang Kongyin composed a long poem after reading it:

"The Essence of Dining and Revelry at Nengxiu Jinglu, written by Liang Wenzhong of Yushan. Among friends, I'd heard snippets but regretted not seeing the whole. General Feng Zhunwan found it by chance and showed it to me. The calligraphy is exquisite, the opinions bold—evident of the author's spirited writing before his illness. It's truly a masterpiece. I composed five quatrains and returned them with this postscript:

'Since Su Dongpo, Hong Beijiang's summer recipes are added to Cantonese greens. After the exile at Stanley annotated it, a year's incense honors Liang's beard.' (Note: Last winter, I inscribed Hong Beijiang's summer menu for Cai Zhefu in Hong Kong.)

'At Xuannan's funeral for Zhang Nanpi, we shared a rainy room. No more Yu Huiruo bringing shark's fin, nor Duan Wuqiao's Huangmi Hu tong feasts—all gone, leaving melancholy.' (Note: In 1909, I was summoned to Beijing, coinciding with Liang's visit to Zhang Nanpi's funeral. We lived at Yuantong Temple, where Yu Huiruo brought shark's fin by rickshaw, and Duan Wuqiao joined from Huangmi Alley. All old friends are gone.)

'Recalling lychees at Lianggezhuang—returning to enjoy them is impossible. The "thirsty dragon, hungry tiger" vividly depicts feasts at Lanzhai.' (Note: After returning south, Liang visited Lanzhai monthly and asked us to plant more lychees before leaving.)

'A lifetime exiled, only "jade congee" pleased; the poet ate yellow croaker daily. These Nengxiu Jinglu pages are worth more than He Zeng's books.'

'A generation's essayist, shark's fin, and braised fish head were your loves. None but I can tell tales of these dashing seniors.'

—Written by Jiang Kongyin of Nanhai at Xiaobai'er Lanzhai, five days after the Mid-Autumn Festival in Dingmao year (1927).

Years later, Ye Gongchuo, a Guangdong native and representative of the Republic of China era's Transportation Faction, also composed a poem with an elaborate preface:

"This manual reveals elegance in eating—your refined appetite knows no bounds. Indulgence isn't vice; hunger drives profound exploration. An old man craves hometown flavors, yet dining reflects statecraft. Looking back at humble meals, I revisit past feasts. Inscribed on Liang Jiezang's *Essence of Dining and Revelry* manuscript. At Mr. Zhunwan's request, I note this was written during the Xuantong era. It shows how, amid frustration, he amused himself like Su Dongpo crossing the mountains, not merely about food. His boldness leaps from the page, making this a precious local record. My family has known him for three generations: I can't match his writing or integrity, nor his dining prowess. When he invited me to Wuchang, he worried I ate too little, though not vegetarian, I ate poorly and couldn't drink, always making him frown. Nearly forty years later, I recall this with sadness.

—Written by Ye Gongchuo in the summer of the 30th year of the Republic of China era (1941).

Roast suckling pig

Liang Dingfen not only left behind this precious recipe but also many food anecdotes, which are enough to shine a light on Lingnan cuisine. In *Roast Pork and Suckling Pig*, Mr. Tang Lusun said, "Grand Historian Liang Dingfen was famous for his love of good food. He had a signature dish, 'Grand Historian Frog', which he taught to Yulaochun on Huiai Street in Guangzhou. This small restaurant with only three to five tables actually became a grand restaurant with carved beams and painted walls within a few years." The transformation of Yulaochun can reflect the influence of Grand Historian Liang's frog dish among the citizens, which was at least no less than that of Grand Historian Jiang's frog dish. Not only frog dishes, but Liang also had unique secrets for roast suckling pig, one of the most characteristic dishes in Lingnan. Mr. Tang said, "There was a small restaurant called Mo Ji in Huangli Alley, Guangzhou, which knew that the sauce and garlic used in Grand Historian Liang's family for roast suckling pig had special secrets." The owner of this restaurant, Mo Youzhu, was originally an elegant person, so he "used a large box of purple and red eight-treasure ink paste from his collection" to learn this secret recipe from Grand Historian Liang, and since then, he has become famous in Guangzhou for his roast suckling pig. It seems that Grand Historian Liang's dishes were not only delicious but also had a tradition of "entering the market". I'm afraid the popularity of "Grand Historian Frog" back then was more influenced by the Liang family. Mr. Tang Lusun also said that the best roast suckling pig in Beiping was also a secret recipe of Liang Dingfen. "Later, the Liang family passed the secret recipe for roast suckling pig to Da Geng, the chef of Kuai Ruomu's family. Kuai lived on Cuihua Street in Beiping. Da Geng's method of roasting suckling pig was no different from the general method, but when you chewed it, it was as crispy as fried shrimp chips, which was indeed unique. Master Kuai was also very proud of this."

All these not only show the Grand Historian style of Guangdong cuisine but also the inheritance of the elegance of Guangdong cuisine.

2.4 The Origin of "Eating in Guangzhou" and Foreign Cuisine

The formation of "Eating in Guangzhou" depends not only on the ingredients from all over the world brought by "Going to Guangzhou" but also on the integration of various regional cuisines brought by "Going to Guangzhou." Xian Guansheng, a Foshan native and food tycoon of the Republic of China era, once wrote that Guangzhou is the political and economic hub of Guangdong Province. Most of the officials who have worked there have always brought their hometown chefs to satisfy their appetites. However, since being an official is not a lifelong career, once they are dismissed and go elsewhere, most of their chefs stay in Guangzhou, opening restaurants or working as chefs in restaurants to make a living. Then he described the origin of Guangzhou cuisine from other provinces: roasted duck and oil chicken are Nanjing-style, fried eight pieces and chicken soup with stuffed stomach are Beiping-style, fried chicken slices and fried shrimp are Jiangsu-style, spicy chicken and Sichuan-style braised fish are Hubei-style, dry-braised abalone and barbecued Yunnan ham are Sichuan-style, fragrant wine fish balls and dried vegetable steamed meat are Shaoxing-style, and there are also Yangzhou-style soup dumplings and shumai in dim sum. In short, "collecting famous dishes from all over the country to form a new Guangdong cuisine shows that 'eating' in Guangzhou is not groundless." (Xian Guansheng, *Research on Guangzhou Cuisine and Dim Sum*, *Food Industry*, No. 2, 1933)

1. The Suzhou Branch of "Eating in Guangzhou"

Jiangnan culture, especially Suzhou and Huaiyang cuisine, has a profound influence on Lingnan culture, especially "Eating in Guangzhou".

In the fifth issue of *Yue Feng* in 1935, there is an article by Gang Sou, *Pearl River Memoirs* (VI) *Food Trivia* (Continued), which talks about the changes in the cooking of shark's fin in Guangdong. It is believed that "the shark's fin cooked in Suzhou restaurants in Guangzhou in the past" all used cooked shark's fin. It was not until a Chaozhou-born official chef surnamed Chen came out that he reformed it into the later popular raw shark's fin cooking method. As a result, "Chef Chen became famous. In official circles, when hosting guests, they would not be happy or show respect unless they declared that they relied on Chef Chen for help." When the host was transferred to another place, he "used his savings to open Yantang Winery on Weibian Street... and official circles flocked to it for socializing." "Later, Tongxingju, Yipinsheng, Guilian Sheng, etc., followed suit." This proves its seniority and just explains the relationship between "Eating in Guangzhou" and Suzhou flavor, because the author also specially emphasized that Chef Chen's Yantang did not "join the Suzhou restaurant trade association." In addition, the previous mention that Suzhou restaurants in Guangzhou all cooked shark's fin maturely shows how much influence Suzhou restaurants had in Guangzhou to establish a "trade association." Before that, the later well-known local famous restaurants in Guangzhou, such as Yipinsheng, especially Guiliansheng, which was famous for shark's fin, had not "come out." From this, it can be inferred that even before the Tongzhi and Guangxu periods, even if there was a reputation of "Eating in Guangzhou", Suzhou restaurants were in power. It was not until after the middle of the Guangxu period that "Taihe Restaurant and Wenyuan in Xiguan rose to compete... Guiliansheng's cooking was excellent and popular for a time."

Shark fin soup

Today, people believe that the most famous person who thinks that "Eating in Guangzhou" is deeply influenced by Suzhou and Huaiyang flavors is Mr. Tang Lusun. In *Unforgettable Tan Family Cuisine*, he said that Tan Yankqing, the owner of the famous Tan Family Cuisine, originally used a chef.

He employed Tao San, a former chef at Yang Shixiang's residence in Xuyi, Jiangsu, whose skills were exceptional. For long-term purposes, he asked his concubine, Zhao Fengli, to learn cooking skills undercover in the kitchen every day under the pretense of assisting. Additionally, his sister Tan Zupei married Chen Gongmu, the grandson of Chen Li, a Lingnan Confucian scholar from an affluent family with profound knowledge of cuisine. She became a female culinary expert and carefully taught her sister-in-law. Thus, Zhao Fengli "combined the culinary arts of Lingnan and Huaiyang, "finally creating Tan Family Cuisine, which is based on Huaiyang cuisine and incorporates Lingnan Chen family techniques, symbolizing "Eating in Guangzhou."

Closer to modern times, memories of old Guangzhou further confirm this. As Feng Han et al. stated in *Guangzhou's Grand Restaurants*, there used to be "grand restaurants, "also known as banquet contractors, with a history of over a hundred years. By the late Qing Dynasty, eight representative restaurants emerged, including Juxin, Guanzhen, Pinrongsheng, Nanyangtang, Yulaochun, Yuansheng, Bazhen, and Xinruihe, all "affiliated with the 'Suzhou Restaurant' organization, mainly serving officials and politicians by contracting banquets." During their heyday in the 1920s-1930s, there were over 100 such restaurants in the city, mostly concentrated in Xiguan, Guangzhou's prosperous area, demonstrating the influence and lingering charm of "Suzhou Restaurants."

Chen Pei, a senior in Guangzhou's food industry, wrote in *Northern Flavors in Guangzhou*, "Yuexiangcun on Hanmin Road (now Beijing Road) and Jufengyuan Restaurant on Yuehua Road operated Suzhou-style food" (*Historical Stories of Eating in Guangzhou*, 41st Volume of *Guangzhou Cultural and Historical Materials*). Jufengyuan was a model of poetic and culinary elegance for Suzhou restaurants during the Republic of China era. After Tan YanKai, the "Gourmet God" of the Republic of China era, dined there, he praised it highly and asked his renowned private chef, Cao Si, to learn and replicate the dishes on the spot, still commending them in his diary:

> April 8, 1924 (March 5th): Crossed the sea with Danfu to the Provincial Governor's Office, met Xiao and Wu, who invited us to Jufengyuan for soup dumplings, other dim sum, and fried sauce noodles, costing 3-4 yuan, paid by Danfu.
>
> June 17, 1926 (May 8th): Ate sesame cakes with Damao, made by Chef Cao imitating Jufengyuan—one salty, one sweet, similar enough that I skipped rice.

Tan Yankai

Regarding the influence of Suzhou-Huaiyang cuisine on "Eating in Guangzhou, "another evidence can be found. For example, during the Republic of China era, Guangzhou's department store industry dominated the country. Although Shanghai's four major department stores emerged later, they can be seen as Shanghai branches of Guangzhou's four major ones. Few know that Guangzhou's department stores were previously called "Suzhou-Hangzhou Sundries"! Why? Since the Southern Song Dynasty, Suzhou and Hangzhou had "prosperous populations, with merchant transactions ten times those of the past," and markets operated day and night. Hangzhou was known as "skilled in craftsmanship, clothing the world." With Guangzhou's single-port trade, goods from Suzhou and Hangzhou flocked south, leading to the saying "Going to Guangzhou," and thus "Suzhou-Hangzhou Sundries" emerged. Interestingly, after foreign goods became popular in China, and with Guangzhou's various products—stimulated by foreign trade—being sold nationwide, inland general stores were called "Guangdong-Foreign (Foreign-Guangdong) Grocery Stores" or "Guangdong Goods Stores." This mirrors how Lingnan cuisine, after fully absorbing foreign elements, formed "Eating in Guangzhou" and spread nationwide.

2. Northern Official Chefs and "Eating in Guangzhou"

Chen Pei's *Northern Flavors in Guangzhou* argues that Guangzhou's northern cuisine originated from official chefs brought by northern officials. Some of these private chefs settled in Guangzhou instead of following officials, opening restaurants that not only spread northern or foreign cuisines in Guangzhou but also significantly influenced the formation and development of "Eating in Guangzhou." Early renowned restaurants like Guiliansheng, Nanyangtang, and Yipinsheng were all run by official chefs, long before "Eating in Guangzhou" gained its reputation.

Contemporaries also discussed the influence of official chefs on the formation of "Eating in Guangzhou," though modern people often overlook it:

> "Eating in Guangzhou" has long been famous. Cantonese chefs, talented and numerous—official chefs, private chefs, restaurant chefs—compete to innovate. So-called Cantonese chefs actually possess the ability to master all flavors. Whether Huaiyang, Suzhou-Wuxi, Sichuan, Fujian, Yan-Lu (Shandong), Manchu-Han, or European-American dishes, they have refined skills in seasoning, thus excelling and gaining global fame. As Guangzhou is the birthplace, there are many food connoisseurs, creating a mutual promotion that has made it a culinary giant. For example, banquets at Zhang Mingqi's, the Viceroy's residence, were luxurious and renowned, producing famous chefs—even titled "kitchen officials"—due to their extensive experience and diverse tastes, making them all-around talents of the time.

This not only emphasizes the influence of official chefs but also highlights Cantonese cuisine's characteristic of inclusiveness and absorbing the best from all. Take the famous official chef Feng Tang as an example:

> Feng Tang entered the Viceroy's kitchen in his childhood and worked there for many years. When he reached adulthood, he even presided over banquet dish innovation. Later, he joined Guiliansheng Restaurant in Guangzhou, creating dishes mostly based on the Viceroy's

secret recipes, which made him famous for a time. Thereafter, restaurants competed to hire him, and he was soon employed by Yuenan Restaurant in Shanghai. Gentry and merchants, after tasting his stir-fries, found them extraordinary, and he quickly became renowned in Shanghai. In recent years, he has been in charge of the kitchen at the Peacock Hall of the International Hotel. Dongya Youyilou, founded by food enthusiasts like Zhang Xiangnong and Wu Quansheng, often invited him to cook, and he was handsomely paid. Diners felt at home, and during grand banquets, Feng Tang would always wash his hands and cook personally.

香港
新華大飯店

An advertisement for Hong Kong Xinhua Grand Hotel

In fact, Feng Tang's status as a high-ranking official chef stemmed from the essence of Cantonese cuisine:

The essence of Cantonese cuisine lies in its ability to cater to all tastes and adapt to local conditions, of which Feng Tang was a master. His fame for stir-fries came from understanding diners' preferences. After banquets, he would often eavesdrop behind the curtain: only when diners finished his dishes would he leave happily; if they lost their appetite, he would ask the host for feedback on saltiness and gather criticisms to improve overnight, showing humility and professional demeanor. No wonder Youyilou is always full, attracted by Feng Tang, the last remaining official chef. It is a blessing for Shanghai food lovers. (New Foodie, *Gossip on Cantonese Cuisine: The Last Remnant of Official Chef Flavor, Star-Studded at Youyilou, Happy Forest*, Issue 16, 1946)

3. Sichuan Restaurants in Guangdong and Hong Kong during the Republic of China era

As China's largest commercial metropolis with a diverse population, Shanghai, sharing the Yangtze River with Sichuan, naturally embraced Sichuan cuisine. In fact, Sichuan restaurants were also common elsewhere, especially in Hong Kong, where they became "the most fashionable dishes"—a surprise to many. Even Guangzhou, seemingly least compatible with Sichuan cuisine, had early and enduring Sichuan restaurants. As early as 1936, Professor Huang Jiyu recorded in his diary:

> September 27: I went to "Jinjiangchun," a Sichuan restaurant, at noon. Qiu Laofu and Dong Dafu came to drink together, and Yan Hua also entered this small eatery... The couplet at "Jinjiangchun" reads,

"Jinli wine first fragrances, should share thousand tubes of Pi bamboo to Lingnan; Jiangnan spring is perfect. May a plum blossom song be sung before the wine." Signed by Dan Maoxin (a Sichuan native).

By the end of the Republic of China era, *Guangzhou Grand View,* published by Tiannan Press in 1948, mentioned several Sichuan restaurants, "Guangzhou's banquet venues, besides some Western restaurants, are mostly Cantonese. However, there are also many Hakka, Sichuan, Jiangsu-Zhejiang, Muslim, and vegetarian restaurants." Among them, Banzhai Sichuan Restaurant at No. 7 Zhonghua North Road and another at No. 10 Xidi Erma Road are confirmed. Especially Banzhai's advertisement, "Visit Banzhai Sichuan Restaurant, a decades-old brand with good taste and fair prices, suitable for group banquets or casual dining, with spacious surroundings and attentive service," demonstrating Sichuan cuisine's long history in Guangzhou. The Dongpo Restaurant's advertisement promoting signature dishes like "Clay Pot Braised Seafood, Sichuan Fried Shrimp and Crab, Dongpo Phoenix Marrow Duck" shows that Sichuan cuisine has won Guangzhou diners' hearts, regardless of the restaurant's origin.

Although Guangdong and Hong Kong are closely linked, Hong Kong, much smaller in area and population, has far more Sichuan restaurants with greater influence than Guangzhou, which is surprising. As early as the 1938 *Hong Kong Guide* published by The Commercial Press, three Sichuan restaurants were introduced: Dahua Hotel, Shuzhen Sichuan Cuisine, and

Guiyuan Sichuan Restaurant. *Greater Hong Kong,* published by Hong Kong Travel Agency in 1941, listed more: in Wan Chai, the Sichuan Cuisine Departments of Yingjing Restaurant and Liuguo Hotel; in Central, Dahua Hotel on the 9th floor of Huaren Building and Yuanlai Restaurant on Des Voeux Road; in Yau Ma Tei, Guiyuan Sichuan Restaurant and the Sichuan Cuisine Department on the 5th floor of Nathan Hotel. An advertisement for Xinhua Grand Hotel stated, "Hong Kong's standard Sichuan restaurant, noble and luxurious, second to none, the best social venue, "reflecting Sichuan cuisine's prestigious status in Hong Kong. In fact, the famous *Travel Magazine* carried a similar advertisement for Xinhua Grand Hotel in its November 1938 issue. As for dishes, "famous ones like Yulan slices, spicy chicken, fried lamb slices, curry shrimp, fried pheasant slices, shrimp with bamboo shoots, and white-braised fish—even ordinary fried chicken is more tender than elsewhere," and "like Cantonese cuisine, they offer clear stewed tonics, "with "caterpillar fungus stewed chicken being unparalleled." It's said that "these cater to Jiangsu and Zhejiang travelers, but many Cantonese also patronize, "which is puzzling. The claim that "due to the domestic war, many northerners have come to Hong Kong, so Sichuan cuisine holds an important place in their diet" doesn't seem entirely accurate.

The above "Guiyuan Restaurant" should be "Guiyuan Restaurant". The success and expansion of Guiyuan Restaurant typically and subtly reflected the popularity of Sichuan cuisine in Hong Kong. At that time, the *Hong Kong Commercial Daily* (Issue 169, 1941) directly titled the exclusive interview with Mao Kangji, the manager of Guiyuan Restaurant, as The Change of *Hong Kong People's Taste: Sichuan Cuisine Has Become the Most Fashionable Dish in Chinese Cuisine: Mao Kangji's Discussion on Cuisine*. The interview originated from Guiyuan's merger with the well-known Cantonese restaurant, the internal restaurant of Kowloon Sihao Hotel. The reason why Sihao Hotel introduced Guiyuan was "completely to cater to the current needs of Hong Kong society", because due to the war, the number of people from other provinces coming to or passing through Hong Kong had been increasing day by day in recent years. Cantonese cuisine, which only suited the taste of Cantonese people, was no longer very suitable for the current needs of Hong Kong society. Since it could suit the tastes of people from many provinces, Sichuan cuisine "became the most popular dish."

Zheng Baohong's *A Hundred Years of Hong Kong's Chinese and Foreign Industries: Food and Entertainment* states, "Since the 1950s, the development of restaurants has entered a golden period. Due to a large number of people from different provinces on the mainland moving to Hong Kong, a large number of Beijing, Tianjin, Shanghai, Sichuan, and Cantonese restaurants opened in various districts of Hong Kong and Kowloon." Therefore, it is also a matter of course that foreign restaurants continued to develop in Hong Kong, and more independently. However, due to Hong Kong's long-term relative isolation from the mainland, relevant historical materials are difficult to find. Special books like *A Hundred Years of Hong Kong's Chinese and Foreign Industries: Food and Entertainment* do not mention them. Ye Lingfeng, however, recorded in his diary the situations of his two visits to Sichuan restaurants on March 20 and July 10, 1970.

4. Foreign Restaurants in Hong Kong

When tracing and discussing foreign restaurants in Hong Kong other than Sichuan restaurants, Ye Lingfeng's diary still provides the primary information: the first he mentioned was Fulu Shou Tea House (Beijing restaurant) on July 5, 1947. This tea house (restaurant) was founded by Zhang Guangyu, the art director of *Star Island Daily* and a famous cartoonist, and his younger brother Zhang Zhengyu, with Zhang Guangyu serving as the manager. According to Mr. Huang Miaozi's oral account, this store was a liaison station for the Communist Party of China in Hong Kong.

The second mentioned was the "Meilijian" Shandong restaurant on September 10, 1949: "Went to Meilijian Restaurant for a small drink with Miao Xiu." Thereafter, he patronized this Shandong restaurant countless times until the end of 1973, more than a year before his death (he died in 1975), with records still in his diary. For example, on March 2, 1973, he said, "Had dinner with Luo, Huang, Yuan, Yan, etc. at New Meilijian tonight. This kind of dinner has been held 99 times so far, and the next time will be the 100th." If all were recorded, it would be impossible to count. As a native of Nanjing, his love for Shandong cuisine is also an oddity.

There were two other northern restaurants he often visited, such as the Tianjin-style Haijinglou and the small Liuxiangguan. In addition, he occasionally patronized Fengzelou. According to Professor Xie Zhengguang, after he was admitted to New Asia College in 1960, he found that Mr. Mou Runsun, a generation of famous teachers, opened his residence every Friday afternoon to welcome students to visit. After the conversation covering various topics, it was a tradition to treat students to dinner at the nearby "Fengzeyuan" Beijing restaurant. Why go to Fengzeyuan? There is a story behind it. As early as in 1954, when Mou Runsun accepted Qian Mu's invitation to transfer from National Taiwan University to serve as the Director of the Department of Literature and History of New Asia College, Tutor of the New Asia Institute, and Librarian, as soon as he went to this restaurant and ordered "stir-fried shrimp with snow peas", after tasting it, he said to the waiter, "Only one person can cook this snow pea and shrimp so well. Quickly invite him out of the kitchen." After meeting for a long time, they hugged each other and wept bitterly. It turned out that the cook was named Alai, a family cook from his hometown of Fushan, Shandong. They fled separately in 1948, one to Taiwan and the other to Hong Kong. After nine years of separation, master and servant met again, and how could they not cry with joy! (Xie Zhengguang, *Remembering My Teacher Mr. Mou Runsun and His Disciples*, *Southern Weekend*, November 5, 2020)

Ye Lingfeng

However, interestingly, as a native of Nanjing, Ye Lingfeng left so many records of northern restaurants in his diary, but only a few records of southern restaurants, which are particularly precious:

> March 3, 1951: I went to Kowloon to watch Zhang Junqiu's play... After the play, Zhang invited me to dinner at the Jiangsu Hotel.
>
> March 17, 1951: I watched *The Story of Horse Trading,* co-starred by Zhang Junqiu, Yu Zhenfei, and Ma Lianliang... After the play, President Lin and his wife invited Zhang Junqiu and me to dinner at Lv Yang Cun.
>
> April 5, 1951: I went to the newspaper office. Zhang Junqiu visited President Lin to discuss the publication of a special issue. President Lin invited us to Jiabin to eat Fuzhou food. The red vinasse chicken and multi-layer lard cake were very good (Note: Jiabin refers to Fujian Jiabin

Restaurant, located at 374 King's Road, Hong Kong).

January 16, 1968: I ate noodles and soup dumplings at Laozhengxing, a Shanghai restaurant. The taste was good.

Appendix: Weng Tonghe's Lingnan Culinary Ties and Tan YanKai's Love for Cantonese Lychees

Weng Tonghe, a "top scholar of the emperor" (champion of the Xianfeng era) and teacher to two emperors (Tongzhi and Guangxu), served as Minister of Justice, Minister of Works, Minister of Revenue, Minister of the General Affairs Office for Foreign Affairs, and Grand Councilor, wielding great power. He was close to Guangdong-born Beijing officials such as Li Wentian, Xu Yingkui, Zhang Yinhuan, and Ding Richang, admiring and respecting them. Before deepening his friendship with Li Wentian (courtesy name Ruonong), he wrote in his diary on May 6, 1860, "Li Ruanang, a compiler from Guangdong, composes grand and beautiful prose. I admire him as a prodigy." Later, they became sworn brothers, "(July 19, 1861) Li Ruonong Wentian and I pledged brotherhood." After inviting Li Wentian to check the feng shui of his residence on October 5, 1887, "I hosted him for dinner and talked at length; he knew much about Macau," leading Weng to praise, "A dominant talent!" Beyond literature and achievements, Weng admired Li's calligraphy and painting. In April 1893, when ordered to write the *Wanshou Temple Stele*, he couldn't, due to a sore arm, he "had Li Wentian write it instead, still using my name", which was a testament to his trust. For Zhang Yinhuan, a successful official through donations and foreign affairs who held a lower rank, though many in court despised him, Weng wrote in his diary, "(November 22, 1895) Zhang Qiaoye (Yinhuan) came for a long talk; his talent truly surpasses mine." Beyond foreign affairs, Weng respected his poetry, "(January 8, 1898) Read four poems by Zhang Qiaoye and Fan Yunmen, truly extraordinary talent." While Weng never directly commented on Zhang's paintings, the master painter Huang Binhong later praised, "Xu Songge and Zhang Qiaoye are excellent painters in the Qianlong and Jiaqing eras." For Xu Yingkui (ancestor of the Xu family on Gaodi Street, Guangzhou), Weng always respected him as a "senior", "(June 29, 1865) Assigned to compile foreign affairs documents with seniors Hu Xiaoquan, Ruilan, and Xu Yunyan Yingkui." "(July 16, 1883) Senior Xu Yingkui visited." Weng called them "Three Guangdong Friends". "(February 27, 1891) At 10 a.m., I attended a gathering hosted by the Three Guangdong Friends: Xu Yunan, Li Ruonong, and Zhang Qiaoye. Guests included Grand Councilors Nanpi and Gaoyang, Songge, and me." Additionally, he interacted frequently with Ding Richang, once praising through others, "(December 10, 1875) Guo Yunxian (Songtao) said only three men currently understand foreign affairs: Prime Minister Li, Shen Baozhen, and Ding Richang."

Weng was also associated with other Guangdong-born Beijing officials like Dèng Huaxi and Chen Lanbin; some even said he recommended Kang Yǒuwei. Once, he got off work early to host a banquet, and all guests were

Cantonese, "(February 18, 1891) Finished work at 12:30 p.m., rushed home to entertain guests—all from Guangdong: Li Shannong Zongdai, Xu Yunan Yingkui, Li Ruonong Wentian, Zhang Qiaoye Yinhuan, Liu Jingjie Shi'an, Weng Liaozhou Weilong." My friend Luo Tao believes Weng Tonghe was key to Guangdong's rise in late Qing politics. In China, dining and drinking symbolize friendship, evident in Weng's frequent banquets and overnight stays with Guangdong officials. Below are food-related entries from his diary:

Weng Tonghe

Zhang Yinhuan

The first record was on October 30, 1865, "Went to Xiancheng Guan (Guangdong Guild Hall in Wangpi Hutong) with Binshi; Li Ruonong invited us to eat fish sashimi. Waited long for Xu Renshan, Pan Boying, Xu Suwen. Seated with Sun Zishou and Guangdong natives Feng Zhongyu, Wang Mingsheng. The fish sashimi was delicious, unlike any I'd tasted." Li Wentian was from Shunde, where fishsashimi remains famous—unbeknownst to many, it delighted the emperor's teacher in Beijing a century ago. He later recorded two more fish sashimi meals at Li's, both memorable, "(November 9, 1880) Attended Li Ruonong's invitation, ate fish sashimi, got slightly drunk." "(November 13, 1891) Went to Li Ruonong's, had wonderful fish sashimi and exquisite dishes."

In those days, fish sashimi wasn't exclusive to Cantonese; coastal people might eat it. For example, he dined at Xu Shouhua's (Jiading, Shanghai; top scholar, Minister of War and Rites, Grand Academician), "(September 11, 1892) Went to Songge's for fish sashimi at 1 p.m.—not good." Comparison revealed the difference—how could it match Shunde's fish sashimi?

Shunde fish sashimi was so superior that others paled in comparison, though Nanhai natives might disagree—and Weng Tonghe likely concurred, "(November 16, 1892) At 10 a.m., attended Zhang Qiaoye's (from Nanhai, now Chancheng District) invitation with Qian Zimi, Xu Xiaoyun, Sun Xiechen, Xu Songge, Liao Zhongshan, and myself. The fish sashimi was exquisite; we enjoyed fine food, talked freely, and lingered until dusk." With Xu Shouheng present, he probably agreed. Weng also ate fish sashimi and fish sashimi congee at Zhang Yinhuan's, "(December 13, 1890) Visited Zhang Qiaoye for fish sashimi congee," a classic pairing in today's Cantonese morning tea.

Guangdong's cuisine and officials' skilled chefs inspired Weng to borrow Li Wentian's cook to entertain guests, boosting the fame of "Eating in Guangzhou." "(September 26, 1866) I invited Song Weidu, Pan Boyin, Zhang Wuqiao, Zhang Xiangtao, Li Ruonong for dinner, borrowing Ruonong's residence and chef." "(February 13, 1891) I hosted Mr. Sun and Southern Study colleagues; Ruonong oversaw the meal, finishing at 1 p.m." Besides Li Wentian's chef, he often enlisted Zhang Yinhuan's, though details are scarce.

Finally, a Lingnan culinary bond: lychees.

"(June 24, 1890) Prince Chun, Zhao Boyuan, Li Xingwu, Wang Liumen, Sun Zishou, Xu Yun'an gifted fresh lychees—Li gave the most." (July 8, 1892) Li Xingwu and Prince Qing sent lychees." "(July 11, 1894) Li Xinwu (eldest son of Li Hanzhang) and Prince Qing sent lychees." These were likely Guangdong lychees: Xu Yingkui was from Guangzhou, and Li Hanzhang (Li Xinwu's father) served as Viceroy of Guangdong and Guangxi, deeply tied to Guangdong.

In comparison, Tan YanKai, resident in Guangdong, documented his lychee love in detail.

A renowned food connoisseur, Tan YanKai was pivotal in establishing Hunan cuisine. His family's dishes endure, with deep Guangdong roots: in 1895, at 17, he accompanied his father (then Governor of Guangdong) and new wife to Guangzhou, where his eldest daughter was born in 1899. From 1923–1926, he served in Sun Yat-sen's government in Guangzhou, recording culinary gems—starting with lychees.

Tan's lychee journey began dreamily. On June 18, 1923 (Dragon Boat Festival), though he didn't note his first lychee, his post-dream poem hinted, "In exile, who knows the festival's beauty? Southern winds ripen red lychees. I long for home-cooked perch, while a foot-long shad accompanies rice dumplings." The next day, invited by Jiang Kongyin to Yanchuntai in Chentang, he wrote, "Ate lychees—small core, thick flesh, called Guiwei, better than usual." This showed he'd tasted lychees before.

The best lychees grew in his Dongshan Jianyuan residence (once a German consulate, now a heritage site). On June 21, 1923, he picked and ate garden lychees, "Better variety than market ones." The next day, he identified them as Guiwei and shared with Liao Zhongkai and Yuanzhu, who praised them.

Famed for his palate, Tan received premium lychees, even from Sun Yat-sen, "(June 24, 1893) At 7 a.m., the Grand Marshal returned from Shilong with Zengcheng lychees, better than Guiwei. Ate heartily, lamenting no Gualv." As Guiwei went out of season, "Ate lychees long—Guiwei gone, Heiye not good." Then Nuomici arrived, "(June 26, 1923) Jiang Xia (Jiang Kongyin's nickname) sent Nuomici; Huang Pan also gave Guiwei. Tasted both—Guiwei tasted best: sweet but not cloying, crisp but not tough, like longan but richer. Wonder how it compares to Gualv?"

Not satisfied with the freshness in the city, on June 27, 1923, he "invited (Jiang) Jieshi to take the Atlantic electric boat to Huangpu" and went to the hometown of his local colleague, Mr. Qimin. "In the lychee forest, there are countless fruits, allowing people to pick and eat. It is said that there are two varieties, Guiwei and Heiye, and Guiwei is still better. The Nuomici is not yet fully ripe, and when Huaili appears, the lychee season will end." It's a pity that "there was a fragrant lychee tree in Huangpu, which was better than Zengcheng Gualv, but it has now been exhausted, which is regrettable." Despite this regret, he still feasted while the lychee season was not over, "(June 26, 1923) Ate a lot of lychees. Recently, eating lychees every day, I realized that eating three hundred pieces is not difficult." More fortunately, he also ate the legendary "Gualv" gifted by the "Gourmet God" Jiang Kongyin. "(July 3, 1923) Jiang Xia sent lychees, saying they were Zengcheng Gualv. After eating them, I found they were between Guiwei and Heiye. The core is large and round, and the inside is crispy and tender, but the shell has no green marks, which is the same as what I ate in the Grand Command a few years ago. They may not be from the old tree." Zhongkai said that Gualv is produced by grafting lychee onto longan trees. The round core, thin skin, and small branches at the stem are all evidence which is probably close to the truth.

Everything has its limits. There is a saying that "eating too many lychees can cause excessive internal heat," and it was said at that time that it could also cause stroke. "(July 6, 1923) Cangbai said that newspapers reported lychee-induced stroke. It turns out that eating too many lychees can cause illness, which makes me cautious." Fortunately, the lychee season of that year was coming to an end, so there was no need to worry about lychee-induced stroke. The next year, the daily lychees were not worth recording, but when he visited Monk Tiechan in Liurong Temple, he heard about a kind of fragrant lychee in Zhaoqing, which was better than Gualv, "(June 6, 1924) Ate a plate of Heiye lychees. The monk said that the most delicious lychees are from a certain county in Zhaoqing. They almost have no core and were tributes in the late Qing Dynasty, better than Gualv, which I didn't know before. Shen Yangong also said that even those who are good at eating lychees can't accumulate a cup of cores when eating fragrant lychees, so you can imagine how small the cores are." This aroused Tan YanKai's appetite again!

Another year later, after eating lychees for two years, Tan YanKai began to evaluate local lychee varieties and even those from the whole country, "(May 18, 1925) I had dinner with Zhesheng, Tiesheng, and others. After dinner, I ate lychees. Guiwei is indeed the best. Ancient people said that Su Dongpo didn't know the goodness of Fujian lychees. Wang Jingwei said that when Zhu Zhuyu first came to Guangdong and ate lychees, they were Da Hebao and Dahongpao, and he lamented that they were far inferior to Fujian's. When he ate Heiye, he said they were just as good as Fujian's. Finally, when he ate Guiwei, he lamented that Fujian's couldn't compare. I don't know which book this comes from, but it can be seen that Fujian's lychees are inferior to Guangdong's, which is beyond doubt." He also wrote *Playful Reply to Wu Tiyun*, highly praising the beauty of lychees, "When the fruits are ripe in the thick shade of ten thousand trees, the flavor of the water village is unforgettable. Why bother with wine to lay down arms? I am planning to exchange my official position for lychees." Su Dongpo said, "Eating three hundred lychees a day, I would not mind being a Lingnan person forever. "Tan YanKai would even resign from his high official position for lychees. With such feelings, he deserved a reward! As expected, he soon ate the Xinxing lychees, which were the aforementioned Zhaoqing fragrant lychees, "(July 27, 1925) I tasted Xinxing County lychees, as small as longan, with plump flesh and small cores, slightly similar to Guiwei. It is said to be a good variety." At that time, Xinxing was a county under Zhaoqing Prefecture, and the production of fragrant lychees was recorded in history: "There is another variety as big as longan, also seedless, extremely fragrant, called Xiangli, produced in Xinxing. However, none are as good as Gualv." (Qu Dajun, *New Words of Guangdong*). Tan Ying, a famous Guangzhou scholar in the late Qing Dynasty who assisted Wu Chongyao, the richest man in the world at that time, in compiling and publishing the far-reaching large-scale documents *Lingnan Yishu* and *Yueya Tang Congshu*, and the father of Tan Zongjun, the founder of Beijing Tan Family Cuisine, who is as famous as Tan YanKai in the history of food and is known as the "Two Tans in the North and South", dedicated the fourteenth of his sixty *Lingnan Lychee Poems* to Xinxing Xiangli, "Xiangli has always been said to come from Xinxing, with jade-like and fat-like flesh that has never been seen before. The flower fragrance keeps assailing people, and it is even more pitifully clear like melting ice." This shows the historical fame of Xinxing Xiangli.

Guilv Lychee

In fact, why is Xinxing Xiangli not as good as Gualv? Ge Zuliang, a Jinshi (a successful candidate in the highest imperial examinations) in the first year of Qianlong and a deputy director of the Ministry of Households, praised in *Eating Xinxing County Lychees in Guangdong* after eating Xinxing Xiangli, "I once was given a basket of fresh lychees in my fairyland journey, and eating them was like drinking jade milk spring. The spiritual energy in the southeast connects with the sea and the sun, and the flavor of the nectar is as clear as shrimp. The purple and blue fruits hang like tame fire, and the crystal-clear flesh surpasses the dew lotus. (Zhang Jiuling's Fu, 'Purple veins and blue texture.' Su Dongpo's poem, 'Fiery clouds tame the fire fruits.') Laughing at the faraway red dust and clean riding, even Bai Juyi's paintings are empty." It means that after eating Xinxing lychees, there is no need to read Bai Juyi's *Lychee Picture* anymore, and Fujian lychees are not worth mentioning.

Lingnan cuisine emphasizes freshness, and lychees are no exception. Tan Yan Kai's perspective on lychees was the same. On the eve of his departure from Guangdong, he repeatedly noted, "(July 3, 1926) Hufang and Xu Da came, so we went to Lychee Bay... Entered Lixiang Garden, which was desolate and vulgar. The owner, Chen Huacun, was ridiculously uncouth, but he picked lychees from the trees to entertain guests, which were quite sweet and fragrant. However, fewer than one in a hundred trees had fruit; was it out of season? After leaving, we boarded a boat and bought lychees, which were not as good as those we had just eaten. Indeed, fresh fragrance is precious." On July 8, "I finally ate Guiwei lychees, which were indeed sweet and delicious. I deeply feared that Dawu would arrive too late." Arriving late, there were still lychees to eat, but they were no longer fresh. In the early Qing Dynasty, Qu Dajun said he had an excellent method to preserve lychees with honey, allowing fresh lychees to be eaten throughout the year, "And I have a method to store lychees: pick intact ones from the tree, leave about an inch of the stem, seal it with wax, then cut off the stem, seal the cut with wax again, and soak them in honey water. After several months, the taste and color remain unchanged. Thus, I can enjoy fresh lychees all year round, and could even live without grains because of them." However, Qu Dajun was not a generation of food gods after all, and his views should not be recognized by Tan Yan Kai. Although his younger brother Dawu returned to Guangdong late and did not directly taste fresh Guiwei lychees, Dawu should have tasted them in Hong Kong and thus approved Su Dongpo's statement that "lychees are like conpoy." "(August 9, 1926) Lv Man, Dawu, and Ximao returned from Hong Kong, saying that Dawu set sail at 5 p.m. yesterday and met Jiang Xia in Hong Kong, disturbing him for a banquet at Nantang Hotel. They also said that fresh conpoy was white, crispy, and delicious, greatly appreciated by Dawu, who believed that Su Dongpo's words comparing lychees to conpoy were not false. I remember having tasted it and also had this view, but I can't remember when it was in the diary."

In fact, whether it is fresh or not keeps pace with the times. In the past, lychees would change color in one day and lose their aroma and taste in three days. A few years after Tan Yan Kai left Guangdong, on July 5, 1930, he ate lychees sent by Hu Hanmin, a senior Guangdong-born member of the Kuomintang, in Nanjing. From Guangzhou to Nanjing, it took at least two or three days, but he still found them very fresh, saying, "Zhan Tang sent excellent lychees, no different from eating them in Guangzhou, "and was so excited that he "inscribed a note to repay him." This was not only due to improved transportation conditions, but also must have had other auxiliary preservation measures; unfortunately, relevant historical materials have not yet been seen.

Chapter 3 Westward Expedition and Northern Expedition: The Golden Age of "Eating in Guangzhou"

Since the single-port trade began in the Ming Dynasty, Lingnan, especially Guangzhou, has been the most prosperous and wealthy region in the world, and the prosperity of its cuisine is unparalleled. However, for a long time, its reputation was not prominent. As mentioned before, during the Xianfeng and Tongzhi periods, it was still restricted to Suzhou restaurants. When we look back today, we find that Guangdong cuisine has a strong Westernized element, especially in the process of expanding outward, which seems to have provided greater help. It may also be that Cantonese cuisine needed to borrow foreign elements culturally to reconcile the influence of Central Plains or Jiangnan traditions to open up a new situation. In the process of expanding outward, we clearly see the boost of culture, including commercial culture, which has finally achieved the great development of "Eating in Guangzhou," especially in Shanghai.

3.1 The Guangzhou Origin of Western Cuisine and the Spread of "Eating in Guangzhou"

The eastward spread of Western cuisine is worthy of attention and discussion not only in the history of Chinese cuisine but also in the history of

Chinese culture. The first credit for the eastward spread of Western cuisine should belong to Guangzhou, which has maintained opening up for more than two thousand years and has long maintained a single-port trade situation since the Ming and Qing dynasties. However, due to Shanghai's later rise, Beijing's imperial capital style, and Guangdong's "silence," this credit and contribution are often deprived and attributed to Beijing and Shanghai. For example, Mr. Bao Tianxiao's *Food Records in Sixty Years* said, "Western food began to be popular in Shanghai, initially called fan cuisine (foreign cuisine), also known as big cuisine. There was none in the interior at that time, so when people from the interior came to Shanghai, there were two things they must try: one was riding a carriage, and the other was eating fan cuisine. These two were both novel things." Mr. Zhao Heng's *The Eastward Spread of Western Wind*, "Fan Cuisine" (*Southern Metropolis Daily*, July 8, 2014) said that Beijing already had it early, "During the Kangxi period, there was a fan cuisine room in the palace to make fan cuisine, and a set of Western tableware was purchased, including various wine glasses, what glasses to use for champagne, wine, whiskey, and white wine; what are fish knives, butter knives, and table knives, which were all clearly distinguished." However, things in the palace are not evidence; besides, where did the Western chefs in the palace come from? Not Beijing, nor Shanghai, only Guangzhou. Generally, the origin of Guangzhou's Western cuisine is often traced back to the establishment of Taiping Restaurant in 1860, which was already much earlier than Beijing and Shanghai. In fact, it should be traced back further to foreign firms and the kitchen servants of Guangzhou merchants.

1. Foreign Hall Cantonese Servants and the Rise of Western Cuisine

Cantonese people learned to cook Western cuisine early on, as there are early records of Cantonese using Western food to entertain Westerners. According to the research of Professors Cheng Meibao and Liu Zhiwei in *Chinese Servants in Western Families in Guangzhou during the 18th and 19th Centuries*, as early as 1769, the merchant Pan Qiguan could entertain foreign guests entirely according to British recipes and etiquette, which is sufficient to rewrite the current origin story of Chinese Western cuisine and also contrasts the neglect of Chinese food. We also know that Western merchants living in Guangzhou were forbidden by the court to bring their families, and allowing them to hire Chinese servants was a leniency. From the foreign documents cited by Professor Cheng Meibao, we never find that Cantonese servants in foreign halls cooked their expert Cantonese dishes, but instead made highly skilled Western food, pastries, and beverages. An Austrian lady observed and recorded, "Breakfast includes fried fish or cutlets, cold roast meat, boiled eggs, tea, bread, and butter... Dinner includes turtle soup, curry, roast meat, ragout, and pastries. Except for curry, all dishes are cooked in British style—though the cooks are all Chinese." In the spring of 1839, when Lin Zexu began banning opium in Guangzhou, one of his measures was to order Chinese servants in foreign halls to evacuate, "(March 24) Suddenly, hundreds of Chinese (estimated at 800) were forced to leave the commercial halls, which became like dead places. In all service work, not even a kitchen helper was allowed to stay. Foreign residents were utterly helpless. As a result, to survive, they were forced to try cooking and cleaning themselves. It seemed ridiculous when we tried to roast a capon, boil an egg, or cook potatoes. Our director, Mr. Green, failed at cooking, producing something like a hard rubber ball. Mr. Loh tried his best, but after burning the bread and boiling eggs into hard 'grape shots,' he gave up..." (Hunter, *The 'Fan Gui' in Canton*) This also shows that without Cantonese servants, these Westerners couldn't even cook.

Chinese-owned foreign firms, due to work needs, also learned to serve Western food for receptions, gradually becoming a fashion. As mentioned, as early as 1769, the merchant Pan Qiguan could entertain foreign guests with British-style dishes and etiquette. In October 1844, Yifan, an aide to the French minister, was invited by Pan Shicheng, one of the most famous merchants at the time, to visit Guangzhou and was served Western food. "They entertained us with European etiquette—that is, a Chinese servant who learned to make some terrible British food." Especially the dessert: the cakes and small, sweet cheeses made by Pan Shicheng's 13 wives, and the even better soup, fully demonstrated the level of Western food made by Cantonese at that time, "They were sweet and delicious—we can't find better words to describe how sweet they were, indicating these small cakes were truly excellent. Incidentally, the soup was even better." (*Inside Canton*: *The Record of a French Minister's Aide's Observations in Guangzhou in the 1840s*) Thus,

Professor Qu Duizhi said in *Collection of Talks on Peop*le, Customs, and Systems, "More than 110 years ago, Guangzhou already had the atmosphere of a concession, and official banquets had taken Western food as a fashion."

2. Shanghai Western Cuisine: From Chinese Servants to Cantonese Chefs

With the opening of Shanghai as a port, the number of foreigners increased daily. The first need was not Western restaurants but Chinese servants who could cook Western food, initially brought from Guangzhou. Later, when Shanghai's "fan cuisine" (Western food) restaurants emerged, Cantonese chefs were naturally the first choice.

According to *Qingbai Leichao*, the first Chinese-run Western restaurant in Shanghai, Yipinxiang, established in 1875, was managed by Cantonese chefs. "Owner Xu Weiquan opened it in the 14th year of Guangxu, with more than 40 rooms of various sizes, hiring famous Cantonese chefs for cooking." In fact, Shenbao's Western food advertisements show that small Western restaurants in Shanghai appeared earlier than Yipinxiang. For example, an advertisement for Shengchang Western Food on December 17, 1873, stated, "Shengchang Western Food is located at No. 3 on the straight street of Laoda Bridge in Hongkou, specializing in self-made gift white hats, various pastries, and undertaking large and small Western meals. Welcome to patronize." Shengchang later became Xinghualou, a century-old Cantonese restaurant still existing today. "Notice: Shengchang, which has been operating Western food in Hongkou for many years and is well-known far and near, has now moved to Sima Road and renamed Xinghualou, opening on the 4th day of the 9th lunar month." (*Xinghualou Notice*, *Shenbao*, September 28, 1883)

Compared to Shengchang, Taiping Restaurant, the first Western restaurant in Guangzhou, opened as early as 1860. Guangzhou's Western cuisine had already adapted foreign styles for Chinese use, outperforming Westerners' own cooking—unlike Shanghai's fan cuisine restaurants, which always played second fiddle. "When I woke again at 10 a.m., I didn't want that cocktail. After washing, I went to the dining room for breakfast. There, we began talking about a luxurious Qing-style feast made with steak. I'd often heard of Guangzhou steak's deliciousness but never tasted it." (*Travel Notes on Canton*, a Famous Qing City, a special report in the New York Times on February 22, 1861, cited in Zheng Xiyuan's *Memories of the Empire: The New York Times' Observations of Late Qing China*).

Shanghai Xinhua Grand Hotel

Guangzhou's superior Western cuisine and chefs made Shanghai's fan cuisine restaurants recruit Cantonese cooks as a draw. An employment ad in the 67th issue of the Shanghai New News on July 19, 1862, explicitly stated, "Seeking a chef, preferably Cantonese." When Tianjin, another major port, developed Western cuisine to meet demand, it also looked to Guangdong cooks: in April 1907, an ad for Tianjin Guanglongtai Chinese-Western Restaurant in the Ta Kung Pao proclaimed, "Newly added French and British cuisine, specially hired top Cantonese fan cuisine chefs from Shanghai, with unique dishes." Thus, Shanghai's Western food (fan cuisine) took Guangdong as its authentic source. In fact, the name "fan cuisine" originated in Guangzhou: "Cantonese drew strict lines between Chinese and foreigners, often prefixing imported items with 'fan' (foreign), hence 'fan cuisine'." (*Observations on Shanghai*, *Jing Bao*, January 9, 1920).

3. Guangdong Restaurants in Beijing and Shanghai: Cantonese Cuisine Advancing with Fan Cuisine

Though Cantonese cuisine was renowned for luxury, it initially dared not flaunt opulence in Beijing and Shanghai. Tastes varied, so early Shanghai Cantonese restaurants were mostly late-night diners; luxurious ones flourished only after the Republic of China era, especially after the Northern Expedition. Early fan cuisine restaurants were mostly run by Cantonese, following market trends—Shanghai locals chased fan cuisine fads, and Cantonese-run late-night diners often sold fan cuisine to attract customers. The 1912 list of major Shanghai late-night diners recorded, "Zhushenju, No. 149 Fujian Road, also serves grand cuisine." The 1918 Shanghai Business

Directory listed 80 restaurants, including the famous Xinghualou Xinji among five Cantonese restaurants, which also operated fan cuisine. *The Shanghai Guide* published in 1919 showed Dongya Restaurant, a major Cantonese eatery, also served fan cuisine. Even in the 1920s, when Cantonese cuisine dominated Shanghai, renowned restaurants on Nanjing Road still offered Western food—for instance, the *Shanghai Treasure* published in 1925 listed Dongya and Dadong Restaurants as Cantonese-Yang hybrid eateries, with the long-famous Xinghualou being no exception. On April 26, 1935, Shanghai Mayor Wu Tiecheng hosted the U.S. Economic Delegation at Xinghualou on Sima Road, serving "high-class set meals, i.e., Cantonese food served Western-style."

Previously, people thought Beijing had no early Cantonese restaurants, but there were actually upscale ones—more "East-West fused" than Shanghai's. Thus, later official summaries in Beijing directly referred to

"Beijing's earliest Cantonese and fan cuisine restaurants" as a combined category. (*Quick Guide to Xuannan Culture*, edited by Zheng Wenqi) Chen Lianhen's Spring Dreams in Beijing described Cantonese cuisine's entry into Beijing in detail: "Cantonese merchants, adept at long journeys, set up shops in the capital like bees around flowers, with restaurants excelling in taste. In Shaanxi Alley, Qiyuan and Yuebolou waved wine flags—their fragrant realms served as apricot blossom villages, lacking only cowherds. Cold dishes included fried roast, roast duck, sausages, and gold-silver liver; hot stir-fries like sweet and sour spare ribs and arhat vegetarian dish; dim sum such as crab meat shumai, fried roast buns, chicken soup dumplings, and eight-treasure steamed rice, etc., some fresh and crispy, others rich and creamy, each dish mastering its craft. Late-night snacks like duck rice and fish sashimi congee were affordable and filling. Winter hotpot was especially delicious: a small stove held a soup pot, with sliced chicken, fish, tripe, and kidneys boiled fresh, dipped in chili oil and vinegar, accompanied by tender spinach. Dandies sitting by flowers, sipping pear flower wine, would have servants buy ingredients to gather around the stove, sipping and chewing at cold-dispelling gatherings—no less enchanting than Luofu Mountain dreams." The most famous was Zui Qionglin Restaurant, a restaurant fusing Cantonese and Western cuisines.

Beijing was like this, and Tianjin was no exception. Until the 1930s, one of the characteristics of Cantonese restaurants was the combination of Chinese and Western styles: among Tianjin's Western restaurants, Dahua

Restaurant was the best, followed by the Pacific Restaurant. "Next to the Pacific Restaurant, such as Zhongyuan Restaurant, Zizhulin Restaurant, Bei'anli Restaurant, Western Food Department of the New Travel Agency, Yanbin Restaurant, Lengxiang Restaurant, Qixiang Canteen, etc., all offer both Chinese and Western food, or take Western food as a sideline and Chinese food as the main business. Except for Zizhulin Restaurant, Western Food Department of the New Travel Agency, and Lengxiang Restaurant, all are Cantonese restaurants." It is specifically pointed out that the reason for this is that "restaurants of the Guangdong school around the country all have both Chinese and Western dishes, and Zizhulin Restaurant and others are just following the example of the Guangdong school." (Wang Shousheng, *Tianjin Recipe: Various Things About Eating in Tianjin*, *Ta Kung Pao* Tianjin Edition, February 24, 1935.) In other words, having both Chinese and Western dishes is the national standard of Cantonese cuisine!

3.2 Beijing: From Zui Qionglin Restaurant to Tan Family Cuisine

Mr. Li Yimeng's *Cross-Regional Operation of the Catering Industry and the Development of Sichuan Cuisine in Beijing* states, "Limited by transportation conditions, people's living standards, and the lack of professional chefs, it is very difficult to establish a catering industry across provinces. Before liberation, only Beijing, Shanghai, Nanjing, and Hong Kong probably had the phenomenon of cross-regional operations." For the cross-regional operations of Cantonese cuisine, Shanghai mentioned several, such as Dashanyuan Restaurant, Guanshengyuan Restaurant, and Datong Restaurant, while Beijing only mentioned the famous Tan Family Cuisine and Liang Family Cuisine in a small alley in Wangfujing, giving the impression that there were no formal Cantonese restaurants. In fact, this is not the case! When Dashanyuan Restaurant, Guanshengyuan Restaurant, Datong Restaurant, etc., were dominating Shanghai, it was indeed the golden age of Cantonese cuisine, especially in Shanghai, but the golden age of Cantonese restaurants in Beijing was much earlier, when Cantonese restaurants in Shanghai were still in the stage of late-night diners.

1. Zui Qionglin Restaurant and the Heyday of Beijing Cantonese Restaurants

The 1935 edition of *Peking Travel Guide* said that although due to the relocation of the capital, the restaurant industry in Beiping had lost six out of ten compared to the heyday of the late Qing Dynasty and the early Republic of China, and restaurants from Hunan, Hubei, Jiangxi, Anhui, Yunnan, Guangxi and other provinces had disappeared, there were still many Cantonese restaurants, including Donghualou Restaurant outside Dong'anmen, with representative dishes such as oyster sauce fried conch, dry-braised bamboo shoots, five willow fish, and braised abalone; Dongyalou Restaurant in Dong'an Market, with representative dishes such as barbecued pork and duck congee; Yiyayi Restaurant in Bamiancao, with representative dishes such as fish congee and duck congee; New Guangdong Restaurant and

Xinyachun Restaurant in Xidan Market. Adding those not recorded and the famous Xiaoxiao Restaurant, derived from Yiyayi Restaurant, it was already very good. What was the scene like in the heyday? Zui Qionglin Restaurant is the most representative.

As early as 1907, the *Shuntian Times* had made lengthy reports on Zui Qionglin Restaurant, first introducing the superiority of its environment:

> The Zui Qionglin Restaurant Chinese and Western Restaurant in Shaanxi Lane recently added a Western-style building in the backyard, which started construction in early June and was just completed this month. It is three floors with three rooms on each floor, all built with red bricks. The doors are all Western-style, inlaid with colored glass, and the interior space is particularly spacious, able to accommodate four large round tables for banquets. There are three large rooms upstairs and three large rooms downstairs, which are civilized, beautiful, and extremely spacious.

Then it introduces the characteristics of its Cantonese and Western dishes:

> Cantonese delicacies: It has always been said that southern dishes are good, and Cantonese dishes are the best in the south. Not to mention Guangdong Province itself, take Xinghualou Restaurant on Sima Road in Shanghai, which has a special rule called late-night dinner, costing only two mao per person, not much money, but very good taste.

Although there are many restaurants in Beijing, Cantonese food was only discovered after Zui Qionglin Restaurant opened, and Beijing people were able to taste it. The dishes of Zui Qionglin Restaurant, including rare seafood, are really unique in cooking and surpass the south of the Yangtze River in taste... The fan dishes of Zui Qionglin Restaurant are all cooked according to the cooking methods of British and French banquets, and are adjusted to the Chinese taste, with appropriate heat and suitable thickness. Therefore, although Yanchun Garden opened earlier, it is not as lively as Zui Qionglin Restaurant; although Dong'an Hotel opened later, it is not as prosperous as Zui Qionglin Restaurant. They are all fan restaurants, but the quality is different.

In addition, it also prepares a variety of Western-style wines, coffee, tobacco, milk, pastries, etc.

Because of its first-class "software", "hardware", and "background", Zui Qionglin Restaurant naturally became a famous restaurant, and even some large political and business activities were held here. For example, the *Spring Ming Dream Talk* of Donghai poet (*New Novel* 1917, Issue 1) said that when the first Congress was convened, after the daily adjournment of the deputies from all provinces, "at the sound of a bell, the deputies in top hats and leather shoes, wearing crystal glasses, with cigars in their mouths, holding cane sticks, got into carriages. With a flick of the brocade whip, the horses' hooves flew, and they had a big meal at Zui Qionglin Restaurant…"

Lu Xun also visited multiple times, "(September 10, 1913) Evening, Shou Shulin came, and we went to Zui Qionglin Restaurant for dinner. There were eight or nine people at the same table, and I mostly forgot their names." "(January 16, 1914) Evening, Gu Yangwu invited me to dinner at Zui Qionglin Restaurant." When Lu Xun went, the national studies master Huang Kan, his classmate from Zhang (Taiyan)'s school, also went, "(June 15, 1913) Attended Zhao Xingfu's banquet at Zui Qionglin Restaurant, with Wang Geng present." "(August 13, 1913) Went to Yaoqing's house to meet Wang Geng, who invited me to dinner at Zui Qionglin Restaurant in the evening. I went to Wang Geng's appointment at night, the place was very noisy, and I left before the meal." "The place3 was very noisy," just shows its full house and great bustle! However, when Tan YanKai visited later, he showed a more prestigious status. Not to mention his achievements and official titles, at least in terms of status in the food industry, it was unparalleled:

> April 26, 1911: Evening, I went to Zui Qionglin Restaurant at the invitation of the Shunzhi Advisory Bureau. Yan Fengge and Wang Guyu were the hosts, with fifteen guests, having Western food. Wang Zhuosheng said he had met at Yu Zhijin's place, but I was completely confused.
>
> May 26, 1911: I went to Zui Qionglin Restaurant to host a grand banquet for councilors with Yuan, Xie, Li, Yu, and Dou, with more than twenty people present.

January 20, 1914: I went to Zui Qionglin Restaurant at the invitation of Chen Zigao and Liu Dihua, sitting with Tang Jiwu, Yan Zhongliang, Deng Zifan, Chen Rongjing, and Zhou Yimou. (*Tan YanKai's Diary*, Zhonghua Book Company, 2018 edition)

2. The New Era of Enchengju

Before Zui Qionglin Restaurant closed, a new generation of Cantonese restaurants represented by Enchengju had already emerged. For example, Taoli Garden, the famous Yang Du said, "Cantonese restaurants once made a large-scale trial in Beijing, that is, Taoli Garden in Xiangchang in the eighth or ninth year of the Republic of China era. There are twenty halls upstairs and downstairs, each with a name. The decoration is exquisite and the layout is spacious, all modeled after the Cantonese style. The guests' tea bowls are all covered, and each bowl is marked with the guest's surname (in Guangdong, to prevent leprosy infection, tableware in homes, restaurants, brothels, etc., all indicate the guest's surname). Various facilities are excellent. Banqueters flocked to it, and its business was extremely prosperous for a time. The whole table dishes are excellent, such as 'Braised Abalone', 'Arhat Vegetarian' (i.e., vegetarian mixed vegetables), 'Braised Shark's Fin', etc." (Hu Gong, *Notes on Capital Cuisine*, *Morning Post*, January 30, 1927) The *Shuntian Times* said, "The President (Feng Guozhang) recently held a banquet in the mansion for Mongolian princes and special military and civilian officials. More than a hundred tables were needed for the morning and evening banquets, which were undertaken by the newly opened Taoli

Garden Cantonese Restaurant in Xiangji. It is said that the President and the princes at the banquet highly appreciated the deliciousness of the dishes." (*The President Appreciates Cantonese Cuisine*, *Shuntian Times*, January 18, 1918) It can be seen that Taoli Garden was opened in the seventh year of the Republic of China era (1918) rather than the eighth or ninth year, and its debut amazed the President, which is the best footnote to Hu Gong Yang Du's various descriptions.

Fried pea sprouts

The later Enchengju gained great fame as a small restaurant due to its authentic Cantonese flavor. "Among the southern restaurants, only the 'Cantonese Restaurant' can maintain the original taste. All oyster sauce, cured meat, barbecued pork, sweet dishes, meat congee, and unique Cantonese dishes can maintain their original appearance. There are also those called Cantonese Restaurants specializing in snacks, such as Enchengju." (Jin Shoushen, *Life in Old Beijing*). Good wine needs no bush, and good food needs no big restaurant. Wang Shixiang's *On Beijing Flavors* said that until the early liberation, Enchengju was still one of the famous "Eight Jus". At that time, there were also the sayings of 'Eight Jus' and 'Eight Buildings' for famous restaurants. The 'Eight Jus' are: Guangheju, Tongheju, Heshunju, Taifengju, Wanfuju, Yangchunju, Enchengju, and Fuxingju."

Enchengju's authentic taste and the effect of celebrities complemented each other. For example, regarding stir-fried vegetarian pea sprouts, Tang Lusun's *On Wine* said, "When Mei Lanfang was in Beiping, he often went to small restaurants with Qi Rulao. Lanfang preferred stir-fried pea sprouts offered by Enchengju in Shaaxi Alley, and Qi Rulao would always ask the waiter to buy four liangs (1 liang=50 g) of Lv Yinchen liquor from Tongrentang to drink while eating. The poet Huang Qiuyue said that famous dishes paired with famous wines can be called the two emerald masterpieces." It also said, "Mr. Qi Rushan from Gaoyang was not only erudite but also a food expert. In those days, in any restaurant in Beiping with a special dish, he would always invite two or three confidants to try it." Enchengju was a "happy discovery" in Mr. Qi Rushan's search for food. "Shaanxi Lane in Beiping is one of the Eight Great Hutongs in the red-light district, where most of the northern singing brothels were concentrated. By chance, Mr. Qi found a small restaurant called 'Enchengju' in Shaanxi Lane, which was Cantonese-style. Not only was it light and lasting in taste, but the dishes were also cheap.

Since then, Enchengju has become a place for him and Mei Wanhua to have a small drink with a few confidants." Enchengju was frequented by celebrities, so much so that some called it the "Little Six Nations Hotel".

3. The Era of Star-Studded Small Restaurants

Any restaurant that indulges in self-admiration can hardly sustain long-term growth. In old Beijing, Cantonese restaurants like Zui Qionglin Restaurant and Taoli Garden earlier, and Enchengju and Jinghua Restaurant later, were never isolated cases. Instead, there was a large number of Cantonese restaurants emerging and fading, but most people were confined to narrow perspectives, "seeing only trees, not the forest." For example, the Tianranju Cantonese Restaurant in Shaanxi Lane, unknown to many, actually has quite a story. As Xu Jun wrote in *Fragmentary Brocades* (*New China Daily*, March 9, 1929), there was once a Tianranju Cantonese Restaurant in Shaanxi Lane where he dined with friends. A guest said, "Tianranju has a couplet: 'Guest visits Tianranju, unexpectedly a celestial guest.' It's quite difficult to match. Later, I saw in a magazine that someone paired it with: 'Person comes to the Foreign Ministry, ministry deals with outsiders.' It can be called neat and proper." But of course, the most storied aspect is that Tan YanKai, the "Gourmet God" of the Republic of China era, visited several times:

> December 3, 1913: I went to Tianranju with Li, Mei, and Wei to eat Cantonese hotpot, drinking until drunk.

December 11, 1913: I went to Tianranju with Li Jiu, Mei, and Wei for Cantonese hotpot, which was still good. There was pure and clear ox penis, but no one dared to eat it, a result of curiosity's folly.

December 15, 1913: I went to Tianranju at the invitation of Long Boyang, waiting long before arrival.

December 18, 1913: I went to Tianranju for Wang Yitang's invitation; the banquet was already half underway.

Fuxiangju, a Cantonese restaurant recorded in the 1922 *Beijing Guide* published by Wenming Bookstore, has never been mentioned by others. In fact, through just three months of Deng Zhicheng's diary from June to November 1926, we can see how many Cantonese restaurants in Beiping during the 1920s were forgotten:

August 5th: I dined at Dongya Cantonese Restaurant in Dong'an Market, which was excellent.

August 13th: I had a small drink at Dongya Cantonese Restaurant.

August 30th: I had dinner at a small Cantonese restaurant named Beiji in Hanjiatan.

November 5th: I dined at a Cantonese restaurant on Wangguangfu Slanting Street, costing 4 yuan and 2 jiao.

November 6th: I dined at a new Cantonese restaurant in Dong'an

Market, where everything was excellent and not expensive.

November 9th: In the evening, I dined at the Cantonese Restaurant with Fei Runsheng.

November 25th: Fei Runsheng and Yang Yonggu came, we dined at Lianji, a newly opened Cantonese restaurant.

November 26th: Runsheng and others came again, and we dined at Lianji.

In the 1930s, many Cantonese restaurants were also mentioned by famous authors. *The Peking Travel Guide* approved by the renowned writer Zhang Henshui listed several Cantonese restaurants and their signature dishes: "Donghualou, owned by Ou Gonghu, opened in January of the 20th year [1931], serving oyster sauce fried conch, Five Willow Fish, braised abalone, and dry-braised fish, outside Dong'anmen; Dongyalou, serving barbecued pork and glutinous rice chicken, in Dong'an Market; Yiya, serving fish congee and duck congee, at Bamiantang; Xinguangdong, in Xidan Market; Xinyachun, in Shaanxi Lane." Among them, Dongyalou was particularly famous. "Their shumai was especially renowned because Chen Sangu from Daliang (in Shunde County) once guest-cooked shumai at Dongyalou during a trip. Their shumai was steamed on aluminum alloy trays, six per plate. The shumai was smooth, moist, and snow-white, allowing the filling color to be seen from the outside. The filling was loose, the skin thin, and it left no residue when eaten. Only Nianghonglu in Hongkou, Shanghai, could barely compare, and even Guangzhou's three major restaurants couldn't make shumai like this!" However, the claim that Dongyalou, "though not very grand, is the only Cantonese restaurant in Beiping," is clearly untrue. (Tang Lusun, *The Memorable Dong'an Market*) Huang Jie, a famous Cantonese scholar and former Peking University professor, once hosted Yang Shuda, Lin Gongduo, and Sun Shucheng at this hometown restaurant: "Dear Yufu [Yang Shuda], tomorrow (Monday, the 17th by the old calendar) at 12 noon, I invite Gongduo and Shucheng to a small dinner at Dongyalou in Dong'an Market. Please come over for a chat." (Huang Jie, *Letter to Yang Shuda*)

Additionally, there was Lingnanlou, where the renowned professor Wu Mi dined and recorded in his diary, "(September 11, 1930) Mi and Xian went outside Langrun Garden, reluctant to part. Finally, we went to Lingnanlou Restaurant, where Xian treated Mi to dinner."

Among Cantonese restaurants in the 1930s, Xiaoxiao Restaurant was more talked about than Dongyalou. Gu Jiegang first mentioned Xiaoxiao Restaurant in his diary on September 2, 1935: "I went to Xinguangdong in Xidan Market for dinner with Lv'an... We went to Xiaoxiao Restaurant in Dong'an Market for dinner." Xiaoxiao Restaurant offered authentic Cantonese flavors, though none of its owners were Cantonese. In his special article *Xiaoxiao Restaurant*, Dong Shanyuan noted that none of the twenty-plus staff in this small eatery, opened in 1934, were from Guangdong, but its three owners all came from Yiya, a Cantonese restaurant: Guo Delin (waiter),

Liu Kezheng (head chef), and Cheng Ming (chef skilled in barbecues and braised dishes), especially Cheng Ming who spoke fluent Cantonese. This truly exemplifies an interesting story in spreading "Eating in Guangzhou"! In fact, Xiaoxiao Restaurant was not small—three floors with private rooms upstairs and open seating downstairs. By 1947, it had expanded by taking over the adjacent storefront, doubling its area to become a more renowned Cantonese restaurant. It continued to thrive into the 1950s and 1960s, only closing in 1968 when Dong'an Market was demolished and merged into the New Market Food Department. (Dong Shanyuan, *Weihui Jisheng: Eighty Years of Dong'an Market*)

Sauce beef

Renowned scholar Deng Yunxiang once followed his father to Xiaoxiao Restaurant, "Two dishes and a soup, or perhaps three dishes—oyster sauce beef, stir-fried squid rolls, and shrimp with crispy rice. The last wasn't stir-fried shrimp but poached shrimp poured over freshly fried crispy rice, hissing loudly with overflowing aroma and rich soup. It was both soup and dish—

delicious and spectacular." "This left a deep impression, making me appreciate oyster sauce's flavor, and I've loved oyster sauce beef since then!" (Deng Yunxiang, *Oyster Sauce Beef*, in *Yunxiang's Food Talk*)

Xiaoxiao Restaurant's fame spread so far that even when eating Cantonese food in Japan, people compared it to Xiaoxiao, "(Yokohama's Nanjing Street) 'Haishenglou' is a Cantonese restaurant serving not only Wujiapi wine but also Guangdong's unique rice wine. Their barbecued pork and roasted meat are excellent—no different from Bei'anli in Tianjin or Xiaoxiao Restaurant in Beijing." (T*he Charming Yokohama*, *Women's New Metropolis*, December 18, 1940)

After the War of Resistance, the newly opened Jinghua Restaurant also flourished. In an exclusive interview with *147 Pictorial*, owner Peng Jinda made credible claims. When asked why Cantonese people are so particular about food, he replied, "First, it's due to prevailing customs; second, Guangdong's proximity to prosperous Hong Kong, where everything is exquisite." When asked about Cantonese cuisine's uniqueness, he said, "Cantonese cuisine uses ingredients other regions discard or consider 'scraps,' transforming them into delicacies; otherwise, it adapts and improves dishes from elsewhere." This echoed Xian Guansheng's views. "Further, Cantonese cuisine is fastidious in every way." "When preparing a banquet, the dishes vary in color and taste—nine dishes can present nine colors and nine flavors." (*Cantonese Talk About Food—An Evening at Jinghua Restaurant in*

Guangdong (Part 1), *147 Pictorial*, Issue 12, 1947) These answers aptly captured Cantonese cuisine's essence, explaining its dominance in Beijing.

3.3 Shanghai: From North Sichuan Road to Nanjing Road

Shanghai's opening as a port after the Opium War was one of Britain's most important moves and a pivotal influence on Guangdong's economic and social development. Soon replacing Guangzhou as China's primary foreign trade port, it saw northern migration of Cantonese compradors, merchants, craftsmen, and service workers alongside foreign affairs and business. Cantonese cuisine followed, evolving from late-night diners and snack shops serving Cantonese migrants to teahouses and restaurants serving the public. Through diligence, adaptive service, and commercial innovation, Cantonese people advanced from North Sichuan Road (their habitat) to Nanjing Road (the commercial hub), outperforming other cuisines to gain national renown, solidifying "Eating in Guangzhou" as a resplendent cultural symbol.

1. North Sichuan Road Era: From Cake Shops to Late-night diners

Shanghai's roots in Cantonese cuisine can be traced back to before the city was opened as a port. Cantonese people, especially Teochew people, were adept at business. Braving hardships, they sailed north on red-headed ships, seizing opportunities in Shanghai even before its opening. Just as Zhang Han of the Jin Dynasty missed his hometown's perch and water shield soup in Luoyang, Cantonese in Shanghai longed for native food, leading to the 1839 opening of "Yuanli" Food Store by Teochew people. This was not a restaurant but a shop specializing in famous Chaoshan pastries. Conditions for restaurants—capital and market—were far from ripe, but the transition from pastries to teahouses was natural, like a prelude to restaurants. Shanghai's first Cantonese-style teahouse, Linanju, opened in 1902, founded by Zhong An, who started with pastries. Linanju set the pattern for Shanghai's "Six Great Teahouses" (Linanju, Tong'anju, Tongfangju, Qunfangju, Yizhenju, Yi'anju), and the later renowned Xinya Cantonese Restaurant followed suit. Teahouses expanded by introducing barbecued sausage, cooked cured meats, and even alcohol alongside pastries, gradually transforming into restaurants offering comprehensive menus.

After Shanghai's opening, its status soared, hosting diverse cuisines with unique heritages and strengths. For Cantonese restaurants to stand out was daunting. Astute Cantonese merchants blazed a trail with late-night diners, an endeavor shunned by inlanders. As *Shanghai Commercial Scenery Poems* noted, "Late-night diners named 'Xiaoye' are opened by Cantonese, their splendid decor attracting guests." Mentions of late-night diners immediately evoked Cantonese establishments. In *Baiyong Shenjiang*, "Where to find evening delight? By a red clay stove. Eating fish sashimi inspires poetry. It's a pity this place is not West Lake." In Shanghai, late-night diners were synonymous with Cantonese restaurants. From Late Qing dynasty to the early Republic of China era, the *Sea Poems* reflected the rise of Cantonese late-night diners, “To enjoy a Cantonese late-night dinner at Xinghualou, each guest gets two courses. Dry and wet dishes to order, do they rival Pearl River flavors?” “Winter’s red clay stove: clear soup with spinach, rich and savory. Sliced fish sashimi, duck, chicken, ideal for driving out the chill.” Cantonese not only diligently ran late-night diners which others avoided, but also prioritized splendid decor and fresh, varied dishes, inspiring literati tributes. For example, an imitation of Bai Juyi’s *Better to Drink Wine* reads, “Better to drink wine to pass the cold night. Red clay stove glows, cabbage soup simmers. Three cups for intoxication, a bite to savor. When the fish is ready, chopsticks hurry in.” “Better to drink wine by the stove. Steaming spinach, round mushrooms. A full belly warms the heart, fresh taste lingers on the tongue. Returning in strong west wind, why not sleep drunk?” (Bi, *Warmth of Hotpot in Cantonese Restaurant on Winter Night*, *Pictorial Daily*, Issue 110, 1909)

Until the 1920s, Shanghai’s Cantonese restaurants remained predominantly late-night diners. In the 41st issue of Shanghai’s *Red Magazine* in 1923, Mr. Shaozhou’s *Comparison of Guangdong Restaurants in Shanghai* listed 14 major Cantonese restaurants in Hongkou, 12 of which were late-night diners, a clear majority. The earliest ones, Guangjixiang and Yizhen Restaurants, were also late-night diners. Late-night diners were the most profitable. “When Weiya opened, it had only one building; now it has expanded to four storefronts. It’s said to make a hefty profit each year—after expenses, it still has a surplus of 3,000 to 4,000 yuan, unprecedented for late-night diners." Their success stemmed from excellent dishes. "Their food is truly top-notch, especially the stir-fried beef, which enjoys great popularity. The same beef is cooked in over a dozen ways—with gravy, oyster sauce, cream, shrimp paste, ketchup, etc. It's too many to list, but all are fresh, tender, and delicious. Chewing slowly releases aroma in the mouth, far surpassing others and never getting tiresome. Once, a friend and I ate nine plates of beef alone—we loved it more with each bite and never grew bored. The braised snakehead fish was also excellent, melting in the mouth like fermented bean curd."

Cantonese ran late-night diners not just to offer filling meals but to serve them as full meals. For example, "Jiangnanchun specializes in Chinese-style Western food, or Cantonese-style grand cuisine." This reflected their shrewdness and pragmatism—occupying the evening consumption gap in Shanghai's internationalization. Robust evening consumption is inevitable in any city's internationalization. Decades later, when Yi Zhongtian saw Guangzhou's thriving late-night market in the reform era, he found it "rare and incredible, "considering it the best representation of "Eating in Guangzhou." "The late night is truly the climax of 'Eating in Guangzhou'." In recent years, with material abundance and rising incomes, more people enjoy late-night dinners, and late-night dinners have become an increasingly popular part of a unique 'Guangzhou scene.' This is rare and unimaginable in inland, especially northern cities, but it's exactly the authentic 'Guangzhou characteristic'."

By the 1930s, Cantonese restaurants had become popular in Shanghai, with late-night diners—their founding feature—still holding a firm place, though evolving into a subcategory. The 1934 *Shanghai Guide* by Shen Bojing and Chen Huaipu stated, "Late-night diners are a subcategory of Cantonese restaurants, smaller in scale but focusing on night markets," listing many famous ones like Yanhualou, Xinghualou, Zuihualou, Changchunlou, Chunyanhua, and Guangyalou—testifying to their indispensability in urban food consumption.

The late-night dinner of Cantonese restaurants has deep roots. Lingnan's hot, humid climate makes morning and night ideal for activities, as seen in Guangzhou's night markets and Tianming Xu (dawn markets) today. Night markets, in particular, have a long history and are incredibly diverse.

2. From Small Eateries to Grand Restaurants

The success of late-night diners spurred the vigorous development of Cantonese restaurants, initially mostly small eateries. *The Miscellaneous Records of Shanghai Local Customs* compiled by the Shanghai Trust Company in 1930 noted that "one-third of all small restaurants in Shanghai are run by Cantonese, featuring beautiful decor and elegant furnishings." The taste must have been as superb as Guangzhou's street food, for the record also said, "Cantonese cuisine wins with flavor, skillful cooking, and elegant settings, hence its popularity. There are many Cantonese restaurants in Shanghai, and they are in vogue. Japanese and Westerners also favor

Cantonese food. A few years ago, Japan sent several renowned chefs to China to study cooking methods and rated Cantonese cuisine as the world's top cuisine."

In fact, some of these small restaurants evolved from late-night diners, and newly opened ones inherited the functions of late-night diners but paid more attention to quality. For example, late-night diners like Dazhonglou advertised that they were managed by famous chefs: "Dazhonglou, a Cantonese late-night diner by Touji Bridge on Zhejiang Road, will hire famous chefs from Guangdong at the end of this month." This quality improvement also implied the desire to grow bigger and stronger. For example, the advertisement of Xihu Lou on Wuchang Road said, "The food of this restaurant has always been recognized by the Cantonese community and is regarded as the best Cantonese restaurant in Shanghai. It is now heard that the business is expanding, and more than ten famous chefs from the four major restaurants in Guangzhou have been specially hired from Guangdong to make delicacies they are really good at, especially Foshan Zhu Hou braised dishes such as fat chickens and fat pigeons, which are special flavors that are not easy to taste in Shanghai, and the price is reasonable and the quality is good." Some small restaurants with good business also began to call themselves giants: "Zuitian Restaurant opposite the Audi An Cinema on North Sichuan Road is the leading giant among the Cantonese restaurants in Hongkou, Shanghai, because it pays attention to cleanliness, which is rare. It specializes in Cantonese food and sells dim sum. It opened last year and had a booming business."

Of course, the best way of eating is to suit the tastes of the public. To develop, Cantonese restaurants in Shanghai must break through the nature of small restaurants and move towards the compatibility of large restaurants, and finally form the so-called Shanghai-style Cantonese cuisine represented by Xinya Restaurant, so as to establish their unique historical status. This is exactly the case, and people at that time also had close observations. For example, Qionglou's *On Chinese Restaurants* in the 4th issue of *Xindu Weekly* in 1943 said that "Cantonese people have a characteristic that they can absorb foreign cultures and give up their prejudices", so "Cantonese food can be popular and attract a large number of diners. I think this may be a reason why Cantonese food has been popular for a while." This kind of inclusiveness has been particularly recognized by foreigners living in Shanghai. For example, the Cantonese food of Xinya is almost regarded as the national food by them, "At present, Cantonese food is the most exquisite in method and the most complex in seasoning, and because it is the first to be influenced by the European style, the method of the food also incorporates the strengths of Western food, so it can cater to the tastes of the general public. Foreigners in Shanghai know 'Xinya' best. They think that the food of 'Xinya' is the national food, but they do not know that the local food is the authentic Shanghai restaurant." (Shu Yan *Nonsense About Eating*, *The Analects* 1947 No. 132)

Soy sauce chicken

The development of new-style Cantonese cuisine is not only reflected in the dishes but also in the new and enterprise-oriented aspects of Cantonese restaurants. According to Mr. Ge Zhengbi's *Grand Hotel* (Issue 4 of *The Masses* in 1943), the catering industry has always been regarded as an industry for peddlers, but through the efforts of Cantonese people, people have come to realize that they must have "progressive ideas", that is, "whether to improve its status and whether to regard it as a 'career'". In the eyes of Cantonese people, "restaurants are a career, a noble career". Therefore, "old-fashioned 'restaurant alleys' and 'old Guangdong' are still welcomed by some people", but they should also keep pace with the times. This is very true. Specifically, this new career and new-style restaurants "should take the 'Xinya Grand Hotel' on North Sichuan Road as the beginning, and make the best use of the characteristics of Western grand hotels in Chinese restaurants." Under this call, "'Xinya', 'Xinhua', 'Jinghua', and 'Hongmian' were opened in a swarm, and then new-style Cantonese restaurants such as 'Nanning', 'Ronghua', 'Meihua', and 'Jinmen' continued to open, which is really a grand view!" And the later ones are "Xinya" and "Xindu". Xinya's products won the honor of "national food", and Xindu became a model of "scientific management". In a word, "the development of new-style Cantonese restaurants to enterprise is the need of the city and the progress of the times".

Shanghai Xinya Cantonese Restaurant

3. Occupying Nanjing Road and Achieving Shanghai Style

Cantonese food is Shanghai-style, and Shanghai-style is inseparable from Cantonese food. *The Miscellaneous Records of Shanghai Local Customs* recommends only Cantonese restaurants when providing dining guides for tourists: "If you live in a hotel along Nanjing Road and do not want to eat in the hotel, you can go to Daya Yuan Restaurant, Xinya Restaurant, and Guanshengyuan Restaurant for tea or meals, which are also run by Cantonese and speak Cantonese. You can also have lunch and dinner in the food and beverage departments of companies such as Sincere, Wing On, and Sun Sun." The most symbolic thing is that major Cantonese restaurants have flocked to Nanjing Road. Nanjing Road is a symbol of the most prosperous and wealthy area in old Shanghai, known as the "First Commercial Street in the Far East"; the land there is very expensive, and you can't stand it without a few skills.

The first restaurants to open on Nanjing Road were undoubtedly Sincere and Wing On. The four major department stores in old Shanghai—Sincere, Wing On, Sun Sun, and Da Sun—were all founded by overseas Cantonese. In 1917, when the Shanghai Sincere Company of the Ma Yingbiao family opened, it set up the Sincere Paradise on the rooftop of the affiliated Dongya Hotel, serving Cantonese meals and Chinese-Western grand cuisine, which became popular for a time. In 1918, when the Wing On Company of the Guo Le family opened, the Tianyun Building on the top floor imitated Sincere's style, and its popularity exceeded that of the latter. When the Sun Sun Company of the Cai Chang family, which had a deep origin with Sincere, opened in 1926, although it also set up dining facilities on the top floor, the trend had passed, and it was difficult to catch up. Therefore, it simply changed the catering department to Xindu Hotel in 1936. However, Xindu Hotel did not forget the rooftop tradition and also opened the "Seven-Story Building" and "Happy Encounter Night Garden" on its seventh floor. Xindu Hotel thus later surpassed others and overwhelmed the crowd. In those days, the wedding banquet of Du Yuesheng, the most famous tycoon in Shanghai Beach, for his son was held here, showing its grandeur. The only one that was difficult to overshadow was the other more powerful Xinya Cantonese Restaurant facing it. Especially after the victory of the Anti-Japanese War, almost two-thirds of the customers of Xinya were Europeans and Americans. When Li Zongren came to Shanghai to entertain dignitaries from all walks of life as the acting president, he used Xinya. Compared with Du Yuesheng's ostentation, how can they be compared on the same day?

In addition to the four major companies and Xinya, Dadong Restaurant was also a Cantonese restaurant with a large number of diners. According to Mr. Cao Juren's recollection, he often went to Dadong Restaurant and thought that the dim sum and dishes were "similar to Xinya. I remember that going to Dadong Restaurant was like going to Longfeng Tea House in Hong Kong, so noisy that it was a headache." Mr. Tang Lusun, who came from the Republic of China era, thought that Daya Yuan on East Nanjing Road was more senior. Daya Yuan was, of course, senior. According to Mr. Cao Juren's record, in the Sima Road era, it had already "dominated one side" and had a good reputation, so much so that famous reporters like Cao thought it was "thundering in the ears". With the opening of a branch of Guanshengyuan on Nanjing Road in 1923 and then the relocation of the head office to Nanjing Road in 1926, the scenery of "Eating in Guangzhou" on Nanjing Road was complete. In just one Nanjing Road, with all these Cantonese restaurants, it was unique and unrivaled. The taste of the Republic of China era, who else but me!

3.4 "Guangzhou Restaurant" Spreads All Over the World and Guanshengyuan Leading

Qu Dajun's *New Words of Guangdong* said, "Guangzhou is a famous county, and many people are engaged in business, following the trend, with incense, sugar, fruits, boxes, ironware, rattan, wax, chili peppers, sappanwood, and palm-leaf fan and other goods, going north to Yuzhang and Wuzhe, and northwest to Changsha and Hankou." The famous work *On the History of Chinese Guilds* by the great historian He Bingdi and Professor Liu Zhengang's *Manuscript on the History of Guangdong Guilds* have all eloquently confirmed this from the perspective of the establishment of guilds. However, while Cantonese merchants competed in various places, Cantonese restaurants were not established in a timely manner. They were only gradually established after the five ports began commercial intercourse, especially after the Northern Expedition and the outbreak of the Anti-Japanese War, when the number of Cantonese merchants and people increased, and the influence of Lingnan culture also became more prominent, and the acceptance of Cantonese cuisine became higher and higher. Due to space limitations, it is impossible to examine the specific situations of Cantonese restaurants across the country one by one. This article only briefly introduces the distribution of the "Guangzhou Restaurant" with regional representation and the Guanshengyuan Restaurant that best represents the golden age of Cantonese cuisine across the country, to see one spot.

1. "Guangzhou Restaurant" Spreads All Over the World

Since taking control of Taotaoju, the current Guangzhou Restaurant is almost the only old catering brand in Guangzhou. Their most influential advertising slogan, "The First Restaurant in Guangzhou, Guangzhou Restaurant, "now more conforms to their identity. From this old brand born in 1935 and its well-deserved advertising slogan, we think of the Guangzhou Restaurants across the country in the golden age of "Eating in Guangzhou" and find an interesting phenomenon: ordinary Cantonese restaurants still dare not use the great name of "Guangzhou", but those who do are generally of strong strength. Through such a combing and investigation, we can also catch a glimpse of the style of "Eating in Guangzhou" at that time from a special perspective.

Cuangzhou Restaurant

First, we came to Nanjing, the capital of the National Government. Before the Republic of China era, the cross-regional food market was very weak. Although Nanjing was an important commercial city along the Yangtze River in the lower reaches, until the Kuomintang regime established its capital, according to media reports at that time, not to mention foreign cuisine, the entire catering industry was lackluster. For example, on September 3, 1928, *A View of Various Aspects of Capital Life* in *Ta Kung Pao* stated, "Nanjing has never been famous for its restaurants. In the city, only around Confucius Temple, there are several restaurants selling food by the river, but they are all small in scale and the food is not good." However, the new atmosphere brought by the establishment of the capital was foreign cuisine, with Cantonese cuisine taking the lead. "Recently, due to the establishment of the national capital, two or three new restaurants have emerged. The most famous ones are the Cantonese Anle Hotel and the Sichuan Shuxia Restaurant.

The food prices are extremely high, especially in Anle, with each banquet costing at least more than 20 yuan, but it is often full of guests, and those in the business have made huge profits." The very official *Municipal Review* 1936, Issue 2, *Eating in Nanjing*, also said that Cantonese cuisine took the lead, "Since the capital was established in Nanjing in the 16th year of the Republic of China era, the number of restaurants in Nanjing has increased greatly like mushrooms after rain. At first, Cantonese cuisine was popular, from the Cantonese Nanyue Company to the early Cantonese cuisine of the Anle Hotel, to the opening period of the World Hotel, and then the Guangzhou Restaurant, Guangdong Restaurant, and the like."

Under the trend, the later ones became more refined. For example, "the Guangzhou Restaurant in Songtao Alley has extremely clean food, and the owner Li Rongji cooks in person. All food lovers in Nanjing flock to it." Who are the ones flocking there? The speaker of the parliament and the president of the examination yuan, "Speaker Luo Junren has always liked Shaoxing wine and can drink three to four catties per banquet. Recently, due to physical weakness, he has slightly reduced, but he likes to eat in small restaurants and often goes alone for a small drink. Xu Gongwu (Chonghao), the secretary general of the Examination Yuan, is also a big fan of this restaurant, saying that it is the authentic taste of Cantonese cuisine. Luo, Xu, and Deng Jiayan all wrote inscriptions at the table." More importantly, Shang Yanliu, the last top scholar from Panyu, who was then working in the Ministry of Finance, "also often went to have a small sip and inscribed a couplet on the wall: 'The mountain top overlooks the sparkling lake, and the red light shines on the seat, making the skin fragrant'" (*Viewing the Wall of Guangzhou Restaurant*, *Jing Bao*, September 4, 1934), which is the best anecdote in the food world.

Such a good restaurant naturally had a large number of diners, including many celebrities. For example, Mr. Huang Kan, a master of Chinese studies who was fond of drinking and bold, had long come to drink heartily, as recorded in his diary, "(September 7, 1930) In the evening, Kuiyuan came, and we went to Qiongyuan to see chrysanthemums, then went to Guangzhou Restaurant to drink heavily." "(September 25, 1930) At night, Yunhe invited me, my nephews, and Menglun to eat at Guangzhou Restaurant in Songtao Alley, and we were very drunk." "(October 8, 1931) In the evening, I drank with my nephews at Guangzhou Restaurant, then watched a movie and returned at midnight." "(September 25, 1932) In the evening, I took my three sons to eat at Guangzhou Restaurant." Under its great reputation, even *Essential Reading for Traveling in Beijing: "Eating" in the Capital*, in the *New Life Weekly* 1935, Issue 63, which mainly reported on the New Life Movement, also praised Guangzhou Restaurant as the best Cantonese restaurant, "For Sichuan cuisine, Empress and Xieying are slightly better; for Zhejiang Shaoxing restaurants, Laowanquan and Liuhuachun are the most famous; for Cantonese restaurants, Guangzhou Restaurant is the best. For larger-scale ones, such as the Central Hotel, Anle Hotel, and World Hotel, they offer various styles, but the Central is better for Sichuan cuisine, and Anle is famous for Cantonese cuisine."

Guangzhou Restaurant

The continuous patronage of celebrities further confirms its status. Chen Kewen, a counselor of the Executive Yuan in charge of party affairs and personnel, not only had friends gather and hold banquets at Guangzhou Restaurant but also ordered banquets from Guangzhou Restaurant for family banquets, with each banquet costing as much as 25 yuan. (*Chen Kewen's Diary*, February 27, 1937, April 10, 1935) When Gu Jiegang was in Nanjing, he also dined here, "(January 28, 1937) Went to Guangzhou Restaurant for a banquet... Tonight's tablemates: Wang Gongmu, Xie Jun, Huang Jianzhong, Lu Yougang, and several others, Yu (above guests), Xin Shujin, Song Xiangzhou (host)." (*Gu Jiegang's Diary*) Even Mr. Zhu Kezhen, who did not like socializing and rarely mentioned going to restaurants in his diary, rarely mentioned Guangzhou Restaurant and even recorded the attendees in detail, "April 10, 1937: At six o'clock, went to Guangzhou Restaurant in response to Lei Jinghuan's invitation, and met Du Guangxun, Li Shucheng, Zhao Damou, Yang Zhensheng, Xunfu, Pi Haobai, etc." (*Complete Works of Zhu

Kezhen, Volume 6, Diary) In this way, together with the Anle Hotel, Guangzhou Restaurant became the leader of Cantonese restaurants in the capital and a must-record in travel guide books, "Cantonese food has also become a hobby of the general people in Nanjing. The famous Cantonese restaurants include the Anle Hotel and Guangzhou Restaurant, which are all very famous." (Ni Xiying, *Nanjing*, Zhonghua Book Company, 1936 edition)

Nanjing was the capital, and Wuhan was also the first relocated capital of the National Government after the Northern Expedition. Later, when the National Government moved westward, it also "resided" in Wuhan. Since the Northern Expedition originated in Guangzhou, how could Wuhan not have a Guangzhou Restaurant? In the 1925 edition of *Hankou Commercial Overview* by Daxin Printing Company, under the "Cantonese Cuisine" category of "Chinese Restaurants," there were as many as 15 Cantonese restaurants in Hankou alone among the three towns of Wuhan. This grand occasion, outside of Shanghai, was no less than that of the later capital Nanjing, with Guangzhou Restaurant prominently listed. In the 1933 edition of the *Wuhan Guide* compiled by Zhou Rongya from the Hankou New China Daily, although the cuisine type is not specified, the confirmed Cantonese restaurants include the following, and Guangzhou Restaurant naturally remains. *The Famous Dishes and Snacks* also introduces the famous dishes of Guangzhou Restaurant:

Xinghualou: Braised Shark's Fin, Sliced Fish in Sauce, Fried

Shrimp Balls, and Combination Dishes

Yanyuelou: Pure Seasonal Fish, Exploded Tripe, Brown Sugar, and Vinegar Radish

Yijianglou: Dim Sum

Wanhualou and Dajichun: White-Cut Chicken, Braised Duck

Guangzhou Restaurant: Barbecue, Roast Duck, Yifu Noodles

Weiya: Raw Sliced Fish, Raw Sliced Sea Cucumber, Squid Pieces

Chinese-Western Restaurants: Fish Congee...

Guangzhou Restaurant, which never missed the list, was also frequented by celebrities. Chen Kewen, a counselor of the Executive Yuan in charge of party affairs and personnel, can be taken as an example, and it is all recorded in his diary, “February 2, 1938, Wuhan: Lusha called and invited me to dinner at Guangzhou Restaurant. The same table included Zhu Lun, Huang Shannong, and Ye Chanzhen.” The diary of Zhang Zonghe, the eldest son of the Hefei Zhang family, is equally elegant: “May 3, 1938: Went home from work at noon. Mr. Ji left a note inviting me to Guangzhou Restaurant... Mr. Ji is from Haimen and works in the Political Department.” Gu Jiegang, a master of history, also dined here, “September 20, 1937, Hankou: Ate at Guangzhou Restaurant. After the meal, I visited Xuezhou with Cheng Bin and met him.” Some schools also chose Guangzhou Restaurant for gatherings, showing its popularity: “The Alumni Association of Wuhan Wenhua Library

College held the first semester meeting of this term at Guangzhou Restaurant on Jianghan Road, Hankou, on May 31..."

Since Nanjing (the capital) and Wuhan had Guangzhou Restaurants, Chongqing (the temporary capital) certainly did too. The 1941 *Chongqing Travel Guide,* published by the Chongqing Service Office of the Social Department, when introducing famous out-of-town Chinese restaurants in Chongqing, highlighted Cantonese restaurants, introducing as many as nine, including Guangzhou Restaurant: Cantonese flavors include Dadong on Linsen Road, Daya Yuan on Linsen Road, Guomin Restaurant on Minzu Road, Qingyise on Minzu Road, Simeichun on Minzu Road, Guangdong Restaurant on Minquan Road, Guanshengyuan on Minquan Road, Guangzhou Restaurant on Minsheng Road, and Taotao Restaurant on Minsheng Road. According to the author's review of documentary materials, there were a total of 24 well-known Cantonese restaurants in Chongqing at that time, which clearly exceeded all lower Yangtze River cuisines except Sichuan cuisine. The development of "Eating in Guangzhou" outward, regardless of chaos or peace, is remarkably impressive and truly worthy of our cherishing and pride.

In the late Republic of China, Guangzhou Restaurants located on Siming South Road (Wengcai River) in Xiamen and Longtou Road in Gulangyu were famous for seafood dishes and Cantonese stir-fries with fine ingredients, exquisite craftsmanship, and light and fresh flavors, such as "Fried Crab in

Fragrant Sauce, " "Fried Osmanthus Shark's Fin, " "Oil-Blistered Shrimp, " "Pigeon Meat Floss, " "Garlic Frog," etc. Dim sum, snacks, and various original stews were particularly popular, and they also left a film industry story. In the winter of 1948, when famous movie stars Bai Hong, Ouyang Feiluan, Yin Xiucen, Guan Hongda, etc., visited the Philippines and passed through Xiamen, they tasted famous dishes and dim sum such as "Steamed Perch, " "Pigeon Meat Floss, " "Arhat Vegetarian, " and "Crispy Fried Shrimp Boxes" at "Guangzhou Restaurant" in Gulangyu and were greatly impressed. Yin Xiucen even signed as a souvenir. This Guangzhou Restaurant had just opened for half a year and was brand new, "Xiamen Guangzhou Restaurant new location opening: Tea noodles, wonton, big buns, home-cooked meals, original stews, No. 452 Siming South Road, Xiamen; large and small banquets, wedding halls, casual dining, welcome, No. 255 Longtou Road, Gulangyu." (*Nanqiao Daily*, March 31, 1948)

Xian Guansheng

Guilin, as a cultural town during the Anti-Japanese War and close to Guangdong, naturally had many Cantonese restaurants. The earliest recorded Cantonese restaurant after the war was the Guangzhou Restaurant noted by Mr. Chang Renxia, a famous art archaeologist, Oriental art history expert, poet, and one of the founders of the Chinese Art History Society, "December 15, 1938 (Guilin): Had dinner at Guangzhou Restaurant." (*Chronicle of War Clouds*, Haitian Press, 1999 edition) Mr. Song Yunbin, a famous literary historian, essayist, democratic personage, and then director of the Guilin Cultural Supply Society (a well-known cultural institution), often went there and found that it was often "crowded with customers, and we had to wait more than ten minutes to be seated." (Song Yunbin's *Guilin Diary*) This shows its booming business!

Xi'an, a city with tastes vastly different from Guangdong, surprisingly also had Cantonese restaurants and a Guangzhou Restaurant. The 1940 edition of *New Xi'an* by Zhonghua Book Company stated that out-of-town restaurants in Xi'an were mostly concentrated on East Street, "Northern-style eateries include Beiping Restaurant, Yushun Lou, and Shandong-style Yixianting; Henan cuisine is represented by Diyi Lou, all on East Street. Southern flavors include Zhejiang Grand Restaurant on Mafangmen, Central Cuisine Society, Nanyuan 456 Cuisine Society, Changan Restaurant on Zhuba Shi, and New Shanghai Restaurant on East Street (all Jiangsu-Zhejiang cuisine). Cantonese cuisine is represented by Guangzhou Restaurant, and Hunan cuisine by Quyuan, both on East Street." An advertisement for Guangzhou Restaurant in *the Northwest Cultural Daily* on August 30, 1938, provided more details: "Seasonal Cantonese cuisine and dim sum, famous roasted pork and cured meats, affordable combination dishes, and luxurious banquets. Address: No. 480 East Street."

Cuangsheng Yuan Restaurant

However, Shanghai, the most developed city outside Guangdong, had no "Guangzhou Restaurant." Upon reflection, perhaps with so many competitors, no one dared to boldly use the prestigious "Guangzhou" label associated with "Eating in Guangzhou." Now, as today's most renowned Guangzhou Restaurant enters Shanghai and targets the high-end market, can it represent the great revival of Cantonese cuisine in Shanghai? Only time will tell.

2. Guanshengyuan Leading the New Era of Cantonese Cuisine

While "Guangzhou Restaurant" spread nationwide, Guanshengyuan

Cantonese Restaurant best embodied Cantonese cuisine's leading strength and golden age across regions. In cities like Wuhan, Chongqing, Kunming, and Guiyang, after the Anti-Japanese War, Guanshengyuan enjoyed great prestige, with even Chiang Kai-shek being a frequent visitor. It served as a benchmark not only for local Cantonese restaurants but for the entire local catering industry. The domestic brand "ABC Mickey Mouse" milk candy, developed by Guanshengyuan in Shanghai in 1943, later repackaged as "White Rabbit Creamy Candy," became a national gift presented to U.S. President Nixon and Soviet leaders. Today, time-honored food enterprises named Guanshengyuan exist in Shanghai, Nanjing, Wuhan, and Chongqing, with those in Shanghai and Nanjing awarded the "Chinese Time-honored Brand" certificate by the Ministry of Commerce.

(1) Rising in Shanghai and Gaining Prominence in Wuhan

Shanghai was the birthplace of Guanshengyuan, founded in 1918 by Xian Guansheng from Foshan. Just two years later, in 1920, Guanshengyuan expanded beyond Shanghai to open a branch in Hankou, another major port:

Our garden pioneered and invented Gravy Beef, Juice Beef, Nanhua Plums, Osmanthus Plum Preserves, Tangerine Peel Plums, Pitted Tangerine Peel Plums, Plum Extract, and Tangerine Peel Pitted Olives—affordable, high-quality, and renowned nationwide. Various beef dishes are perfect for satisfying hunger or accompanying wine; various fruits are delicious, fragrant, and can quench thirst and stimulate saliva. Convenient for travel and daily use, easy to carry, and ideal for gifts or entertaining guests. A branch is specially set up near Houcheng Road in Hankou. We welcome your patronage. (*Shanghai-Hong Kong Guanshengyuan Special Hankou Branch*, *Shenbao*, November 23, 1920)

Choosing Wuhan first was, as Mr. Tang Lusun described in *Food of Three Towns in Wuhan*, "Located at the thoroughfare of nine provinces, along the natural barrier of the Yangtze River, and a hub of water transportation, Wuhan has been an open port since early times, attracting merchants from all over. Materials from southwest provinces are also distributed here, so it boasts a complete range of delicious foods from all provinces, comparable to Shanghai." Meanwhile, Cantonese restaurants were scarce, making Guanshengyuan a pioneer. "Around 1931, there were almost no Cantonese restaurants in Wuhan. Later, a Guanshengyuan opened in Hankou, followed by a branch in Wuchang." The 1933 *Wuhan Guid*e published by Hankou New China Daily specifically listed 14 Cantonese restaurants with addresses, placing Guanshengyuan first, indicating its leading position. The Hankou branch of Guanshengyuan was hugely successful, expanding to three branch stores, one factory, and one distribution office in the city, with two branch stores and one factory in Wuchang, and a special summer branch in Lushan, Jiangxi. Subsequently, Guanshengyuan opened branches in Nanjing (with three branch stores, one factory, and one distribution office), Hangzhou (with branch stores and a West Lake pleasure boat), Tianjin (with three branch stores, one factory), and franchise stores in Beijing and other places.

With the full outbreak of the Anti-Japanese War in 1937 and the Japanese attack on Shanghai on August 13, steamships on the Yangtze River were commandeered for military use. At this critical juncture, Xian Guansheng decided to transport machinery, equipment, and over 180 tons of raw materials from Shanghai to the inland along the Yangtze River using wooden sailing boats, again prioritizing Wuhan. A canning factory was established on Hu Linyi Road in Wuchang, producing various canned foods. Wuhan Guanshengyuan entered its prime, becoming not only the top Cantonese restaurant in Wuhan but also the top Chinese restaurant. As noted at the time, formal banquets and high-level receptions in Wuhan often took place in Cantonese restaurants, "and among the largest Cantonese restaurants, including the Guanshengyuan food department, there were two. It seems that in the general impression, Guanshengyuan ranked the highest." In what ways did Guanshengyuan's supremacy manifest? For example, after the September 18th Incident, when the international investigation team visited Wuhan, "food became the biggest issue—Chinese or Western? After much discussion, it was decided to have Guanshengyuan handle the catering. Although they couldn't accommodate everyone, banquets were set up in the western restaurant across the street, with food and drinks provided by Guanshengyuan. Normally, whether the chairman, committee members, or mayor hosted banquets, Guanshengyuan seemed to be the designated dining venue. Even bankers, educators, etc., had to host guests at Guanshengyuan; otherwise, it seemed insufficient to show respect." (Hubei Native, *Guanshengyuan on*

Jianghan Road, *Food Industry*, Issue 9, 1934) Records indeed show numerous political figures and celebrities visiting Wuhan Guanshengyuan. For instance, Weng Wenhao, a renowned geologist and later President of the Executive Yuan of the Kuomintang, was invited to dinner at Guanshengyuan by Li Zhengqing on December 5, 1937, when he served as Minister of Economic Affairs of the National Government. (*Weng Wenhao's Diary*, Zhonghua Book Company, 2014 edition)

(2) Holding Fast in Chongqing

Around the Wuhan Campaign in 1938, as the National Government further relocated west to Chongqing, Guanshengyuan followed. This development can be seen in travel guides of the time. The 1993 edition of *Chongqing Travel Guide* briefly introduced restaurants, especially out-of-town ones, listing only a few. The only Cantonese restaurant mentioned was Zuixia Restaurant on Xiaoliangzi. However, the 1944 edition, while still brief, included several more Cantonese restaurants: "Cantonese cuisine includes Guanshengyuan and Guangdong Grand Restaurant (both on Minquan Road), and Nanjing Restaurant (at Fuxing Road intersection)." Except for Sichuan cuisine, other cuisines only mentioned Zhenji and Wufangzhai (Beijing-Shanghai cuisine) on Minzu Road. This highlights the prominent position of Cantonese cuisine and Guanshengyuan in Chongqing. Two versions of the *Chongqing Guide* compiled by Yang Shicai introduced Cantonese restaurants similarly but with different emphases, both led by Guanshengyuan: Douyou

Street in 1939 and Minquan Road in 1942. Lu Sihong's *New Chongqing* emphasized that "Chongqing has so many restaurants that they seem to exist every five steps," and "during lunch and dinner, every restaurant is packed," while also highlighting Cantonese restaurants, "So-called Xiajiang restaurants, covering various regions, such as Guanshengyuan and Daya Yuan, are famous for Cantonese cuisine." The 1941 *Chongqing Travel Guide* published by the Social Department's Chongqing Service Office prominently introduced nine Cantonese restaurants when listing famous out-of-town Chinese restaurants in Chongqing, with Guanshengyuan naturally included.

In any case, the largest and most famous Cantonese restaurant in Chongqing at that time was undoubtedly Guanshengyuan. "On every Sunday morning, the bustling scene at Chongqing Guanshengyuan was probably unimaginable to those in the isolated island [Shanghai]. There was not a single empty chair at the tables. Many people stood by the pillars, waiting for a chance to sit down. As soon as someone paid the bill and left a chair, it was occupied in a split second. The ancients said 'the mat is not warm enough,' but here it's 'the mat is not cool enough.'" Due to the fact that "all guests were from the upper class," it was imagined that Guanshengyuan branches nationwide were no different, "From 7 to 10 in the morning, such a scene unfolds across the country." (Artist, *Sketch of Chongqing Guanshengyuan*, *Yihai Weekly*, Issue 20, 1940) Such a renowned restaurant naturally attracted frequent visits from Mr. Gu Jiegang, as detailed in his diary. How could Chen Kewen, a native of Guangdong and Guangxi, be absent? Chen Kewen's last record of visiting Guanshengyuan in Chongqing is particularly precious: "July 27, 1939: At noon, invited by Liu Changyan and Guo Songnian, I had lunch at Guanshengyuan in the city with Zhuqiu. This was the first time to eat at a restaurant in the city since the surprise attack on May 3. Now there are only two restaurants in the city, which close after 11 am every day, presenting a desolate scene. After the surprise attacks in May and June and the recent two-night raids, there is hardly a single intact house in the city." In other words, when enemy planes had bombed the city into ruins and other restaurants dared not or refused to operate, Guanshengyuan became one of the only two remaining businesses—and certainly the only large restaurant—still open. With such dedication, how could it not become the benchmark for Cantonese restaurants and even the entire catering industry in Chongqing?

Mr. Ye Shengtao regarded Guanshengyuan as an important reference for his banqueting life: On the night of May 5, 1942, "Xianglin hosted a banquet in the name of Kaiming (Bookstore) at Guanshengyuan. Having not eaten Cantonese food for a long time, I quite enjoyed it. A banquet cost 300 yuan, which was not expensive by current standards." In a letter dated January 11, 1938, he wrote, "I have been to Brother Li Songye's wine shop, which has two floors and sells warm wine. It has eight tables, similar to Guanshengyuan, and is quite tidy." He also used Guanshengyuan as a reference to introduce a friend's wine shop. In a letter to a friend on October 8, 1938, when talking about the famous Chongqing restaurant Shengsheng Garden, he compared it to Shanghai Guanshengyuan, "It is structured like the Shanghai

Guanshengyuan farm. On the 2nd of this month, I dined there with Jiegang, Yuanshan, and Xucheng for a gathering of four primary school friends from 32 years ago." (Ye Shengtao, *Sichuan and Me*) This shows the status of Guanshengyuan Restaurant in his mind.

Mr. Liu Jie was very frugal and strict in his studies, rarely visiting restaurants. During his time in Chongqing, he naturally had few records of visiting Cantonese restaurants, but he visited Guanshengyuan relatively many times—about 10 times—which seemed to foreshadow his later settlement in Guangdong. (*Liu Jie's Diary*, Elephant Publishing House, 2009 edition) Mr. Mei Yiqi, President of Tsinghua University and Chairman of the Southwest Associated University's Administrative Committee, occasionally visited Cantonese restaurants in Chongqing due to work. He mentioned Guanshengyuan twice and Guangdong Restaurant twice, and the guests were all renowned figures. For example, on May 26, 1941, "At 7 pm, invited by Lin Bozun to Guanshengyuan, with Minister Weng (Wenhao), Wu Huafu, Bao Huaguo, Wang Pu, and others." (*Mei Yiqi's Diary of Southwest Associated University*) Chang Renxia visited Guanshengyuan twice while passing through Chongqing, "March 6, 1941: Morning, entered the city and dined at Guanshengyuan with Mr. Zhou (Shixian)." "July 6, 1944: Morning, invited by Tao Xingzhi to breakfast at Guanshengyuan." (*Chronicle of War Clouds*)

Mei Yiqi

Even after the victory of the Anti-Japanese War, the media still reminisced about Chongqing Guanshengyuan and mentioned that Chiang Kai-shek had visited, "Guanshengyuan has a farm in Caohejing, which will invite journalists to visit. Guanshengyuan can be regarded as China's first Cantonese restaurant. After the war, branches moved inland, and a farm was set up in Chongqing, which was quite a romantic story at the time, as Chongqing ladies and gentlemen liked to visit this Shanghai-style countryside. One day, Chairman Jiang also visited there and felt thirsty. Seeing a tea room set up by Guanshengyuan Farm, he went in and ordered a cup of coffee. The waiters were particularly attentive when they saw Chairman Jiang. At that time, prices had risen, and an ordinary cup of coffee cost about 100-200 yuan. Chairman Jiang refused to eat for free and insisted on paying the bill. Finally, the bill came, and Chairman Jiang was very satisfied." (*Chairman Jiang Visits Guanshengyuan: Xian Guansheng's*

Mooncake Theory, *Southeast Wind*, Issue 20, 1946) When Chiang Kai-shek's prestige was at its peak due to the victory of the Anti-Japanese War, the media probably would not have spread rumors. This shows how prestigious Guanshengyuan truly was.

Chengdu and Chongqing now belong to two different provinces, but they were both part of Sichuan in the past. When examining the grandeur of Cantonese cuisine and Guanshengyuan in Sichuan at that time, Chengdu cannot be overlooked. As stated in the guidebook *New Chengdu* of the time, "Although Sichuan cuisine is not as magnificent as Cantonese cuisine, in terms of snacks, Guangdong cannot compare to the past. Sichuan cuisine was once confined to Chengdu, while places like Chongqing and Wanzhou were far inferior to Chengdu in variety." However, Cantonese grand cuisine still had the upper hand. Thus, the book records two Cantonese restaurants: the Guangdong Economic Flavor Tofu Pudding Restaurant on Fuxing Street and Guanshengyuan on Zhengkejia Alley. (Zhou Zhengying, *New Chengdu*, Fuxing Bookstore, 1943 edition) Another guidebook also mentions Guanshengyuan on Zhengkejia Alley, calling it "the largest Cantonese restaurant in the city, with comprehensive facilities and clean sanitation." (*Chengdu Guide* compiled by Shanchuan Publishing House, Shanchuan Publishing House, 1943 edition)

(3) Advancing into Kunming

With the outbreak of the Anti-Japanese War, the rear area flourished.

Chongqing became the temporary capital, while Kunming became a crucial rear area: on the one hand, marked by the westward relocation of the Southwest Associated University, it became one of China's most important cultural hubs; on the other hand, it later became a key rear and forward base for the Allied forces in the anti-Japanese war. Assuming these two roles, people from all walks of life converged in Kunming, which presented a prosperous scene for a time, and restaurants have always been a symbol of prosperity, so Cantonese restaurants were certainly indispensable. On the one hand, Guangdong and Yunnan are both in the Great Southwest, as viewed by the new Confucian master Zhang Junmai in *The Shift of the Core Elements of the Chinese Nation in History and the Responsibilities of the Southwest*; on the other hand, due to their geographical proximity, there were many interactions, and Cantonese people not only had a gourmet palate but also financial means, as observed at the time, "(Southwest Associated University) also had dandies and ladies in fancy clothes squandering money—especially those with Cantonese accents." (Mu Wenjun, *Southwest Associated University Today*, *Student Friend*, Issue 4, 1940) Among these Cantonese restaurants, Guanshengyuan was the most representative.

Kunming Guanshengyuan had a thriving business with a constant stream of customers, but what deserves recording is undoubtedly the poetic and bohemian gatherings of celebrities from all walks of life, especially renowned scholars. According to historical records, the first to visit was the great historian Gu Jiegang on August 31, 1939, "Went to Guanshengyuan for dim sum with Zizhen, Changhua, and Xiangbo... This morning's tablemates: Xu Changhua, Dai Xiangbo (guests above), Yu and Zizhen (hosts)." Note: According to the recollections of those involved with Guanshengyuan, it had not yet opened at this time! Obviously, the memories are unreliable, and Gu's diary should be taken as the standard. In this case, Gu can be regarded as the authentic first customer to taste Guanshengyuan's "first soup." Unfortunately, he soon moved to Chengdu and Chongqing to visit Guanshengyuan there.

Zhu Ziqing

The next great celebrity recorded to have dined at Guanshengyuan was Mr. Zhu Ziqing on October 24, 1939, not long after its opening, "Attended the wedding of E Cun's daughter at Guanshengyuan. The groom was an officer. The food was good." Starting well with a new experience, he visited five or six more times later, but only until 1942. (*Zhu Ziqing's Diary*, Petroleum Industry Press, 2019 edition) Why didn't he record any visits in the following years? It's impossible that he didn't go at all, but professors and administrators of the Southwest Associated University mostly only recorded visits up to 1942 or 1943. Why? Even if they didn't go voluntarily, passive socializing was inevitable. For example, Professor Zheng Tianting, the general affairs director of Southwest Associated University, should have had many social engagements, but he only recorded two or three visits during the opening period, all with top university figures or famous professors:

> October 8, 1939: Half past six, I went to Guanshengyuan for a casual dinner invited by Master Menglin.
>
> October 11, 1939: Six o'clock, I went to Guanshengyuan to host a public banquet for Wen Zao, Bing Xin, and their husband, and Jin Fu with Shen Tian and Xue Ping.
>
> November 26, 1939: Because Master Menglin and I invited the young masters to dim sum on the 24th, I got up early, waited for others at Caisheng Lane at 7:30. At half past eight, I walked to Guanshengyuan on Jinbi Road for Cantonese dim sum, which Cantonese call "drinking tea." (Zheng Tianting's Diary of Southwest Associated University, Zhonghua Book Company, 2018 edition)

Finally, it is well put, "Having Cantonese dim sum, which Cantonese call 'drinking tea'." Without this clarification, many out-of-towners would hardly understand. For instance, Gu Jiegang wrote about visiting Cantonese restaurants for "dim sum" multiple times but never mentioned "drinking tea".

It should be noted that Cantonese "tea drinking" is vastly different from that in inland areas, focusing on dim sum with tea as a supplement. The dim sum is so delicious that it not only fills one's stomach but can even overstuff, far from being just a "snack" to satisfy a craving. Instead of getting tired of it after overeating, one would want to go again next time, and it's available all day, often open until 2 a.m. Mr. Mei Yiqi, one of the three giants of Southwest Associated University and President of Tsinghua University, had more social engagements and recorded about ten visits, but only up to 1943. (*Mei Yiqi's Diary of Southwest Associated University*, Zhonghua Book Company, 2018 edition)

Zhang Zonghe and his wife

Certainly, the one who visited Guanshengyuan the most and embodied the poetic and bohemian spirit was perhaps Mr. Wu Mi. As a bachelor, he often dined out; being in love, he frequently treated others; and as a renowned professor, he was often invited. His first visit to Guanshengyuan was remarkable. "November 17, 1939, I went to Guanshengyuan for a banquet hosted by A. L. Plad-Urquhart, and was introduced to his sister, the new British Consul General in Kunming, H. I. Prideaux-Brune. The dishes were abundant, and the wine was good. However, I deeply felt that in recent public banquets, I was almost the oldest in age but seated last (like tonight, others were all presidents, directors, and deans of the university, while I was just a professor)." Although this banquet triggered Wu Mi's sense of inferiority, "It increasingly shows that I have failed in this world and should not be attached!"—the level of the restaurant and the high standard of the banquet were fully demonstrated.

In addition to Mr. Wu Mi, Mr. Zhang Zonghe also left several records of visiting Kunming Guanshengyuan in his diary. Despite his aristocratic background, Zhang Zonghe lived in the Southwest and held an ordinary teaching position, leading a financially strained life. However, from these records, we see both his generous demeanor as a noble son. For example, "November 24, 1942: Rushed to Guanshengyuan at 5 o'clock, spent 260 yuan, but was not satisfied." It should be noted that three months earlier, Wu Mi spent only 140 yuan on a birthday banquet here. On the other hand, it reveals Guanshengyuan's survival strategy in difficult times, catering to all budgets, where his family of three could fill up with a plate of fried noodles and several dim sum.

(4) Guiyang and Others

Guangdong and Guizhou are connected by the Pearl River. In 2006, Lin Shusen from Guangdong governed Guizhou and promoted the construction of the Guiyang-Guangzhou Railway, shortening the "distance" between Guizhou and Guangdong. Especially after its official opening in 2014, the slogan of making Guizhou, particularly Guiyang, a backyard garden for Guangdong resounded loudly. In recent years, more and more Cantonese have indeed traveled, traded, and even settled in Guizhou. Few know that the Cantonese have long been the main visitors to Guizhou, especially Guiyang. Since the Qing Dynasty, Guangdong Street, Guiyang's most famous commercial street, got its name because Cantonese merchants operated general merchandise, jade, and marine products there, "With the market's expansion and prosperity, merchants from Jiangxi, Hunan, Sichuan, and Yunnan also came to Zhu (Guiyang) to trade, mostly settling on Guangdong Street." (Zhu Linxiang, Zhu Zhiguo, *Commercial Activities on Guangdong Street Before Liberation*, in *The Changes of Guiyang's Commerce*, Guizhou People's Publishing House, 2012 edition)

However, the peak of Cantonese migration to Guizhou likely occurred during the Anti-Japanese War, a period that remains unmatched to this day. As Guizhou was a major rear area at the time, many public and private institutions, especially military organs and factories, were stationed in Guiyang. Particularly after Guangzhou fell in 1938, numerous personnel and institutions from industrially developed Guangdong relocated to Guiyang. A December 18, 1945, *Shenbao* report stated that there were approximately 10,000 Cantonese personnel and technicians serving in U.S. military agencies in Guiyang, with families totaling around 50,000. Their mass return after the agencies disbanded became a social concern due to resettlement challenges. The total Cantonese population in Guiyang was likely numbered 80,000 to 100,000. In the early days of Guangdong Street, cross-regional food markets were underdeveloped, so Cantonese restaurants were rare; local flavors were mostly provided by Guangdong Guilds. But such a massive flow of people and goods during the war inevitably spurred the rise of Cantonese restaurants. Within just a few years, 16 verifiable Cantonese restaurants emerged in Guiyang, some of which were among the city's premier hotels (see my article *Connected by a River: Cantonese Restaurants in Guiyang during the Republic of China era*, Shuwu 2022, No. 2). Comparing this to Tianjin, where only 17 named Cantonese restaurants were documented over a century (see my article *Gateway to Guangdong: Cantonese Restaurants in Tianjin during the Republic of China era*, *Yangcheng Evening News* January 13, 2021), it exemplifies a spectacular spread of "Eating in Guangzhou." The most prominent was Guanshengyuan, opened on May 25, 1941, at Dashizi Sanshan Road in the city center with a 200,000-yuan investment. In 1943, Xian Guansheng stayed in Guiyang for a year, meticulously planning business development and strictly implementing regulations (Bai Tianbai, *Cantonese Restaurants in Guiyang Before Liberation*, *Selected Historical*

Materials of Yunyan, the Eighth Volume).

Celebrity mentions of Guanshengyuan first appeared in Ye Shengtao's writings. When traveling from Chengdu to Guilin via Guiyang in 1942, he noted on May 18, "Song Yushu invited Yu and Binran to have dim sum at Guanshengyuan." Zhang Zonghe, who frequented Cantonese restaurants and Guanshengyuan in Hangzhou, Shanghai, Wuhan, Chongqing, and Kunming, recorded post-war visits to Guiyang's Guanshengyuan in his diary. Though his evaluations were moderate, Xian Guansheng's post-war focus returned to Shanghai, naturally affecting Guiyang's operations—Zhang still dined there repeatedly, indicating its acceptability.

Additionally, Tianjin and Lushan each had a Guanshengyuan. Sun Limin and Yu Zhihou's *Overview of Tianjin French Concession* (*Tianjin Historical Materials Selection 22nd Volume*) states, "Southern-style shops include three Daoxiangcun stores (Senji, Mingji, Linji), as well as Guanshengyuan, Jinyangchun, Guanglongtai, etc."

Appendix: General Li's Wine Crosses the River

In China's long feudal society, wine bans were imposed for various reasons, such as grain shortages, tax issues, and what would today be called discipline and work style problems. However, Lingnan was essentially free from such bans throughout history. Theoretically, this provided unique advantages for the development of wine-making techniques and craftsmanship in Lingnan, as well as the accumulation of wine culture. Wine-making first requires high-quality grain and water. Lingnan's hot and rainy climate allows many areas to have three harvests a year, ensuring an abundant grain supply. The region's unique topography is dotted with "spiritual springs and sweet liquids" (as described by Fan Duan'ang), with Qu Dajun's *New Words of Guangdong* listing many examples. Abundant grain, excellent water, and good yeast are essential. Lingnan's rich plant resources mean herbaceous materials for yeast are readily available. The precious Wencao, for instance, was used to make wine with a unique flavor, as noted in Yang Fu's *Records of Southern Foreign Oddities* from the Eastern Han Dynasty, "Wencao used in wine-making perfects its taste. Buying this herb with gold is not considered expensive." Under Lingnan's favorable grain, water, and climatic conditions, ancestors could even make yeast by simply "pounding rice flour and mixing it with three to five medicinal herbs" (Qu Dajun's words). Thus, how could Lingnan not produce good wine, produce it in abundance, and produce it early? Luofu Jiuyun, a representative of Lingnan fine wines, outshone Jiannanchun in Li Zhao's *Supplements to the History of the Tang Dynasty*. It was already a world-renowned wine as early as in Zhang Hua's *Ode to Extravagance* during the Jin Dynasty. Jiannanchun is now highly renowned and claims to have been created in the Tang Dynasty, yet Luofu Chun remains obscure—is this not a strange phenomenon? Additionally, Lingnan's four-season flowers and widespread fruit forests inspired ancestors to use them for winemaking. As Qu Dajun said, "Almost everything can be made into wine:

longan wine, orange jelly wine, winter white grape wine, spring red fairy grass wine, monthly yellow osmanthus wine, and lychee shaochun—all are noble wines." Furthermore, the Hundred Flowers Wine from the Western Han Dynasty and the Plum Blossom Zhou mentioned by Ji Han in the Jin Dynasty, which intoxicated Western Han scholar Lu Jia and Dongfang Shuo, have longer histories and more legendary colors. These flower and fruit wines, endowed by nature, are unmatched elsewhere.

Lychee wine

In recent times, since lychees are most renowned in Lingnan, lychee wine has also dominated here. Especially, materials on the spread and value of lychee wine are almost exclusively from Lingnan. Examining the history of lychee wine production and its northward spread using newly excavated historical records—particularly its popularity in literary circles from the mid-late Ming Dynasty and its status as imperial wine in the early Qing Dynasty—

holds significant importance not only for agricultural and lychee history research but also for the study of food culture history, especially Lingnan wine culture history.

1. The Origin of Shaojiu (Distilled Liquor) and a Brief History of Lychee Wine Production

The earliest reference to lychee wine comes from the mid-Tang Dynasty poet Bai Juyi's *Wine at Lychee Tower*, "Newly ripe lychees glow like cockscombs; newly opened shaojiu exhales amber fragrance. I wish to pluck a branch and pour a cup, but who can share this at West Tower without guests?" As Zhang Xuan, a famous Ming Dynasty scholar, wrote in *Doubts and Illuminations*, "In my hometown, lychees are often soaked in shaojiu. Even when making lychee wine, shaojiu is used, a practice that has prevailed since the Tang Dynasty. Bai Letian's poem proves this." However, strictly speaking, this material cannot be fully trusted, as it involves correctly interpreting the poem: Was it about soaking fresh lychees in shaojiu, using lychees to accompany wine, or making lychee wine with lychees and shaojiu as Zhang Xuan understood? The exact answer is hard to determine, but it at least provides imaginative space for later lychee wine brewing, at minimum, the brewing of Lingnan lychee wine, as interpreted by Zhang Xuan from Bai's poem.

Furthermore, during the transportation of Lingnan lychees, shaojiu was often used for preservation. For example, Wang Lin, a Zhejiang scholar who became a Cabinet Secretary during the Kangxi-Qianlong period, praised the preservation function of wine-soaked lychees in *Ming Mountain Wine-Soaked Fresh Lychees*, "Peeling light red lychees is not rare; the combination with deep green wine is truly delightful. The scarlet shells still resemble phoenix eggs, and the jade-like flesh maintains its divine beauty. Superior to the millennial fruits of the Jasper Garden, it wouldn't require the post horses that tired for Yang Guifei." He believed that if this technique had been used in ancient times, the imperial post horses wouldn't have been exhausted for lychee delivery. Another example is Wang Su of Jiangsu in the Qianlong era, who described in *Record of Bestowed Lychees* that lychees were presented to the emperor by using shaojiu immersion for preservation, "When do lychees from the hot region arrive? Wrapped in red silk and fine gauze. The sound of bells startles as they're presented, their radiance shimmering through the curtain. Groups of purple-red lychees pile up; peeling them reveals ice-like slices. The jade-like juice in the bowl can't be poured fast enough; the nectar slides down the throat. The immortals of the sea mountains have great drinking capacity, especially granted a Yaochi banquet. Drinking for ten days without waking, the spring scenery of Lingnan always graces their faces. (Fresh lychees are pickled in wine for tribute.)" This practice continued until the late Qing Dynasty. Zhang Wenxiang loved fresh lychees. When governing Hubei, he ordered the magistrate of Zengcheng, Guangdong, to buy ten thousand lychees, soak them in sorghum wine, seal them in porcelain jars, and send them to Hubei. When the jars reached Wuhu, they were intercepted by the tax office and confiscated. The tax official at the time was Yuan

Zhongjie Gongchang. Suddenly receiving an urgent telegram from Zhang, over a hundred words about the lychee case, Yuan knew the lychees had been eaten by inspectors, so he purchased replacements to make up for them." (Xu Ke, Zhang Wenxiang's *Love for Lychees*, in Qing Dynasty Unofficial Records)

Another piece of Tang Dynasty historical material about lychee winemaking, though different from later practices, consistently attributes it to Lingnan: "When Li Wenru of the Tang Dynasty went to Changle Long, his servant hid lychees in a jar, which Li didn't know at first. During the sweltering summer, fragrance emanated from the jar, and the pulp overflowed. He added qu (yeast) and japonica rice to it, and after three days, wine was formed, more fragrant than pepper and cinnamon. Many people imitated this, inspiring the *Lychee Wine Song*." (Tongzhi *Shaozhou Prefecture Gazetteer*) Japonica rice refers to rice made from japonica rice; pepper and cinnamon refer to pepper and osmanthus wine, representing fine wines. This is the traditional fermentation method for qu wine, not the shaojiu brewing method mentioned by Zhang Xuan later. This also implies that the "shaojiu" in Bai Juyi's poem likely refers to heating wine, as distilled shaojiu was introduced from abroad starting in the Yuan Dynasty, with Cantonese people being among the first to adopt it. As Qu Dajun wrote in *New Words of Guangdong*, "There is also a type of 'big cake shao,' made by steaming distiller's grains in a tin steamer and draining the juice. It is extremely hot in nature; excessive consumption harms the spleen and kidneys, often causing phlegm and foot problems, even death, which should be prohibited. Huang Taiquan once commented on this. According to records, the method of shaojiu originated in the Yuan Dynasty. Siamese people would rebrew shaojiu with exotic fragrances for two to three years; drinking a few cups would make people drunk, called 'A Zhao Ji Jiu.' The Yuan Dynasty is said to have learned this method from foreigners." This shaojiu technique still exists in rural Hunan and Guangdong. Qu Dajun also dedicated an entry to "fire wine" (another term for shaojiu):

> Cantonese call newly distilled shaojiu "wine head;" mixing it with water makes "he jiu" (mixed wine), consumed by the poor. The best shaojiu on the market uses fine cakes, followed by big cakes, called "fine cake shao" and "big cake shao." The excellent ones are "Longjiang shao," which tastes good after three to four years of aging. However, excessive drinking causes phlegm and foot problems. Phlegm originates from the stomach; shaojiu is steamed with fire, formed from fire's sweat, so it ignites easily and has an extremely hot nature, the leftover harm from the Yuan Dynasty. Siamese wine is rebrewed twice, smoked with sandalwood until dark, then sandalwood is added, sealed with wax, and buried for three years to remove fire qi before consumption. This is the most potent shaojiu, called "fire wine," which can cure chronic diseases and kill insects when drinking one or two cups. However, all shaojiu in Guangdong is fire wine, also called "qi jiu" (qi meaning vapor), with an overly pungent taste. Its qu is made from galangal, mountain citrus,

smartweed, etc., mixed with beans and rice. Xinhui and Xiangshan use almond, called "herb qu," which is toxic. Panyu has more sugar shao and yam shao, the lowest-grade wines.

Lychee

Since all "shaojiu" in Guangdong is this "fire wine," there is no doubt that lychee wine is either this fire wine or made from it. Thus, Qu Dajun further noted, "For lychee wine, locals bring brewing tools under a tree, and use lychees to stew wine, completing it in one night"—that is, using Lingnan fire wine and lychee pulp through a special "bi" (stewing) process. According to the "Lychee Wine Recipe" in Xu's Penjing cited in Deng Qingcai's *Comprehensive Record of Fujian Lychees* from the Ming Dynasty, the method fully aligns with Guangdong's shaojiu brewing: "Use three dou of lychee pulp and one jin of shaojiu cake noodles, mix well, and place in a large basin. After fermenting for a day, transfer to another large basin and ferment for another day, then distill according to shaojiu methods. Bury the wine in the ground for two days to remove fire qi; it becomes fragrant and delightful."

Lingnan's four-season floral and fruit abundance meant "almost anything could be made into wine." Especially in the Song Dynasty, with no wine bans and "prosperous people," "every household brewed wine, competing to create exotic varieties, "leading to a succession of famous wines that "eminent scholars exiled here often favored." By the Ming and Qing dynasties, with the introduction and improvement of shaojiu (distilled liquor) techniques, lychee wine flourished, becoming a paragon among wines. By then, not only Lingnan but also Fujian, another lychee-producing province, made lychee wine similar to Guangdong's. "Shunchang Snowflake Fire Wine, infused with lychees and aged for ten days, is rich, gorgeous, and deep, like Xi Shi drunkenly leaning on a jade bed or Dazhen emerging from a hot spring. Sealed with mud, when opened a year later, the room fills with the fragrance of fresh lychees." (Song Biyu, *Lychee Manual*)

2. A Brief Discussion on the Northward Spread of Lychee Wine

The northward spread of lychee wine can be traced to Wei Xian's Farewell to Chen Luya, Grand Counselor, "Two years in an ancient temple with deep trees; how many kindred spirits in White Gate's carriages? Your poetic obsession will leave a legacy; my homesickness rests on a plain qin. We often drank together on lychee wine at midnight, protected by lotus robes from the wind. Suddenly, I board a spring-river boat once more; peaches and plums say nothing; I seek them only in dreams." Note: Wei Xian (birth-death unknown), styled Weidu, was from Fuqing, Fujian. A Jiajing 23rd year (1544) civil servant, he served as a Ministry of War official and the Surveillance Commissioner of Guangxi, among other posts, and he was the author of *Zhenjiang Hall Collection*. Later, in Tang Xianzu's classic play *The Peony Pavilion: Encounter*, when Liu Mengmei bids farewell after obtaining travel expenses from Imperial Envoy Du Bao, "[Sheng (Male Role)] If so, free from parents or spouse, I bid farewell now. [Jing (Painted Face Male Role] Attendants, bring scholarly gifts and prepare wine. [Chou (Clown Role)] Guangnan loves lychee wine, while north winds blow elm pod money. Wine arrives, as do scholarly gifts. [Jing] Sir, please accept these travel expenses. [Sheng] Thank you! [Jing offers wine]" Though lychee wine's northward spread was then only in writing, as imperial envoy wine, it should have already been transported to northern China. Later, Gu Qiyuan of Nanjing, a Tanhua (third-place scholar in the imperial examinations), served as the Left Vice Minister of the Ministry of Personnel and concurrently as Hanlin Academy Scholar-Official, listed lychee wine among national famous wines in his 1618 self-published Conversations of a Guest, indicating its long-standing prevalence and acclaim in Jiangnan, "I am not good at drinking, unable to finish three small cups each time, yet I rejoice at the sight of wine and greatly at the mention of fine wine. Throughout my life, I have tasted: the Forbidden City's 'Full Hall Fragrance,' officials' 'Inner Method Wine,' Beijing's yellow rice wine, Jizhou's job's tears wine, Yongping's Sangluo wine, Yizhou's Yi wine, Cangzhou's Cang wine, Daming's Diao wine and Jiao wine, Jinan's Autumn Dew White Wine, Taihe's Tai wine, Magu's Shenggong Spring Wine, Lanxi's Golden Plate Dew Wine, Shaoxing's bean wine, Guangxi's mulberry mistletoe wine, Guangdong's lychee wine, Fenzhou's lamp wine, Huai'an's bean wine and bitter wormwood wine, Gaoyou's Wujiapi wine, Yangzhou's snow wine and Xixian wine, Wuxi's Hua family Dangkou wine and He family pine flower wine, most of which excel in color and taste."

Later, Song Biyu stated, "South Sea people brew with Heiye lychees, equally renowned in Jiangnan as Guangxi's mistletoe wine, "citing Xin'an Cheng Mengyang's *Lychee Wine Ode* in praise, "Don't you see Du Ling's old guest among princes, left hand plucking light red, right clutching green? To this day, in Huanhua's poems, spring wine and lychees shine together. Who mixed with ingenuity to brew lychee into spring wine? Heavy green and light red blend indistinctly, falling into my hand from thousands of miles away. Romantic Sima with a frosty beard, jade plates spread with tens of thousands of delicacies. Heaven sends rare things to comfort enthusiasts, flying hundreds of pots from Yu Ridge. I'm the poorest drinker here, a spoonful reviving my parched poetic heart. When the silver jar opens, its aroma is robust; the jade cup reflects a clear, almost invisible hue. Northerners hear that wine is like milk, while the Wu people drool over pearls. The host's love for rarity brings extra joy; behind golden screens emerge flower-like beauties. Comparing their grace to wine's splendor, no need to trace silk robes and jade skin. If youthful faces transformed into wine, who could support us as we topple like jade mountains? Don't you see Su Dongpo devouring hundreds of lychees in exile, boasting of this livelihood for his post? How much better are these three wonders before us: fruit as sauce, horse as nectar. I only regret ancients never saw you—why shouldn't we rejoice?" Note: Cheng Jiasui's *Songyuan Langtao Collection* also preserves this poem, titled *Impromptu Lychee Wine Ode for Lord Yin's Guests*, with a self-note after "Heaven sends rare things to comfort enthusiasts, flying hundreds of pots from Yu Ridge", "Wine from Xuwen County, Guangdong, specially sent by Cao Gaozhou of Taicang with two bottles." This indicates that lychee wine was abundantly produced in southern Guangdong, of excellent quality.

What further enhanced lychee wine's reputation in Jiangnan were the poetic and drinking gatherings centered around Qian Qianyi, a high-ranking official in the late Ming and early Qing dynasties and a leading literary figure. Qian Qianyi, a Tanhua in the 38th year of Wanli in the Ming Dynasty, served as Minister of Rites and was one of the leaders of the Donglin Party. Later, he surrendered to the Qing Dynasty and became Minister of Rites, dominating the early Qing literary scene. Leveraging his prestigious status, he had disciples and former subordinates across the country. When Huang Dake, a student returning to Lingnan, Qian Qianyi presented him with a poem to request wine, fully demonstrating his love for lychee wine, "Remember when the lychee wine is ripe, send me a full jar despite poverty." To ensure Dake sent the wine, Qian repeatedly urged him not to use poverty as an excuse and to send it in full jars. Of course, given Qian's wealth, he would not let Dake give it for free, but this not only showed their close relationship but also his greed for Lingnan lychee wine. With Qian's status, he could taste any fine wine in the world, yet his deep attachment to lychee wine naturally highlighted its exceptional quality. This was further demonstrated in Qian's poem *After Seeing Dake Off* after Huang Dake's departure, "Holding hands at the thatched gate by autumn water, tears fall looking south to Wuyang. Among rustling poplars are many good friends, and among spirited martyrs are old acquaintances. I can't bear to pour old tears while washing my face, but I'm glad to still have a free body. Brew lychee wine again next year, and compete with pine wine in the small spring." "Tears falling when looking south to Wuyang" certainly expressed their teacher-student bond, but it was also likely related to missing lychee wine, as the concluding lines said, "Brew lychee wine again next year, and compete with pine wine in the small spring." Pine wine was a famous ancient wine, as mentioned in the poem *Returning to Pei Mingfu's Residence* by Li Shangyin, a great poet of the late Tang Dynasty: "Borrow a dou of pine wine to accompany you in washing away worries." Compared with pine wine, lychee wine was worthy of being listed among ancient and modern famous wines.

What is less known is that these two poems by Qian and his later Preface to *Chen Qiaosheng's Poetry Collection* embodied the sorrow of his unfulfilled ambition to restore the Ming Dynasty after surrendering to the Qing. Especially in the preface, he began by saying he did not know Chen Qiaosheng and wrote the preface only because Chen was the younger brother of Chen Zizhuang. His relationship with Chen Zizhuang was no more than "etiquette first, "yet "they held hands and poured out their hearts like brothers, "so "even though I had never met Qiaosheng, I regarded the younger brother of Nanhai as my own brother." Inspired by loyalty and righteousness, and with "old age in winter, a hundred feelings converging, "he was fortunate to "drink lychee wine, "then "happily picked up the pen, with a dim cold lamp and rustling window paper, as if under the influence of divine beings." Beyond the poetic and bohemian charm, there was a generous and tragic spirit, leaving a precious record of Jiangnan-Lingnan cultural exchange alongside the history of lychee wine.

Qian Qianyi also had a poem *Huang Sheng from Lingnan Sent Me a*

Wine Manual to Brew Lychee Wine; *Yiren and Zunwang Each Drank a Cup, and Yiren Composed a Poem, So I Hastily Responded*, describing the scene of drinking lychee wine with Liu Rushi and his most valued grandnephew Qian Zunwang, "Lingnan lychee wine surpasses crane-shaped goblets in postal delivery. We admired its deep green color, yet couldn't finish a full cup. It instantly melted green on the teeth, and fragrance began to fill the intestines. I still pity the Qujiang Ode for failing to praise this nectar." The poem uses multiple allusions to describe the excellence of lychee wine, praising it beyond measure.

He once took out the lychee wine stored for years to bid farewell to Fang Wen, a gifted scholar known as one of the "Three Poets of Tongcheng, "and praised it boastfully. Only true love would lead to such disregard for formal etiquette, "...I have Yangcheng lychee wine, sent by an old friend from Lingbiao to celebrate my birthday. The rim of the jar can thank the world, but the surface should only be shared with good friends. Sealed for a year, it's opened for you—don't hesitate to drink a full cup at the crossroads." (Qian Qianyi, Farewell to Fang Erzhi Returning to Jinling) Fang Wen was deeply moved by this banquet and wrote *Mr. Qian Mu Zhai Invited Me to Drink Lychee Wine and Composed a Song Afterward*, "A guest came from Wuyang City, carrying a jar of lychee wine, saying it was brewed from lychee pulp for Mr. Qian of Yushan. Mr. Qian has kept it by his bed for a long time, waiting for good friends to drink it. Hearing of my arrival, he happily ordered the maid to open the wine. I had never tasted fresh lychees before, but now I know their flavor. Its color is like jade dew on a cold day, and its fragrance is like when light red lychees are first peeled. He repeatedly urged me to drink from an ancient porcelain cup, showing such love for me. How can I repay him? Only with a prescription—village wine for deafness plus iron arrows." He also wrote *Farewell to Qian Mu Zhai* to express his gratitude again, as mellow and lasting as lychee wine, "When I visited Yushan in the hot summer, I knocked on Mr. Qian 's door nine out of ten days. He spared no lychee wine, and walking through the path was like entering a Peach Blossom Spring. Ancient sages traveled thousands of miles lightly, and heroes valued a word to repay kindness. Looking back reluctantly at parting, we agreed to meet again in winter."

We know that since the late Tang Dynasty, Jiangnan has gradually become the economic and cultural center of China, which has had a profound impact on Lingnan culture. Especially since the Ming and Qing dynasties, Lingnan culture has directly taken Jiangnan as its model. In particular, Qu Dajun received the support of Qian Qianyi and Zhu Yizun, two leading figures in the literary world, during his critical growth period. Qu himself was deeply grateful, "Fame arose from the praise in the literary field; even before crossing Meiguan, the fragrance had spread." However, just as "teaching and learning promote each other, and the student surpasses the master, "Qu Dajun, as a commoner from remote Lingnan, first obtained the support and even praise from the leaders of the cultural center. The most important positive impact was that "the Wusong scholarly circle's Wengshan

School found its elegant leaders in these two gentlemen" (*Ode on Repeatedly Receiving Letters from Friends*), in turn influencing Jiangnan culture and becoming mentors and friends with Jiangnan literary giants. The story of lychee wine is no different. Having received unsparing high praise from Jiangnan literary masters, Lingnan scholars naturally took pride in treating guests with it. Qu Dajun composed the long poem Lychee Wine (written at Prefect Wang's banquet), highly praising the beauty of this Lingnan specialty, and calling "brewing wine with lychee flowers an immortal recipe."

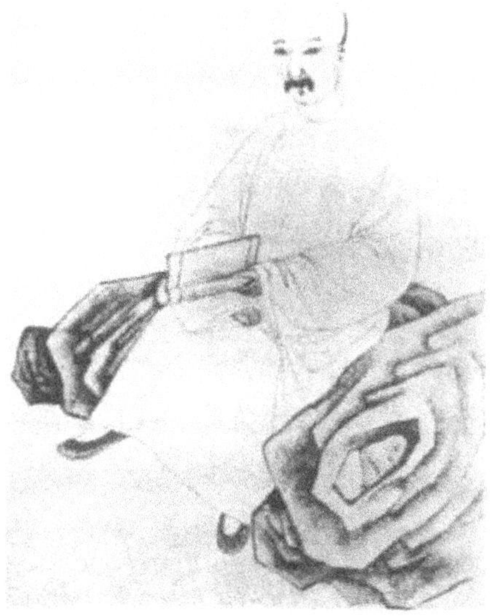

Liang Peilan

Chen Gongyin, one of the "Three Great Masters of Lingnan," praised lychee wine no less than Qu Dajun. His *Lychee Wine* (chanted at Prince Qian's banquet in Huizhou) states, "Its power to invigorate the mind and enhance wisdom remains, and its ability to beautify the complexion is even more complete." It is truly an immortal product. Liang Peilan, another of the

“Three Great Masters of Lingnan, “invited friends from Jiangnan to farewell banquets with lychee wine, “I have lychee wine, but you refuse to come. With infinite feelings of parting, I see you off at Yuewang Terrace...” (Sending Wang Yuzhao and Zha Deyin Back to Yuhang). Liang Peilan not only proudly used lychee wine to send off friends in his hometown but also took it to other regions to entertain them, winning great praise, “Born from the cinnabar of the hot mountains, growing alongside the jade-like elders of Huatian. Regardless of silk ribbons and red robes, it leaps into the crystal palace (stored in a glass bottle).” “Sweeter than jade dew and richer than milk, its flavor truly rivals fragrant jade. A single drop feels like an enlightenment, not exchanging hard work for Yiliang.” (Chen Dazhang, *Liang Yaoting Brought Lychee Wine from Lingnan and Invited Us to Drink; Composed with Lu Xinzhai, Guo Moxu, and Wei Yuping*). The time and place of this gathering are unknown, but the poet Chen Dazhang was from Huanggang, Hubei, a Jinshi of the Kangxi Wuchen period, selected as a Shujishi, and resigned to care for his elderly mother. Thus, the location was either Hubei or Beijing. Regardless, as documented, under the advocacy of literati from Jiangnan and Lingnan, lychee wine began to spread north beyond these regions. In the late early Qing Dynasty, Wang Shizhen, a new literary leader and Minister of Punishment from Shandong, composed the poem *Lychee Wine* to highly praise it, marking the clear success of lychee wine’s northward spread, “Red through cicada gauze wrapping jade skin, the brewed fragrance surpasses lotus. In Tianbao, Sichuan post horses delivered lychees, vainly causing the palace to lose teeth.”

Later, Wang Mo, a native of Baodi, Hebei, who served as the Prefect of Huizhou, wrote *Lychee Wine* with a contrast and climax approach: Guangdong is good in all aspects except wine, but lychee wine is exceptionally good, rarely comparable to ancient and modern famous wines, and was delivered to Beijing via fast post as a tribute, "The elder loves drinking and has a good complexion; it arrived in Beijing after two months of rapid delivery." Gong Hongli, a Jinshi of Kangxi, compiler of the Hanlin Academy, and editor at Wuying Hall, couldn't help but passionately compose Lychee Wine: *Composed with Others at Lord Xincheng's Banquet* after drinking lychee wine at a banquet in the capital, "...Sun-baked and rain-soaked, it can't be preserved; through snow and ice, it reaches the capital. White jade as pulp lacks fragrance, and clear frost syrup can't match its whiteness. How can we taste such sweet and sour nectar? There's been no such recipe since ancient times. Accidentally obtaining a volume of wine scriptures, I surpass Yidi and Dukang. I've long relied on broken inkstones, only getting drunk at the Minister's banquet. While he serves the world like ginger and cinnamon, he loves this pure flavor. I once traveled through Fujian, sighing at empty branches in the wind. Suddenly seeing duck-green waves in the unsealed mud, saliva flows at the goose-yellow milk. Alas, Yongyuan and Tianbao have seen many changes, but Boyou and Linfu have different evaluations. Just let me drink a dan in one go, not asking about side growth in the red dust."

Later, lychee wine became an essential precious "gift" for Cantonese people or those who had served in Guangdong when traveling north. "Why ask about Cantonese attire when meeting? Just bring a unique famous wine. Pouring light white like plum blossom color, savoring the delicate red lychee fragrance. Stopping cups to talk about the journey for thousands of miles, washing away sorrows with nine rounds of drinking. Pearls and jade are useless; winning friends a drunkard's cup" (Wang Shixiang, B*rother Yangting Just Returned from Guangdong and Offered Lychee Wine to Guests*). "Brewed wine brought from east of Yuling, clear as jade and particularly rich. One jar makes me drunk, as if I were on the four hundred peaks of Luofu" (Yu Wen'ao, *Lychee Wine*).

The most remarkable achievement or successful identity of lychee wine's northward spread was becoming a tribute. For example, Cao Yin, the grandfather of Cao Xueqin, the author of *Dream of the Red Chamber* and someone who received Kangxi's southern tours four times at home, said in *Shi Xunjiang Composed a Farewell Poem and Enjoyed Gifted Lychee Wine; This Is to Express Gratitude*, "Who plucks deep green and light red, with spring following the south wind for thousands of miles. Local products have always followed tribute, with poetry cylinders the first to arrive by post. Pitifully knowing my love for food, sending it to ease grief in vain. The color and fragrance remain unchanged when poured, with flowers in bloom beneath the eaves scattered in the evening smoke." Furthermore, it became a national gift. The King of Portugal dispatched Messire Medeiros and others to present a memorial to congratulate and respectfully wish the Emperor good health, with ceremonies identical to those of the 59th year. Tributes included local products... The Emperor specially bestowed upon the King ginseng, imperial silk, porcelain, foreign lacquerware, lychee wine, bud tea, paper, ink, silk, lanterns, fans, sachets, and other items, with varying rewards for the envoys." (*General Dictionary of the Qing Dynasty*) Granted such imperial honor, the lychee wine's reputation became untouchable for later generations. Thereafter, countless poems and praises of lychee wine emerged, too numerous to list here.

Chapter 4 Each in Its Glory: Chaoshan Cuisine and Hakka Cuisine

Chaozhou and Meizhou in eastern Guangdong, historically known as Chaoshan or Lingdong, often gave an impression of integration. Although the terms "Chaoshan people" and "Hakka people" later emerged, their mutual influence remained profound. Chaoshan and Hakka cuisines also influenced each other. For example, Chaoshan beef balls, a representative Chaoshan food, originated from the Hakka. Additionally, since both Chaoshan and Hakka people typically traveled by sea from Shantou, moving south or north without often passing through the provincial capital, Chaoshan and Hakka cuisines—mutually influenced yet each has its own unique characteristics—differ significantly from the Cantonese cuisine centered on Guangfu. This led Mr. Tang Zhenchang to argue that excluding Chaoshan cuisine from the "Eight Great Cuisines" was truly inappropriate, making a special account worthwhile.

4.1 The Early Rise of Chaoshan Cuisine

Lingnan cuisine is renowned worldwide for "Eating in Guangzhou, "even internationally. Within Guangdong, however, there is a saying, "Eating in Guangzhou, flavor from Chaoshan." Due to the ethnic group's long-term colonization of Southeast Asia, they excel in utilizing Southeast Asian spice resources—the early trade route between Europe and Asia was commonly known as the "Spice Route." The most typical example is Chaoshan brine, which often uses a dozen or even dozens of spices. How could this not make Chaoshan cuisine unique! As early as the mid-late 1980s, Professor Huang Shusen, a leading figure in Lingnan culture, believed that as the new vanguard of Cantonese cuisine, Chaoshan cuisine "will 'advance north' at a speed of 500 li per year." Today, top restaurants in the capital definitely include Chaoshan dishes.

1. Fang Shu's *Chaoshan Miscellaneous Odes* and the Origins of Cantonese Cuisine

Han Yu's *First Taste of Southern Cuisine: Presented to Yuan Shiba, Assistant Law Officer*, has no relation to Chaoshan, which is regrettable. However, Fang Shu's *Chaoshan Miscellaneous Odes* by modern author Fang Shu is highly valuable. Published in the first issue of *Youth Magazine* (1915), hosted by Chen Duxiu, this poem is a rare classic in my years of researching Lingnan food culture history. Alongside Han Yu's poem and Zhao Yi's *Playful Ode on Eating Frog*, it stands as one of the most important early documents on Chaoshan cuisine. Fang Shu (style name Liuyue), a native of Wuwei, Anhui, was a descendant of Fang Bao, the founder of the Tongcheng School, and a juren in the 20th year of the Guangxu reign. Gifted in poetry, his surviving works were compiled by descendants into *Selected and Annotated Poems of Liuyue* (Huangshan Bookstore, 2014). Appreciated by Li Hongzhang, he was invited to serve in his residence as a tutor and was friendly with Chen Duxiu. Having served in Lingnan, he authored two volumes of *Lingnan Ode Manuscripts*, which "vividly depict Guangdong customs." *Chaoshan Miscellaneous Odes*, though published in 1915, was actually written during his 1892 visit to Chaoshan at age 36. Below is a brief explanation of its food-related verses:

Chaozhou marinated meat

"Job's tears can combat miasma, while asafoetida often accompanies meals." In Lingnan's miasmic regions, coix seed treats miasma, and asafoetida (a spice native to India) often accompanies meals.

"Even in mid-winter plagues, decoct dou lou po." Even in Lingnan's winter fevers, dou lou po (Storax, with effects of resuscitation, foulness elimination, depression relief, phlegm resolution, and pain relief) is decocted for prevention.

"Bitter bamboo shoots grow disjointedly, while banana flowers bloom in sequence." Bitter bamboo shoots emerge gradually, and banana flowers bloom in turn.

"Squeaking mice on the feast, inch-long self-breaking worms." "Feast mice" refer to candied baby mice, still alive and squeaking when eaten, coated in honey; "self-breaking worms" are mudskippers, which break into inch-long segments when ripe, delicious when cooked.

"Flounder flying like swallows, riding the sea breeze." Flounder leaps from the sea like swallows, with tender, white meat, delicious and fatty, replenishing qi.

"Raising cups to serve blood clams, shouldering shovels to plant oyster beds." "Blood clams" (ark clams), small shellfish living in shallow sea sand, are delicious. Liu Xun's *Records of the Lingnan Region* (Tang Dynasty) states, "Guangdong people particularly value them, often grilling them for wine, commonly called 'heavenly roasted meat'." Famous writer Gao Yang believed they are blood clams, "blanched half-cooked, mixed with scallion, ginger, soy sauce, or fermented bean curd brine"—delicious. "Planting oyster beds" means cultivating baby oysters in coastal tidal flats.

"Picking moon shells on island reefs, splitting clams to reveal white fat." *The Dietary Materia Medica* states that moon shells (thin, translucent bivalves) "maintain phlegm digestion; mixing with raw pepper sauce makes them delicious, aiding in digesting all foods and inducing hunger." Cui Yuxi's *Food Classic* adds that they "benefit the large and small intestines, treating blockage, jaundice, and thirst." Clams, another bivalve, include the "Xi Shi's Tongue" variety, praised as "the world's first delicacy" and "crown of flavors."

"Crystal plates hold candied melon, brush pens, script sugar frost recipes." "Candied melon" refers to preserved fruits, a thriving industry in Chaozhou, popular at home and abroad. "Brush pens" write "sugar frost recipes"—refined white sugar, symbolizing Chaozhou's excellence as a renowned sugar-producing region with diverse, high-quality cane varieties worthy of documentation.

"After spreading ash on bitter grass, eels ride the tide with fins raised. Eels climb hills, fish could be sought in trees." - Huang Zhong's *Sea Discourse* (Ming Dynasty) details trapping eels with ash when they ride tides to graze, "Giant eels, as thick as millstones, 1.6-1.7 zhang long (about 5.5 meters), have spear-like mouths and serrated teeth, attacking humans in groups. They climb hills with high tides to graze, leaving trench-like paths, their saliva glowing at night. Sailors spread thick ash on paths; eels get stuck, growing tired. Coastal people kill and eat them—their inch-thick skin yields delicious meat." Catching eels on hills is as odd as finding fish in trees.

"Crabs pickled in salted beans, garden veggies stewed in pots." - Small crabs (pangqi) were thought to be toxic, causing vomiting/diarrhea, so some Cantonese fed them to ducks. But Chaozhou cooks transformed them: Qu Dajun's *New Words of Guangdong* notes soaking in saltwater for two months, boiling the brine, adding citrus peel, creating "exquisite flavor, "praised in verse, "Like garden veggies in custom, daily served sticky-white. Reduced fishiness in fresh water, quick-cooking from salt."

Raw seafood

From these verses, Chaozhou's distinctive foods align with Lingnan's culinary mainstream—perhaps why traditional Chaozhou food literature rarely stands alone. Yet their cooking methods intrigued Fang Shu, who wrote, "Reading Erya isn't a flaw; others may laugh at my gluttony." With such delicious Chaozhou food, homesickness fades.

2. Miscellaneous Writings from the Dream Factory Initiates Chaozhou Gongfu Tea Narratives

Chaozhou's most symbolic food is Gongfu tea. Regardless of its origin, the earliest classic description comes from Yu Jiao's *Miscellaneous Writings from the Dream Factory* • *Chaojia Romance* • *Gongfu Tea* (Qianlong-Jiaqing period, Shaoxing):

"Gongfu tea brewing follows Lu Yu's *The Classic of Tea*, with more exquisite utensils. The stove resembles a bamboo tube, 1.2-1.3 chi (about 0.4 meters) tall, made of fine white clay. Yixing kiln teapots are best—round, flat-bellied, with a protruding spout and curved handle, holding half a sheng. Cups and plates are mostly porcelain, painted with landscapes/figures, highly detailed, likely ancient but unmarked. Each set includes one stove, pot, and plate; cup numbers vary by guests. Cups are small, plates full-moon shaped, with clay filters, palm-leaf brushes, paper fans, and bamboo tongs—all simple and elegant. Old, fine pots/plates/cups are as precious as jade, rare on ordinary boats. First, boil spring water in a kettle with fine charcoal. When it first boils, add Fujian tea to the pot, cover, pour hot water over the pot, then pour and sip slowly. The aroma is stronger than chewing plum blossoms, unappreciated by boisterous drinkers." (Yu Jiao, *Miscellaneous Writings from the Dream Factory*, Volume 10, *Chaojia Romance*)

Fang Zongyi, a native of Dingyuan, Anhui, who served as the Salt Transport Commissioner of Guangdong and Guangxi and concurrently as the Governor of Guangdong during the Tongzhi and Guangxu reigns, also regarded Gongfu tea as a classic famous tea. "Its price exceeds Longtuan tea cakes, and its rarity surpasses the tips of sparrow tongues. The host is truly hospitable, frequently adding live fire. Chaozhou Gongfu tea is not as sweet and fragrant as this. Junshan tea is still inferior, while Yangxian tea can barely compare." (*Bitter Pearl Tea from Wuyi Mountain, Each Hu Demands Sixteen Taels of Silver*). The Gongfu tea mentioned by Fang did not refer to the tea-making method but to the tea leaves themselves. This Gongfu tea likely refers to Chaozhou-produced Daizhao tea, also known as yellow tea. The *Chaozhou Prefecture Gazetteer* of the Shunzhi period, Volume 1, states, "Fengshan tea is excellent, also named Daizhao tea and yellow tea." *The Da Qing Yitong Zhi* of the Jiaqing period also records, "Daizhao Mountain is thirty li southwest of Raoping County. Locals plant tea there, commonly known as Daizhao tea. It is also called Hundred Flowers Mountain due to the continuous blooming of various flowers throughout the four seasons." Lan Dingyuan (1680-1733), a Zhangpu native of Fujian who once served as an official in Chaozhou, mentioned in his *Illustration of Raoping* County, "Daizhao Mountain produces local tea, and Chaozhou Prefecture is renowned for Daizhao tea." Le Jun (1766-1814), a Linchuan native of Jiangxi who once traveled to Lingnan and stayed in Chaozhou, composed *One Hundred Songs of the Han River*, which also includes an ode, "At the top of Hundred Flowers Mountain and the nest of Fengshan, tea pickers sing arm in arm every year. My elder sister picks tea while I pick ting (a kind of grass), wondering how bitter or sweet it is." He self-annotated, "Hundred Flowers Mountain in Raoping, also known as Daizhao Mountain, produces tea called Daizhao tea. Fengshan tea comes from Chaoyang, and the leaves of camellia sinensis are called bitter ting. Cantonese people always add a little ting when brewing tea for a better taste." Certainly, the most beautiful ode comes from Qiu Fengjia, who returned to Lingdong, in his *Sixteen Miscellaneous Poems of Raoping*, "Ancient caves are deep in clouds, locking a hundred flowers; fragrant springs fly to nourish thousands of households. The spring breeze brings out the Yuexi girls to pick Daizhao tea in the mountains."

In modern times, the best account of Gongfu tea comes from Xu Ke (1869–1928) of Hangzhou. In 1927, he consecutively wrote two articles and five additional notes, documenting his experience of enjoying Gongfu tea in Shanghai, leaving precious literary materials for both Gongfu tea and Chaozhou cuisine. His first article, *Double Narrative of Tea and Meal*, states:

> "In Shanghai's banquet customs, there is 'double narrative of harmony and wine'—harmony and wine refer to drinking and gambling. Today, I experienced the double narrative of tea and a meal. On the 20th day of the 11th month in Dingmao (1927), I visited Chen Zhian (Bin) and Meng'an (Zhang) of Chaoyang at their residence. Having long heard that Chaoshan people value Gongfu tea, and having been acquainted for years, I requested to experience it. The host said, 'In Chaoshan, those who appreciate Gongfu tea typically have a page boy handle the tea affairs. Since there is no page boy today, I will do it myself. Please don't laugh at my inexperience.' He then drew water to boil on a small stove and arranged the tea set on a table. The tea set included a 'guanzai' (as Chaoshan people call the teapot, which is very small,

similar to the sesame oil pot of Zhejiang people), placed on a five-inch-diameter plate with a round mat underneath to prevent the pot from slipping. There were four tiny cups, placed on a six to seven-inch-diameter plate. Additionally, there was a large bowl for pouring water. When the water in the small stove boiled, he poured it over the empty pot, empty cups, and their surroundings. After a while, he poured the water into the large bowl, filled the pot with Wuyi Tieguanyin tea, and immediately poured the tea into the four cups. When pouring, it must be done in several batches to ensure the tea in the four cups is of even concentration; one cannot wait to fill the first cup before pouring the second. When drinking, a cup is finished in two sips. The first sip should be slow to savor the taste; the second sip should be slightly faster to avoid the tea becoming lukewarm. After drinking, one can also smell the fragrance from the cup. When adding tea leaves to the pot for one brew, boiling water can be added seven to eight times (after seven to eight times, the leaves are poured into a large pot, and boiling water is added to drink, which still has flavor)."

The classic Gongfu tea-drinking method we know today is exactly as described. Some say today's Gongfu tea is an overly garish later version, but from this article, it is clear that this was indeed the original method. The Chaozhou Gongfu tea ceremony was already well-formed and mature. As an intangible cultural heritage, it has likely been very well preserved. After drinking Gongfu tea, the subsequent Chaozhou cuisine also had distinct characteristics:

> "The host served two brews, satisfying my desire. Then came the meal, which included both Shanghai and Chaozhou dishes. Lobster slices were dipped in orange oil (sweet and sour taste), fried hairtail in white sauce, stir-fried cuttlefish with celery, stir-fried kale (also known as olive vegetable), all Chaozhou dishes. There was also a hotpot purchased from a Chaozhou restaurant (Chaoshan people also call it 'bianlu,' which is very different from Guangzhou's). The hotpot contained ten ingredients: fish dumplings (fish meat as the skin, stuffed with pork), fish strips (sliced with red filling), fish balls (Chaoshan custom values firm fish balls), squid, herring, pig stomach, pig lung, fake fish maw (i.e., pork skin, also found in Shanghai), Chaoyang cabbage, and Jiaozhou cabbage. The soup was clear, oil-free, and tasteless, pleasing those who prefer a light diet. Enchanted by the tea and satisfied with the lunch, I, having been a guest in Yangcheng twice and frequently enjoying Guangzhou's tea and dishes, finally tasted Chaoshan flavors, deeply grateful for Zhian and Meng'an's hospitality."

Kongfu tea

At the end of the main text, three additional notes are attached, all valuable documents regarding Gongfu tea and Chaozhou cuisine:

"On this day, Chen Julai (Xue) of Pinghu was also present, saying that Xia Yizi (Tongxian) of Jiangdu was fond of tea appreciation, sharing the same hobby as Ouyang Shizhi (Zhu) of Xiangshan. They collected more than ten kinds of tea, including those with a lotus fragrance, and even co-owned a tea garden in Shanghai with Shizhi."

Zhian mentioned that Chaoshan people traditionally enjoy taro rice at the Beginning of Winter, adding pork, squid, and shrimp. Farmers particularly value this, as it serves as a well-deserved reward after a year of hard labor in the fields.

Meng'an stated: Chaoshan people have three meals a day, differing from Guangzhou's two meals. They have congee in the morning and rice for lunch and dinner; some also have congee at night, called "night congee, "unlike Guangzhou's "midnight snack." He also noted that Chaoshan rice preparation differs from Jiangsu-Zhejiang: rice is first cooked into congee, then the dry part is scooped out as rice. Xu Ke commented: This is what I call killing two birds with one stone. Meng'an added: Though Chaoshan is known for wealth, some poor families even have congee for all three meals.

Tea utensils can be stimulating and often disrupt sleep, especially Tieguanyin. After drinking two brews, Julai said, "You'll surely stay

> awake tonight." However, when returning from the Chen family at 4 PM, I took a nap and didn't wake until dusk, sleeping soundly. (*Collected Notes of Kangju*, No. 154, Shanxi Ancient Books Press, 1997 edition)

This Chen Julai was a renowned seal engraver praised as the "first in 300 years." His manuscript *Random Memories of Anchi Figures*, serialized in *Wanxiang* for seven years by the famous writer and scholar Shi Zhecun, was hailed as *A New Account of the Tales of the World* in the Republican era. It includes an article *Record of Chen Meng'an*. From this, we know they enjoyed such exquisite Gongfu tea and Chaoshan cuisine due to their wealthy family background. Chen Meng'an upheld Chaoshan traditions, valuing culture despite wealth, which likely prompted him to invite Xu Ke and Chen Julai. Especially after studying under Kuang Zhouyi, one of the four great masters of the late Qing Dynasty, his academic progress made him a Shanghai celebrity, bringing honor to Chaoshan people—unfortunately, little known today.

Shortly after, Xu Ke visited Chen Meng'an with Cheng Zida, again treated to Gongfu tea and Chaoshan cuisine. The tea and dishes differed from before, worthy of note:

> Six days after the Laba Festival in Dingmao, I visited Zhian and Meng'an with Elder Cheng Zida, who served Gongfu tea. There was a teapot from Siam, made of sand like Yixing ware, pale in color, with seal characters on the handle. From afar, it resembled a Mansheng pot.

> At noon, we were invited to stay for lunch, served unprecedented dishes: stir-fried beef with chili sauce (from Siam, possibly mixed with fish), dried ti fish (a kind of slippery long fish) (Chaoshan people call all dried meat "pu"; ti fish is ideal for pu, tasting inferior fresh) stir-fried with pork, duck pu (duck soaked in soy sauce, then smoked with sugarcane peel. Chaoshan sugarcane differs from Guangzhou and Tangxi varieties; Shanghai substitutes with Chongming sorghum stalk peel), and hotpot with black carp heads and bamboo shoots, oil-free, also a Chaoshan dish. (*Collected Notes of Kangju*, No. 155, *Gongfu Tea*)

While Xu Ke appreciated Chaozhou Gongfu tea, he did not overly praise it. The true tribute to Chaozhou Gongfu tea comes from Piao Qiong's *Tea Houses in Hong Kong*, which directly names it the best in China, "Among Chinese, Chaoshan people in Guangdong truly excel in tea appreciation. During my three years in Shantou, I found Chaoshan people extremely particular: they use tiny clay cups only five fen tall, not large bowls, with exquisitely small teapots. When guests arrive, only one cup is served. Tea is as strong as coffee but not bitter, leaving you longing for a second cup. It is a pity the host allows only one. We Chinese gulp tea down in one sip, but Chaoshan people place the cup to their lips and savor it drop by drop—they drink tea to appreciate, not to quench thirst." (*Hong Kong Random Memories IX*, *Shanghai China Weekly*, 1930s, Issue 90)

A few years later, Shan Shi's *Tea and Cantonese* echoed this view. The article first states broadly that Cantonese are ardent tea drinkers, taking Guangzhou as an example: "The Cantonese obsession with tea is evident in the number of teahouses, tearooms, tea shops, and tea-loving masses. In Guangzhou alone, there are over 160 teahouses, 130 tearooms, no fewer than 60 tea shops, and more than 700 tea snack and noodle shops..." The article then turns to praise Chaozhou Gongfu tea, "But while Guangzhou people drink tea, they pale in comparison to Chaoshan people. I observe Chaoshan people drink tea with great propriety. At home, when guests arrive, they serve tea on a tray with small cups. If the guest is an expert, they sip slowly, savoring every drop—only then considered knowledgeable. Downing it in one gulp marks an amateur. Chaoshan teapots are particularly exquisite: the more tea stains, the more valuable. A rare treasure needs no tea leaves, yet still tastes of tea. Some even judge wealth by teapots—owning a stained teapot is a matter of pride. Such is their reverence." (*Social Sciences*, 1937, Issue 6)

The praise for Chaozhou Gongfu tea has continued unabated, repeatedly lauding Chaoshan people as the epitome of tea connoisseurs in Guangdong. "We often observe that Chaoshan people are extremely particular about tea-drinking, using exquisite small teapots and cups as tiny as babies' mouths. Unlike those who guzzle tea like digging a well to quench thirst, they leisurely savor it. In contrast, Guangdong people use large pots or cups, regarding any water turned yellow as tea. Even after multiple infusions, when it turns pale and tasteless, they still drink it without care." (*Three Movements of Cantonese Tea-Drinking* by Tianxiang, *Happy Forest*, 1946, Issue 12)

3. The Shanghai Story of Chaoshan Cuisine

Mr. Tang Zhenchang, a renowned Shanghai scholar, stated, "Chaoshan cuisine is absent from the Eight Great Cuisines, perhaps considered part of Cantonese cuisine. This is incorrect. Standard Cantonese cuisine cannot encompass Chaoshan cuisine's characteristics, as any food lover knows. Look at Hong Kong, where Chaoshan restaurants abound—why label them as Chaoshan rather than Cantonese? In old Shanghai, there were many Chaoshan restaurants, later almost extinct, only reviving in recent years, though inauthentic. Some even lack Gongfu tea, excusing that tea sets aren't prepared. Still, Shanghainese enjoy tasting it." (Tang Zhenchang, *The So-Called Eight Great Cuisines: One Aspect of Culinary Chaos*, *Yong Sun Collection*, Liaoning Education Press, 1995, p. 26) These words both highly praise Chaoshan and reveal Shanghainese affection for its cuisine.

However, Chaoshan cuisine gradually became known in Shanghai's mass media after the 1920s–1930s. Xu Ke's account in 1927 wasn't published immediately. In my humble view, an early report on Chaoshan food is Ming Dao's *Chaoshan Tea Snack Shops* in *Shanghai Common Knowledge* (1928, Issue 46), but it only mentions tea snacks, not meals, and states such shops were rare in Shanghai:

> "Shanghai has countless tea snack shops, roughly divided into Suzhou, Guangdong, Ningbo, Chaoshan, etc. Let me first discuss

Chaoshan tea snack shops, which are few in Shanghai—only Bolanglin on Fifth Avenue and Fuzhen on Zhejiang Road's Zhengfeng Street. Their products include over ten kinds: pomelo peel, winter melon candy, lard fudge, peanut brittle, lard soft peanut candy, etc. Pomelo peel and soft peanut candy are unique—pomelo peel, usually waste, becomes delicious when processed, while soft peanut candy is exceptionally fluffy, tastier than elsewhere. During Mid-Autumn Festival, they sell Chaoshan-style mooncakes, a distinct Shanghai variety."

Two years later, Chaoshan cuisine began entering Shanghai's food scene. The first advertisement in Shanghai's renowned *Shenbao* (November 3, 1930) wasn't for a Chaoshan restaurant but for the Pacific Western Restaurant on Avenue Edward VII, adding Chaoshan dishes, acknowledging Chaoshan cuisine's previous obscurity, "Shanghai has all kinds of cuisine except Chaoshan, a great pity..." Of course, this was biased; as Xu Ke mentioned, the Chen brothers had ordered Chaoshan food from a restaurant. A week later, a soft advertisement claimed Shanghai had only one decent Chaoshan restaurant, whose quality paled compared to the Pacific's new offerings:

"The largest Chaoshan eatery in town is Xudexing in Mantingfang, founded by a Chaoshan native surnamed Xu, locally known as 'Old Xu Zi' rather than by its sign. The dishes are exquisitely delicious, less oily than Huizhou and Ningbo cuisines, fresher than Guangzhou food. But due to a lack of promotion, only Chaoshan people dined there, rarely outsiders.

> Now the Pacific Restaurant has hired renowned chefs to add Chaoshan dishes, with cooking and presentation far superior to Xudexing, winning universal praise. Their shark's fin is particularly outstanding." (*Food in Hancheng* by Tianxian, *Shenbao*, November 11, 1930)

For advertising needs, exaggeration was necessary. The same day's ad cited famous Chaoshan director Zheng Zhengqiu, claiming no authentic Chaoshan cuisine existed in Shanghai:

> "The Pacific Western Restaurant on Avenue Edward VII recently added Chaoshan dishes and hosted a press banquet last night. Mr. Zheng Zhengqiu introduced Chaoshan cuisine, stating that Shanghai has all cuisines except authentic Chaoshan. The Pacific's new offerings are unparalleled, especially shark's fin, richer and more nourishing than elsewhere. Each bowl of Chaoshan shark's fin takes three days to prepare." (*Zheng Zhengqiu Hosts Banquet at Pacific Western Restaurant: New Chaoshan Dishes*, *Shenbao*, November 11, 1930)

Fish dumplings

Although the advertisement was biased, Chaoshan cuisine had not gained significant fame in Shanghai and could be said to have a weak influence. By 1935, when magazine articles with dedicated sections on Shanghai's Chaoshan food emerged, there were still only a few Chaoshan restaurants. The best among them remained the old-fashioned Xudexing, which was renowned for its flavors but shabby decor:

> "Now let's talk about Chaoshan cuisine, which is a type of Guangzhou cuisine. However, despite both being Cantonese, the flavors of Guangzhou and Chaoshan are absolutely different. There are very few Chaoshan restaurants in Shanghai. Apart from a few on North Sichuan Road, they are rare in the International Settlement. As far as I know, in Mantingfang on Fifth Avenue, there is a Xudexing Restaurant, which is a formal Chaoshan establishment. Although its interior furnishings are extremely shabby, it enjoys a great reputation. The Tongle Building on Avenue Edward VII is also a Chaoshan restaurant...
>
> The most famous dishes in these restaurants include a hotpot. The hotpots served in other regional restaurants usually contain standard ingredients like meatballs, sea cucumbers, pickled vinasse, sliced meat, shredded chicken, ham, egg dumplings, and shrimp, which never change. However, Chaoshan hotpots have a unique flavor, featuring fish meat dumplings, shrimp and egg buns, and Chaozhou taro as the base, which is fragrant and crispy, making it endlessly appetizing. Moreover, it is not

expensive, costing only about one yuan. Readers might as well give it a try, and you're guaranteed to be satisfied. As for stir-fried dishes, seafood such as lobster, conch, blue crab, and herring are Chaoshan specialties." (*A Porridge and a Meal: Eating in Shanghai by Shicai*, *Life Ten-Day Journal*, 1935, Issue 6)

From this article, it can be seen that Shanghai people used to regard Chaoshan restaurants as a type of Cantonese restaurant. In that case, Mr. Tang Zhenchang need not be too concerned about Chaoshan cuisine not being recognized as an independent category. Perhaps this is another reason why Chaoshan restaurants were not prominent or developed in Shanghai; since Cantonese food was available, there was no need to seek out Chaoshan cuisine. Guangzhou cuisine features "bianlu" (hotpot), while Chaoshan cuisine prefers "nuanguo" (warm pot), generally following similar trends. "Last winter, I went to a bookstore on Fourth Avenue with a Chaoshan classmate. Passing by a Chaoshan restaurant, my classmate felt homesick and insisted that I join him for a 'Ten Sceneries Warm Pot' of Chaoshan cuisine. Unable to refuse, I went in with him." (*Chaoshan Dialect* by Chen Tianci, *Shenbao*, January 25, 1937)

However, there were "exceptions." The *Shanghai Guide,* published by Zhonghua Book Company in 1934 (authored by Shen Bojing and Chen Huaipu), and the *Shanghai Tour Guide,* published in 1936, both highly praised Chaoshan cuisine. The latter, in the third chapter, *Daily Life and Diet*, introduced various cuisines and restaurants, listing Chaoshan cuisine separately and placing it before Cantonese cuisine, stating, "Chaoshan cuisine is a branch of Cantonese cuisine, entirely different from Guangzhou cuisine." Nevertheless, when introducing Chaoshan restaurants, the list was still short: "Such restaurants are only found on North Sichuan Road, along with Tongle Building (on Rue du Consulat in the French Concession) and Xudexing Restaurant (on Guangdong Road, i.e., Mantingfang on Fifth Avenue). Their specialties are mostly seafood dishes like 'stir-fried lobster,' 'stir-fried conch,' and 'stir-fried blue crab,' with winter warm pots being the best. The warm pots contain 'fish meat dumplings,' 'shrimp and egg buns,' and 'Chaozhou taro,' etc., with a unique flavor. 'Jingdong Cuisine' is also excellent and can be sold separately, about 30-40 cents per can."

4.2 Dominating Guangdong and Hong Kong

Chaoshan is a coastal area where people rely on the sea for their livelihood—some became sea merchants, while others turned to piracy. Sea merchants sailed red-headed ships north to Shanghai and Tianjin, and south to Hong Kong and Southeast Asia, with Hong Kong and Southeast Asia being the main destinations. Thus, while Chaoshan restaurants were not popular in Shanghai, in Singapore, Southeast Asia, it was, "Inviting others to a restaurant for drinks, Chinese are unlike locals. Ordering dishes requires a chef, half are Chaoshan and half Guangzhou." (*Singapore* from *Overseas Bamboo Branch Poems* by Shengchu, *Qiaosheng*, 1942, Issue 6) In contrast,

Guangzhou, the provincial capital, was not a stronghold for Chaoshan people—there are few records of Chaoshan activities and even fewer reports on Chaoshan restaurants during the late Qing and Republican periods.

According to Chen Guoxian's *Unique Chaoshan Flavor*, the famous Chaoshan chef Zhu Biaochu rose to prominence after taking charge of Chaoshan cuisine at the Overseas Chinese Building in 1957, making Chaoshan people feel at home and gaining international fame. Favored by Premier Zhou, he was even invited to serve as an "imperial chef" in Beijing. However, when the Zhu brothers first came to Guangzhou, they only opened "Zhu Ming Ji, "a food stall at the intersection of Huifu East Road and Dafosi Street, mainly selling Chaoshan fish noodles, claypot rice, and occasionally catering for banquets. The reason for this small-scale operation was that there were no proper specialized Chaoshan restaurants in Guangzhou at the time, primarily due to the insufficient concentration of Chaoshan people and the lack of a suitable market environment.

Fried oyster

In addition to the Zhu brothers' Zhu Ming Ji, another small shop named "Qiaohe" on Yide East Road carefully operated authentic Chaoshan snacks such as fried oyster pancakes, stir-fried koay teow, and satay beef, also gaining a reputation. Apart from this, even the scenario of hiring renowned Chaoshan chefs to handle newly added Chaoshan dishes, like the Pacific Western Restaurant in Shanghai, was rare. Among the more famous ones during the Republic of China era, the Shamian Victory Building topped the list. Due to the manager being a Chaoshan native, renowned Chaoshan chefs were specially hired to refine Chaoshan dishes and pastries, significantly paving the way for Chaoshan cuisine. Later, the new Nanyuan Restaurant opened in Haizhu District in 1963, and in 1964, it employed the Chaoshan master chef Li Shulong, who began serving Chaoshan-flavored dishes. However, as Mr. Li had previously practiced his craft in Chaoshan and Fujian, he was unfamiliar with the Guangzhou market, ultimately limiting his influence. (The 41st Volume of *Guangzhou Historical and Cultural Materials*)

This also illustrates the importance of the market for the development of the catering industry, especially for spreading its reputation. Truly authentic Chaoshan cuisine had to wait until the reform and opening-up period, particularly after the construction of highways. Since Chaoshan cuisine primarily features seafood, some seafood varieties are unique to Chaoshan, while others are not supplied by seafood merchants elsewhere. Therefore, when you visit authentic Chaoshan restaurants today, they all boast about fresh seafood deliveries—large hotels have their own transportation channels, and small restaurants also contact fixed early-morning buses to ensure timely arrival. Furthermore, only with the reform and opening-up, the economic development of Guangdong, and the growth of Guangzhou's catering market, which has generated a sufficient number of diners, can authentic Chaoshan cuisine be effectively guaranteed to survive.

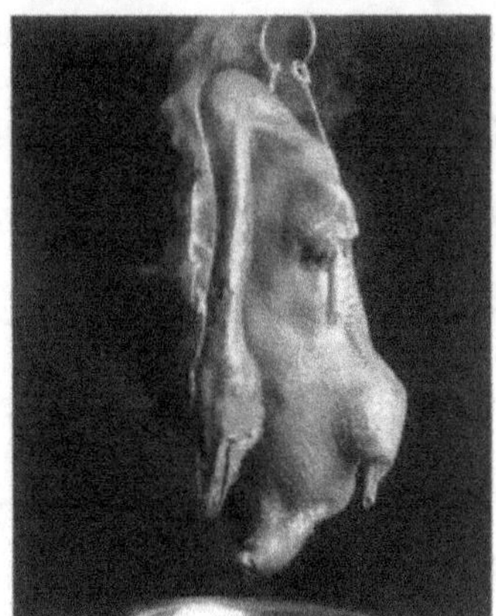

Marinated goose

One of the most iconic specialty dishes in current Guangzhou Chaoshan restaurants is braised goose, especially the goose head, while the characteristic of Cantonese cuisine is roasted goose. Broadly speaking, Chaoshan cuisine features more braised dishes and fewer roasted meats, while Cantonese cuisine has more roasted meats and fewer braised dishes. From this perspective, the differences between Chaoshan and Cantonese cuisines are quite significant. The tradition of Chaoshan brine, especially braised goose, has a long history. For example, Chaoshan people often use braised geese for ancestor worship and religious ceremonies during festivals, while Guangfu people use chickens, as previously mentioned. Chicken heads are considered as toxic as arsenic, and Guangfu people mostly avoid them; roasted goose heads are also tough and tasteless, but braised goose heads are a flavor prized in Chaoshan cuisine. Unlike Guangzhou's roasted goose, which uses small black-maned geese, Chaoshan braised geese use Shitou geese from Chenghai, weighing 20 to 30 catties, known as the "World Goose King." With a large head, the goose head with the neck can be cut into a large plate. The braised goose head is tender and full of flavor, enjoyable even for the elderly. The lion-head-shaped fleshy nodules on the forehead and cheeks are extremely plump, with a special fatty aroma. Therefore, the larger the goose head, the better. In the past, these large goose heads were often taken from breeding male geese raised for three to four years. Now, due to market demand, some people specifically raise male geese for two to three years. Such top-grade large goose heads can cost hundreds to thousands of yuan! Of course, the "flavor from Chaoshan" is not only the taste of the goose but also the flavor of the brine. Chaoshan brine uses high-quality stock as the base, adding more than twenty kinds of spices, including some precious ones, as well as unique ingredients like southern ginger (known as Chaoshan ginger) and lemongrass introduced from Southeast Asia. Chaoshan brine is often regarded as the secret of Chaoshan flavor, and it is difficult for outsiders to master the art of brine preparation. In recent years, Chaoshan food expert Cai Hao has advocated pairing braised Shitou goose heads with single-malt whiskies from England, such as 30-year-old Glenmorangie. This combination is undoubtedly a delicious treat, where the aroma of the goose bones, the fruity scent of the wine, and the spicy fragrance of the seasonings blend seamlessly, leaving a lingering aftertaste. However, such high-aged wines are already extremely expensive, and the resulting goose heads are even more "fit for the gods, rarely tasted on earth". Once the "head" achieves perfection, the "liver and intestines" ascend to heaven. Driven by braised goose heads, Chaoshan braised goose intestines, and goose liver have also become table treasures. Well-prepared goose liver even aims to compete with French foie gras! Abalone sauce, goose paws, or Liaoning sea cucumber with goose paws are classic dishes; Raoping's goose blood soup, paired with bean sprouts, pickled cabbage, and scallion heads, is extremely tender and delicious.

From braised goose, we can see a key difference in seasonings between Chaoshan and Cantonese cuisines: Cantonese cuisine relies primarily on soy sauce, a feature profoundly influencing its characteristics, as described in the Qing Dynasty poem *Guangzhou Bamboo Branch Lyrics* by Hu Zijing, "Foshan's charm lies in its rural style, where pigeon meat smells fragrant at Sanpin Tower. It's said Zhu Hou's secret recipe owes half its sweetness to fermented bean paste." In contrast, Chaoshan cuisine rarely uses soy sauce, favoring brine and dipping sauces instead. Cantonese cuisine combines ingredients complexly, while Chaoshan cuisine serves them separately in a wide variety, with countless small dishes on one table: fish sauce, red soy sauce, orange oil, plum paste, satay sauce, salted lemon, salted sour plum, southern ginger paste, garlic (scallion) oil, chive brine, sanshen sauce, Puning bean paste, ginger rice with black vinegar, etc. When serving congee, it is accompanied by pickled vegetables, radish preserves, olive vegetables, and more. Fish sauce, indispensable in Chaoshan cuisine, is made by brining fresh river fish until rotten, then steaming and refining, offering an extremely delicious alternative to soy sauce. However, its fishy odor makes it hard for outsiders to adapt. Satay sauce, introduced from Southeast Asia, imparts a unique flavor to Chaoshan specialties like satay beef and skewered dishes. As Confucius said, "One does not eat without the proper sauce". Chaoshan cuisine embodies this strictly. A simple beef ball soup, besides being sprinkled with fish sauce, pepper, fried garlic in lard, winter vegetables, sesame oil, and chopped coriander or lettuce, is served with a small dish of satay sauce for dipping. Even white-cut chicken, a common dish in both Chaoshan and Guangzhou, differs in condiments: Chaoshan style typically includes sesame oil, bean paste, fish sauce, orange oil, and a handful of raw coriander in the center of the plate. When serving other main dishes, different condiments are paired: steamed lobster with orange oil, steamed crab with ginger vinegar, dry-braised wild goose with plum mustard, clear-braised giant catfish or soft-shelled turtle with red soy sauce. The variety of sauce dishes is spectacular, dazzling both the eyes and the taste buds.

The famous Chaoshan dish minglu xiangluo (open-fire conch) requires perfect timing to achieve a crispy and fragrant texture, a skill so tricky it's called a "secret family recipe." In fact, since the best conch comes from

Chaoshan, it has always been a signature Chaoshan dish. Zhu Biaochu featured it at Guangzhou Huaxia, Li Shulong at Guangzhou Nanyuan, and it was already a renowned Chaoshan specialty in 1930s Shanghai—listed alongside stir-fried lobster and blue crab as the three signature Chaoshan dishes in *Shanghai Guide* (1934, Shen Bojing & Chen Huaipu, Zhonghua Book Company).

4.3 Returning to Chaoshan

Premium dishes like abalone, sea cucumber, shark's fin, dried scallops, and conch may represent a culinary school, but they are the tip of the iceberg, requiring a deep foundation below. Returning to Chaoshan, the birthplace of Chaoshan cuisine, this depth becomes evident.

Guangdong has more mountains than plains, with the Pearl River Delta and Chaoshan Plain as a rare land of fish and rice, unmatched in prosperity. Zhou Yuanhao of the Ming Dynasty wrote in *Sequel to Jinglin Records*, "Only counties in Guangzhou Prefecture are wealthy, followed by Chaozhou." Thus, after Guangzhou, Chaozhou leads in cuisine. In recent times, while the Pearl River Delta saw rice fields converted to mulberry plantations, the Chaoshan Plain has maintained intensive farming, reflected in its meticulous rice-based dishes. Additionally, confined to their region yet engaged in commerce north-south and even in Southeast Asia, the Chaoshan people have developed a highly regional cuisine, distinct from Guangzhou's inclusive food culture.

1. Chaoshan's Rice Cake Delights

Despite being a land of fish and rice by the South China Sea-East China Sea coast with abundant seafood, Chaoshan has faced population pressure on limited land in recent times. While not as opulent as Guangzhou (once the "Southern Treasury" of the imperial court), its cuisine excels in intricacy. Take rice-based snacks: the variety of guo (rice cakes) rivals Guangzhou's "Sunday dim sum, "a testament to Chaoshan's culinary finesse. This precision originates from their "farming like embroidery" tradition, mirrored in Chaoshan embroidery, Gongfu tea, and woodcarving—all meticulous, hence their dishes and dim sum blend rustic ingredients with refined craftsmanship.

Fried guotiao

Start with guotiao (rice noodles). Chaoshan guotiao, steamed from rice flour and cut into strips, resembles Guangzhou's Shahe noodles but has a longer history, appearing at least in the Ming Dynasty as sacrificial offerings and daily food.

In the Qing Dynasty, as large numbers of Chaoshan people migrated overseas, Chaoshan guotiao (rice noodles) took root in the overseas Chinese communities of Southeast Asia. Along with Fujian noodles and Hainan turtle beer (coffee), it became one of the most popular foods in Southeast Asia. In Malaysia and Singapore, "guotiao" is written as "KUE TEO" in English based on the Chaoshan pronunciation, and in Hong Kong, it is transliterated as "Kwai Tiu" in restaurants. In Paris, guotiao soup is known as "Phnom Penh Guotiao, "actually introduced by Cambodian refugees after the 1970s. Guotiao can be served in soup or stir-fried, each with distinct flavors.

Besides guotiao, there are guojuan (rice noodle rolls) and changfen (rice noodle sheets), similar to Guangzhou's changfen but more meticulously made with richer ingredients like eggs, mushrooms, shrimp, squid, greens, and pumpkin, particularly famous in Hongyang, Puning. Apart from these three main types, the renowned jianmiwan (pointed rice balls) can be considered a variant, shorter than guotiao and pointed at both ends. There are also regional subvariants: for example, zhanmiwan (glutinous rice balls), shaped between guotiao and jianmiwan, is the freshest type. Thick rice batter is poured onto a perforated wooden board, squeezed into 70–80°C hot water to cook, then scooped up, rinsed, and dried, served in a rich soup for a fresh, refreshing taste. Guozhi (rice paste) is a mixed rice noodle dish: 70% rice batter and 30% sweet potato batter are spread on a pan, baked, dried, cut into strips, cooked into a paste, sprinkled with light brown brine, and served with braised intestines, meat, eggs, tofu, etc., hot and delicious—an excellent breakfast choice. Without the brine, it is dry guo.

There are also various guogao (rice cakes). First is chaoguo gao: refined white rice cakes are cut into small pieces, fried with fish sauce and sweet soy sauce until golden, then mixed with fresh kale, shrimp, pork, snake meat, eggs, etc., seasoned with satay sauce, chili sauce, rice flour water, and soup, resulting in a crispy exterior and soft interior, complex flavors, and rich nutrition—filling enough as a snack. Xianshuiguo are small, white, boat-shaped rice cakes served with Chaoshan radish preserves, unique in flavor. Caitouguo is similar to Guangzhou's turnip cake but more flavorful with added coriander, garlic flowers, peanuts, pepper, etc. Gantongguo and yuguo use sweet potato flour for the skin, with dried tubers (gantong) or taro as fillings. Jiucaiguo is stuffed with chives. Shuijingqiu (crystal balls) have translucent starch skins with clear fillings in various flavors. Pingpangguo has a traditional skin but unique fillings: originally black sesame, sugar, and crushed peanuts, later added with red bean paste, taro, betel nut crumbs, and scallion oil.

Among the guo, sunguo (bamboo shoot cake) is distinctive and relatively upscale, as the saying goes, "Even beggars crave sunguo"—similar to "toad wanting to eat swan meat." Chaoshan produces excellent bamboo shoots, especially summer shoots, a rarity among shoots. There is also modou (cuttlefish) roe guo, rare due to limited roe production, only available in Shantou and the surrounding areas.

Beyond guo, there are other rice pastries: for example, juan is made by wrapping glutinous rice mixed with fragrant swallow nests, shrimp, pickled pork, chestnuts, lotus seeds, taro, and lotus corners in beancurd skin, seasoned with celery and turtle sauce, steamed and optionally fried, delicious. Luotangqian, also called ruanguo, is a dough made from peanuts and sesame powder, steamed and cut, beneficial for tonifying qi, stopping diarrhea, and warming the spleen/stomach. Mirun is made from glutinous rice, sugar, maltose, and lard, crystal clear and white, sticky but not tooth-gluing, sweet but not cloying, fragrant and refreshing. Nuomi (sticky rice) ci are widely available, while glutinous rice-stuffed lotus root includes peanuts, red dates, lotus seeds, red beans, and brown sugar. Shuce gao is white and crystal-like, shaped like books. Yamuniang, famous after appearing on CCTV, resembles tangyuan but has far superior fillings; the dry-fried version is called Phoenix Spring.

Cooked and chilled fish

"Make guo for the season". Chaoshan guo is not only an important origin of Chinese dim sum but also a sacrificial offering for worship. Chaoshan has many seasonal guo, such as hongqu guo (red yeast rice cake) for the Kitchen God Festival, jiao guo (fermented cake), and baifan tao (white rice peach), etc.

During the Spring Festival, there is shuqu guo, made by boiling shuqu grass into a soup, mixing it into the guo skin, wrapping the filling, pressing it into a mold, and steaming it on leaves; during the Lantern Festival, there are "three cages together" of sweet guo, jiao guo (fermented guo), and caitou guo, symbolizing sweetness, prosperity, and good luck; during the Qingming Festival, there is puzi guo, made by mashing young leaves and green puzi of the puzi tree, mixing them with rice flour, sugar, and baking powder into a paste, pouring it into a ceramic bowl, and steaming it over high heat in a xianshui guo steamer; during the Dragon Boat Festival, there is zhi guo, made by using the extract of gardenia (a Chinese medicinal herb) and ginger from herbal stores, which is heated at high tempreture and soaked, and mixing it with glutinous rice paste; during the Zhongyuan Festival, there is wange guo (i.e., xiao guo); during the Mid-Autumn Festival, there is laoma palace zongqiu, which is shaped like a zongzi but made very differently. First, the soaked glutinous rice is put into a pot, stir-fried with lard and an appropriate amount of high-quality fish sauce until the rice grains are crystal clear, fragrant, and smooth, mixed with sweet and salty double-fillings, then wrapped in bamboo leaves and salty grass, tied into a hexagonal sphere, and cooked; another seasonal snack for the Dragon Boat Festival, zhutou zongzi, is even more unique: fresh pig hind leg meat and part of the head skin must be selected as raw materials, seasoned with fish sauce, soy sauce, sugar, sorghum wine, and more than ten kinds of spices such as star anise, chuan pepper, clove, cinnamon, big anise, and small anise, wrapped in tofu skin, placed in a special wooden mold, and pressed to squeeze out the lard and water, with a distant and lingering fragrance. The richness of "making guo for the season" also has a factor of "preventing seasonal diseases". For example, shuqu guo can prevent spring cold and cough, hongqu guo can aid digestion and invigorate the spleen, caitou guo can remove evil heat, mai guo can facilitate defecation and nourish the liver, and zhi guo can aid digestion, increase appetite, and dispel diseases. It is particularly worth mentioning that Chaoshan Sun Guo is definitely a special snack that is not easy to eat. First, fresh bamboo shoots are put into guo (dumplings), which is rare in the world; second, Chaoshan spring (summer) bamboo shoots are only on the market in May and June, which is even rarer.

Under the "power" of guo, other noodle snacks and pastries are also called guo. For example, "mai guo" is made by mixing unrefined flour with sugar and baking it into a paste. Another example is cao guo, which is mainly made of wheat snow flour, actually a kind of starch jelly. In addition, there are countless kinds such as houhe guo, caiqian guo, jiandan guo, midou guo, cenggao guo, you guo, guotiao juan, gui guo, qianzai guo, yutou guo, xiaomi guo, modou luan (cuttlefish egg) guo, etc., no less than a hundred kinds; no other place has so many kinds, and no other "land of fish and rice" has so many kinds, and all are exquisite; besides guo, there are also many kinds of pastries and buns, which are equally exquisite. Creating novelty from the ordinary best shows the Chaoshan people's unremitting pursuit of the way of eating and continuous creation of the realm of eating, which is the foundation for Chaoshan food to lead the trend.

2. The Fish Flavor of Chaoshan

The Chaoshan Plain is a land of fish and rice. In fact, when talking about rice (guo), we have already mentioned fish: the fillings of many guo either have fish or use fish sauce. Another example is shumai in other places, while Chaoshan xiaomi uses "rice", such as shrimp. Another example is the famous casserole porridge, which must have fish, shrimp, crab, etc. Some snacks literally have rice or noodles, but they are purely made of fresh fish. For example, fish dumplings, although named dumplings, have nothing to do with the noodles of traditional dumplings or the guo of Chaoshan dumplings; only have the shape of dumplings; their dumpling skins are made of sea eel meat, with only a little sweet potato flour used as a coagulant. The most unique is fish rice, which is completely made of fish, as rice, which is hard for outsiders to imagine. Fish rice was originally a cooking method invented by boat people to preserve seafood in a local way. The raw materials are economic fish such as barracuda and "nage fish" (called "dog stick fish" in Guangzhou); good fish are reluctant to be eaten as rice. Of course, in today's high-end Chaoshan restaurants, superior fish such as humphead wrasse and eastern star grouper are also used to make fish rice. Although the fish are ordinary and the production seems simple, just cleaning the fresh fish, loading them into a basket, cooking them, and cooling them, there are still subtle particulars. For example, the fish must be fresh, the basket for loading the fish must be new, and the key is that the salt water for cooking the fish is a high-concentration salt water with a formula, so that the cooked fish rice has a sweet taste and a bamboo fragrance, which can almost represent the seafood delicacies of Chaoshan.

Now people certainly do not use fish rice as a meal, but in the past, it was indeed used as a meal, especially for the "boat dwellers" who "make a living by boats and collect seafood" and "do not eat grain"; when Yang Wanli, a great poet of the Southern Song Dynasty, was an official in Chaozhou, he had a poem *Boat Dwellers*, "Heaven has assigned a water life, teaching them to ride the waves from childhood. Cooking crabs as food, they do not know rice, weaving bananas into cloth without needing yarn." Mr. Ye Hanzhong, the inheritor of the intangible cultural heritage of Chaozhou Gongfu tea, also agrees with this statement and believes that the rise of Gongfu tea is related to relieving the greasiness of fish rice.

In addition to fish rice, pickled crab roe, pickled blood clams, pickled razor clams, pickled shrimp, pickled small flat crabs, pickled mantis shrimp, pickled red-spotted swimming crabs, and clam stir-fried with basil, salted clams, salted mantis shrimp, etc., possess more regional characteristics and thus greater representativeness than those high-end varieties. Some ice-cut pickled products are even hailed as "seafood ice cream". Eating customs also classify shellfish and crabs like clam meat, blood cockle meat, frozen red crabs, frozen crayfish, etc., together with barracuda fish rice under the category of fish rice.

In an era when fish rice is no longer treated as a staple, it sometimes paradoxically serves as one. In some larger diners (night congee stalls, similar to Guangzhou's late-night diners), there are often more than twenty varieties of fish rice, including high-end fish like ma you fish, white pomfret, and yellowfin seabream, sold at very low prices. With such high quality and low cost, tasting this and that until full without realizing it—isn't fish rice better than regular rice?

The fish flavors of Chaoshan lie in their fish-specific preparations. For example, while steamed groupers are common elsewhere, boiling them in sour plum soup is unique to Chaoshan; stewing dried fish with dried radish strips is also a distinctive feature. Steaming tongue sole or boiling it with bean paste, cooking hairtail with green garlic and chili, all are Chaoshan methods. Small squid are mostly blanched in Chaoshan, while elsewhere they might be cooked "meiji" style. Pomfret can be steamed or braised elsewhere, but never cooked with cucumber, like in Chaoshan. Other dishes include ma you fish braised with preserved vegetables, banded gizzard shad cooked with pickled vegetables or dried radish, sand catfish cooked with pickled vegetables or dried radish, nude moray eel steamed with plums or in soup, puffer fish cooked with celery and chili, red-eyed fish cooked with green garlic in soup, carangoid fish semi-fried and semi-boiled, (dragonhead fish soup with vermicelli and minced meat, etc. Throughout China's coastlines, no other region offers such diverse and colorful fish dishes.

The Chaoshan region in Guangdong, rich in delicious sea fish, also boasts exquisite fish sashimi, no less than that of Guangfu, though it receives less attention. The *Chenghai County Gazetteer* of the Jiaqing period states, "Chenghai abounds in fish, and locals excel at making fish sashimi, which is as white as clouds and snow, served with vinegar and other condiments, called 'fish sashimi'. Oyster and shrimp sashimi follow similar methods." The 1934 *Shantou Guide* records 20 "fish sashimi congee restaurants" in downtown Shantou.

3. Vegetable Flavors of Chaoshan

No other region has transformed rice into hundreds of guo (rice cakes) like Chaoshan, nor has any region crafted ordinary sea fish into such rich and exquisite fish rice as Chaozhou. Yet that's not all. No other region has elevated side vegetables and fruits to superb dishes like Chaozhou, forming the deepest foundation for Chaoshan cuisine to stand as a major culinary school.

Chaoshan cuisine values vegetables first as a cultural necessity. For example, Chaoshan banquets always include two sweet dishes: one as the first sweet course and one at the end, symbolizing a sweet life from start to finish. Sweet dishes here are diverse and use special ingredients. While common vegetarian ingredients like sweet potatoes, taro, pumpkin, ginkgo nuts, water chestnuts, lotus seeds, citrus, pineapples, and beans are used, fatty pork and streaky pork can also be made into top-tier dishes. Representative vegetarian sweet dishes include pumpkin and taro puree, sweet lotus seeds, braised ginkgo nuts, and sweet and sour stir-fried pork. Of course, seafood is central to Chaoshan cuisine, prepared in a light style called "pure sweetness" by locals. This "sweetness culture" roots in "Chaobai", Chaoshan's traditional white sugar, which, along with "Chaolan" (blue-printed fabric) and Chaoshan tobacco, dominated Chaozhou's foreign trade after the Qing Dynasty lifted maritime bans, especially monopolizing the domestic sugar market for over 200 years. Culture often embodies material desires; sweetness is a cultural root for Chaoshan people, primarily expressed through sweet vegetarian dishes. Just as Chaoshan people refined coarse local sugar into white sugar, they also transform ordinary vegetables into light, delicious, and nutritious dishes, giving vegetables a status equal to meat in Chaoshan cuisine.

Because Chaoshan cuisine emphasizes vegetables, there is a saying of "Three Treasures of Chaozhou": preserved radish (caipu), pickled mustard greens, and fish sauce. First, regarding caipu, "Once caipu is served, Chaoshan flavor arrives." Caipu takes precedence in Chaoshan cuisine. Caipu is essentially dried radish, which exists everywhere, but Chaozhou's is particularly excellent, especially when well-pickled. For example, "Gaotang

Caipu" from Raoping, with an amber color, thick flesh, and crispy texture, is sold not only nationwide but also exported to Southeast Asia, Europe, America, and the Middle East. Next, pickled mustard greens, a product of pickled leaf mustard, hold a distinguished position in Chaozhou. In the past, on the Lantern Festival night, women would go to the fields to "sit on leaf mustard" to pray for "choosing a good husband tomorrow, "highlighting its importance. Mustard greens are crucial to Chaoshan flavors, as seen in dishes like eel with pickled mustard greens, pickled mustard greens with oyster soup, and pickled mustard greens with clam soup. The taste of pickled mustard greens has become the most representative flavor of Chaoshan, and "ham and mustard greens casserole" is a high-end delicacy. Chaoshan people traveling abroad always miss the hometown flavors of caipu and pickled mustard greens, which have long been major export products. Some aged caipu, such as those preserved for 30 or 50 years, cost tens of yuan per catty, far more expensive than meat. Such aged caipu, served with congee, cleanses the stomach, offering both deliciousness and health benefits.

Chaoshan people also have a type of pickled vegetables, including pickled oysters and other "garden substitute" raw pickled seafood. In the past, during poverty, pickled oysters, like caipu and pickled mustard greens, were daily "mixed pickles" for "accompanying congee, "meeting the minimum physiological need for salt. Oysters, however, were luxuries for "enjoyment" rather than "filling the stomach" for survival. From this perspective, gourmet food can be understood as home-cooked dishes that cannot be eaten often due to economic, technical (cooking skills), or cultural reasons.

Common Chaoshan pickles and caipu include preserved vegetables, olive vegetables, winter vegetables, black olives, bean paste ginger, salted plums, salted eggs, scallions, salted garlic, pickled mantis shrimp, pickled clams, pickled crabs, pickled freshwater crabs, raozi pu (preserved fruit), kale stems, pickled carambola, salted barracuda, threadfin, pickled cucumber, etc., mainly served with Chaozhou white congee (chaozhou mi), totaling over 100 varieties, unimaginable elsewhere. A renowned hotel in Shantou even promotes mixed pickles as a highlight, presenting 100 exquisitely prepared varieties under the name "Hundred Birds Worship the Phoenix."

"The best fish are Spanish mackerel and pomfret, the best vegetable is kale flower stems, and the best opera is *Su Liuniang*." The tender flower stems of kale are compared to high-quality fish like Spanish mackerel and pomfret, as well as Su Liuniang, the finest traditional Chaoshan opera. Stir-fried beef with kale in satay sauce or simple stir-fried kale are classic Chaoshan dishes. Among the regional greens which are popular throughout Guangdong, besides Chaozhou kale, there are Shuidong (Dianbai) mustard greens and Zengcheng late-season bok choy. Basil, commonly known as "Nine-Layer Tower" and hailed as "Jinbuhuan (irreplaceable herb)", is the most treasured seasoning herb for Chaoshan people. With "Jinbuhuan," clams, once considered cheap food for feeding ducks elsewhere, are stir-fried into a famous Chaoshan dish.

"Thorn flowers, white and spreading / Young sister brings rice to the field / Wish elder brother a good harvest / Beat a gold hairpin heavily... Thorn flowers, white and floating / Young sister brings rice to the farm / Wish elder brother a good harvest / Beat a pair of gold hairpins heavily." The Chaozhou ballad *Thorn Flowers*, with the flavor of the *Book of Songs*, sings of bitter thorn hearts, once a favorite of Chaozhou people. Hu Puan's *General Customs of China* in the early Republic of China records, "Bitter herb, also known as bitter thorn, is a wild grass growing luxuriantly. During Qingming, women and children carry small poles and bamboo baskets, picking as they go, then washing and cooking with bean sprouts. It is said to clear blood and detoxify." Today, under the trend of environmental protection and health preservation, it is highly valued, popular in dishes like fried eggs with bitter thorn or boiled in clear water, though hard to obtain as a wild plant.

Motherwort, known for making gynecological medicine, is turned into a table delicacy by the Chaoshan people. "Blanched motherwort" or "blanched pearl flower vegetable" is often ordered. Mei Mao (Wang Jiemei), a Chinese American painter from Hangzhou, is obsessed with Chaoshan cuisine and visited Shantou twice in a month, claiming he "must eat motherwort," playfully highlighting its allure with a double entendre. Most remarkably, hemp leaves, from China's oldest and most widely cultivated crop for "men plow, women weave," have become a dish indispensable even in top Chaoshan restaurants.

Huguo Cai

Of course, the top dish is Huguo Cai (National Protection Vegetable). Nowadays, Huguo Cai is mainly made from sweet potato leaves and is said to have a history of more than 700 years. It is said that when Zhao Bing, the last emperor of the Southern Song Dynasty, fled south to Chaozhou after being defeated in battle, he had nothing to eat in his haste. Locals presented him with a soup made from fresh wild vegetable leaves. The young emperor, too hungry to be picky, ate it and repeatedly praised it, saying, "In the crisis of the Great Song Dynasty, this little sweet potato leaf can also help me. I will confer the title of 'Huguo Cai'!" This soup may have existed long before, but after this, following popular preference, villagers became more attentive, making it more and more delicate and flavorful. Extending to amaranth, spinach, water spinach, and houhe cai (called qiongdie cai in Guangzhou), all can be used in dishes, becoming one of the preferred soups in Chaoshan banquets and a typical symbol of refining common vegetables in Chaoshan cuisine. The usual practice today is to cut the top one-third of fresh sweet potato leaves to ensure tenderness, remove the thick veins and fibers, finely chop them with a knife, soak and press them dry with alkaline water, then simmer them with concentrated chicken soup, supplemented with northern mushrooms and ham paste. The result is as green as jade, very beautiful, with a fresh and smooth taste and rich nutrition. Some even make various shapes, such as a Tai Chi pattern in green and white on the surface of the bowl, which can be called the best of Chaoshan cuisine.

The most distinctive Chaoshan dish, even praised by *A Bite of China*, is seaweed. Most of the seaweed sold in Guangdong markets comes from Chaoshan. In Guangzhou, we mostly use it to make soup or sushi, but in Chaoshan, it can be stir-fried, boiled, or roasted, making it a delicious home-cooked dish. It can be stir-fried with celery, blanched with pearl oysters, fried with eggs, or made into egg rolls, or directly roasted. If used to make baked rice, it is even more delicious than sushi.

4. Night Flavors of Chaoshan

The nightlife of Cantonese people is well-known, and Guangdong's late-night dinners also "defy health risks" and remain popular. During the Republic of China era period, as mentioned before, in Shanghai, "late-night dinner represented 'Eating in Guangzhou.'" Since the new era, Chaoshan restaurants have been aggressively expanding into major cities like Guangzhou and Shenzhen, making late-night dinners relatively rich and upscale. In the past, late-night dinners usually consisted of stir-fried rice noodles, oily vegetables, and two bottles of beer. However, in Chaoshan restaurants, there are seafood casserole porridge, stir-fried clams and other seafood, various braised dishes, and of course, some rice cakes. But if you return to Chaozhou or Shantou, Guangzhou's late-night dinners pale in comparison. In some large night congee shops, several long tables are arranged in a row, with all "daleng" (cold dishes) displayed on them. The variety is so extensive that it is dazzling. Just the fish rice alone includes more than a dozen types, such as red-eyed fish, ma you fish, di zi fish, pomfret, red fish, parrot fish, red crucian carp, and nage fish. There are also a lot of braised dishes like Longjiang pig's trotter, braised pig's large intestine, fat goose liver, and braised streaky pork. Traditional dishes such as green garlic braised cuttlefish, pickled cabbage, crucian carp, and pan-fried Spanish mackerel, fresh small yellow croaker, large pomfret, live eel, and stir-fried shrimp and crab are served on the spot. Meat dishes like pork-stuffed bitter gourd and fried spare ribs are interspersed, not to mention green vegetables and mixed pickles.

Chaoshan late-night food stall

Nowadays, Chaoshan night congee stalls are no longer solely dominated by "daleng" but are integrated with traditional seafood stalls, offering more stir-fried dishes than "daleng." For example, fresh fish such as small yellow croaker, large pomfret, stone horn fish, banded gizzard shad, live eel, spaghetti eels, golden flower fish, and light turtle fish, as well as various shrimp and crab, are ordinary supplies. Together with seasonal vegetables, they tantalize the taste buds with their beauty and affordability.

Such nutritious delicacies, accompanied by Chaozhou white congee ("mi") cooked with sticky soft rice that is "harmonious water and rice, soft and smooth as one." "A nap after congee is wonderful." In this splendid night congee stall, some ordinary ingredients also become upscale. For example, there is a cold joke about a red crab, "How did the bear die? Stupidly, how did the red crab become expensive? Frozen to be expensive." Red crab has loose meat and much water, with almost no meat to eat, which can be called "chicken ribs". But after freezing, its meat becomes delicious, and its price soars.

4.4 Eating from the Mountains and the Essence of Hakka Cuisine

Guangzhou is the provincial capital. In the past, when transportation was inconvenient, the cuisines of various regions and ethnic groups in Guangdong were often displayed through Guangzhou or integrated into Cantonese cuisine represented by Guangzhou or Guangfu cuisine, making Cantonese cuisine what it is. Among them, Hakka cuisine (or Dongjiang cuisine) is particularly typical.

1. Contributing to the Style of National Cuisine

There was a saying among Guangzhou people in the past, "The Hakka occupy the landlord's place." That is to say, although the Hakka are guests, they live everywhere and even become the host. In terms of the way of eating, they can both export and absorb, having a long-term mutual influence on Cantonese cuisine.

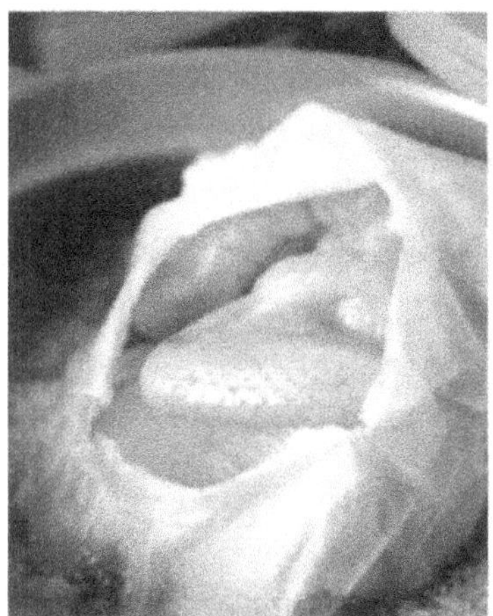

Hakkas salt-baked chicken

For example, Shahe Fen (rice noodles), now one of the representative dishes of "Food in Guangzhou," was created by the Hakka people. According to the elderly Mr. Lao Saiban, more than a hundred years ago, some Dongjiang Hakka people who engaged in stone masonry moved from Wuhua County to settle in Shahe, Guangzhou. Each of these households had a stone mill, using it to grind rice into a slurry with water, and steaming it with Baiyun Mountain spring water to make Shahe Fen that was thin, chewy, refreshing, and smooth. Later, besides self-consumption, they opened shops to sell it. Due to its affordability and deliciousness, it was loved by everyone, and the business thrived, gradually becoming a famous snack. Another example is the representative dish "Eight Treasures Salt-Baked Chicken" by Shunde's Xiao Liangchu, a national banquet chef, which is based on the famous traditional Hakka dish "Dongjiang Salt-Baked Chicken." In fact, from the multiple salt-baked chicken recipes recommended by Wu Huizhen, a famous socialite in the Republic of China era, the early influence of Hakka cuisine can be faintly seen, along with the characteristics and new ideas of Guangfu cuisine: salt-baking can serve as a tonic instead of medicine, with fragrant chicken and tender meat, absolutely not greasy, preserving the original quality and flavor. The cooking method: first, take a fat hen, pluck it clean, wipe it dry inside and out with a cloth, then rub it evenly with rose wine and hang it to dry. Use a clay casserole produced in Shiwan (i.e., a thin clay pot), thinly spread raw salt produced in Haitian inside the pot, place the whole chicken in it, add more raw salt to cover the chicken, then cover the pot tightly and place it on the stove to bake slowly for about fifty minutes. It can then be taken out to eat, half crispy, soft and smooth, with fragrant skin and meat. However, there are two points to note when cooking: the chicken should be dry, as any moisture will make it taste bitter; the fire should be slow and even to prevent the clay pot from bursting before the chicken is cooked.

Some rub honey, spices, etc., inside the chicken belly, which adds fragrance but is too complex, not as good as the pure taste.

There is another very special Hakka chicken dish in Guangdong that is difficult for outsiders to learn: Hakka Niangjiu Chicken, cooked with natural red glutinous rice sweet wine, which is very beautiful; the wine is fragrant and the meat is tender, with an excellent taste; and it has profound nourishing effects, as it was originally mainly made for women during confinement. In addition to the famous salt-baked chicken and niangjiu chicken, there are also braised chicken, slow-baking chicken, smoked chicken, roasted chicken, braised chicken, fried chicken, etc., enriching Guangdong's chicken dishes.

Some scholars believe that Hakka flat rice crispy chicken and rose wine-baked double pigeons further inherit the distant Central Plains traditions. Flat rice chicken is made by stuffing flat rice into the cleaned chicken cavity, first steaming and then frying, with a golden color, crispy outside, and tender inside, and a strong fragrance. Flat rice is actually glutinous rice steamed into rice, placed in a basket, covered with a damp cloth, and dried in a ventilated place, making the rice grains flat and small, hence the name flat rice. Because of this, it has the function of regulating qi and stimulating appetite, making flat rice crispy chicken a traditional Dongjiang famous dish. As for rose wine-baked double pigeons, the method is to clean and dry the two pigeons, place them spread out in a clay bowl, put two bamboo chopsticks horizontally under the pigeons to leave a little distance between the pigeon bodies and the bottom of the bowl for heat circulation; take a cup of rose wine and place it between the two pigeons, then put the whole thing into an iron pot, cover it with a clay basin, and heat the pot over medium heat. When the pigeons are cooked, half a cup of clear wine remains in the cup, but the wine taste has completely disappeared, while the pigeon meat is fragrant with wine. It is generally believed that the Hakka people originated from the Central Plains, preserving their traditions, and the same is true of their cuisine; it is said that the system of flat rice can be seen in the *Biography of Yu Zong in the Southern Qi Dynasty*, which may be credible. (Preface to *Guangdong Hakka Cuisine* by Zhang Xiusong, Guangdong Science and Technology Press, 1995 edition)

Another example is Hakka preserved mustard greens, which are one of the widely used auxiliary materials in Cantonese cuisine. Wu Huizhen, a celebrity in the Republic of China era, introduced Cantonese Cuisine Cooking Methods in a column in the Shanghai magazine Home, often mentioning it. In the past, at the famous Dongjiang Restaurant on Zhongyou Street in Guangzhou, many people traveling overseas did not ask for abalone, sea cucumber, shark's fin, or dried scallops when they returned home, but specifically asked for preserved mustard greens with braised pork, in order to evoke some childhood memories. The deep hometown concept of the Hakka people has enabled Hakka cuisine with strong flavor to still occupy a place in the central region of Cantonese cuisine, which is mainly light, and has lasted for a long time. Zhou Jianzhang's book Old Flavors still says that preserved mustard greens are elegant dishes served at state banquets.

Another iconic event of "Hakka people occupying the landlord's place" is the naming of Guangzhou Dongjiang Restaurant. Founded in 1946, it was originally called Yunlai Pavilion, later renamed Ningchang Hall, and was approved to be renamed "Dongjiang Restaurant" in 1972, which was the only case at that time where the restaurant name was characterized by the regional cuisine. Due to its traditional Dongjiang flavor being highly favored, it was extremely popular for a time; the original "Dongjiang Salt-Baked Chicken" was particularly sought after, dominating the scene. Its dishes are characterized by using poultry as the main ingredient, with prominent ingredients, simple and generous cooking, and rich flavors. It has ten famous dishes, including Dongjiang Fragrant Crispy Chicken, Braised Sea Cucumber, Refreshing Beef Balls, Red Fermented Pork Soaked Double Limbs, Seven-Colored Mixed Casserole, Eight-Treasure Stuffed Tofu, Dongjiang Roll, Preserved Mustard Greens with Braised Pork, Dongjiang Big Round Hoof, Pickled Vegetable Belly Slices, etc., in addition to Dongjiang Salt-Baked Chicken. Its "Eight-Treasure Stuffed Tofu" can be regarded as the best of the now-famous Guangzhou Hakka stuffed tofu. It uses pork, squid, shrimp, winter mushrooms, salted fish, dried sole fish, and chopped scallions to make the meat filling, which is stuffed into tofu, fried to a golden brown over medium heat, placed in a clay pot padded with "vegetable hearts," added with seasonings and superior soup, and slowly cooked before serving. This dish is fresh, fragrant, tender, and rich in flavor.

Hakka cuisine not only influences Guangfu cuisine but also Chaozhou cuisine. For example, the famous Chaozhou beef balls originated from the Hakka people. Some believe they were introduced from Meixian and Xingning during the Anti-Japanese War, but they were only served as snacks and could not be served on grand occasions, unlike the clear soup beef balls of Dongjiang cuisine that can be served at banquets. Of course, Hakka cuisine is also fully borrowed from Chaozhou cuisine. The most ingenious is creating the excellent Gongfu Soup by drawing inspiration from Chaozhou Gongfu tea. Gongfu Soup does not use a stewing cup or casserole but a teapot. Chinese herbal medicines such as ganoderma lucidum, wolfberry, and angelica, together with ingredients such as farm chickens and lean meat, are put into a teapot and slowly steamed for several hours until they become as pure as tea. Naturally, soup bowls are not used for drinking soup, but small tea cups are used, just like drinking Gongfu tea, with a mellow taste and lingering fragrance. At Chaoshan banquets, where Gongfu tea is drunk, old fire soup is basically not consumed, and instead, freshly cooked beef balls, fish ball soup, or tofu fish soup are more common. The Hakka's five-finger peach soup is also unique.

Perhaps the most proud moment for Hakka cuisine is when Zhang Bishi from Dabu, Meizhou, founded the Changyu Grape Wine Company in Yantai in 1892. The two leading figures of Guangdong people, Sun Yat-sen in martial arts and Kang Youwei in literature, both paid tribute to it: in 1912, Mr. Sun Yat-sen inscribed "Pin Zhong Li Quan" (meaning excellent wine) to show his appreciation; Kang Youwei visited and stayed there in person and presented a poem, "Sipping Changyu wine, transplanting Fengtai peonies. Writing new verses again, happy to meet and make it home." A century-old store remains young—can we not be proud?!

2. Dim Sum as Main Dishes

Another skill of the Hakka people is turning staple foods and some mountain specialties, such as green vegetables or wild vegetables, into dimsum-like banquets, which greatly enhances the Hakka cuisine. This is "ban (rice crispies)." For example, Pingyuan's Huangban is made by soaking a mixture of glutinous and indica rice in water filtered from high-quality plant ash for several hours, processing it into rice slurry, cooking it into a soft and tough ban dough over low heat, taking it out and steaming it in a copper basin, and then putting it into a mortar to pound into ci, resulting in golden, fragrant, and tender Huangban; its yellow color comes from the bayberry leaf juice in the plant ash. Another example is Weijiao Ban, which is suitable for all ages. Marshal Ye still remembered it when he returned to his hometown at the age of 80 and specially requested to taste it. The production of Weijiao Ban is simpler: grind japonica rice into a slurry, add "alkali sand," and steam it; it can be eaten with "red flavor" made by boiling brown sugar and a little soy sauce or dipped in "garlic flavor". There is also Laoshu Ban, popular in Dabu, which is actually a kind of noodle made with a board, named because both ends are pointed and resemble mice. It is elegantly called Yinzhen Fen by the Hakka in Hong Kong and Mitai by the Hakka in Taiwan. There is also a "Zhulong Ban," which is actually a rice-made vegetable bun, named because its shape resembles a bamboo cage for pigs. Originally, it was just a white rice ball carried for food when working in the mountains, but now, with conditions to pay attention, it is wrapped with various fillings and becomes a delicacy.

There is also a Rending Ban, which is made by kneading a mixture of glutinous and non-glutinous rice flour with water into a cylindrical strip about 15 centimeters long and steaming it thoroughly in a cage. It is mostly used as an offering, symbolizing family happiness and prosperity, and is mainly popular in the Dabu countryside.

Hakkas rending ban

There is also a Liangshu Ban. First, grind rice into rice slurry with water, add fried pork, mushrooms, squid, crushed peanuts, and shrimp bran, add appropriate salt, then pour into a large pot and stir-fry over high heat, turning and pressing frequently to prevent sticking to the pot. After it becomes a paste, squeeze it into ping-pong-sized balls with hands, boil them in water, add chopped green onions and celery, and mix well with seasonings such as pepper and monosodium glutamate.

There is also Luobo Ban, or Cai Bao Guo, similar to the turnip cake in the Guangfu region. There is Yezi Ban, where glutinous rice flour mixed with red bean paste is wrapped in bamboo leaves smeared with lard and steamed. The dish combines the fragrance of bamboo leaves, glutinous rice, red bean paste, cooked oil, and sugar, offering a fivefold aroma.

There is "Xianren Ban," similar to jelly, which cools the body and relieves summer heat. When eaten, it is mixed with honey and sprinkled with banana syrup, tasting sweet, refreshing, and refreshing. The best is made in Zijin, Heyuan.

In Jiexi, a Hakka area now belonging to Chaoshan, there is Niaozi Ban, named for its bird-like shape. Stuffed with dried tofu, scallions, garlic, shrimp, and lean pork, it rivals Chaoshan guo in color, aroma, and taste. In the county town of Heping, more than 50 shops are making this ban, with over 10 concentrated on Qinghe Road and Hexi Fourth Road, known as "Niaozi Ban Street." Its prosperity stems from local love and export demand.

There is also Jiuceng Ban, with alternating salty and sweet layers, offering a unique taste.

Yizi Ban has a special name and a long history, with unknown stories behind it. Stuffed with meat slices, squid shreds, scallions, and ginger, it is delicious and suitable for all ages, deeply loved and praised.

The main ingredient of Lvdou Ban is not mung beans (only 1 part), but a filling of 4 parts brown sugar, 1 part orange cake, shredded meat, longan meat, and melon slices, with 3 parts glutinous rice for the skin, wrapped in banana leaves and steamed. Sweet, fresh, and fragrant, it is known as "gold in sand."

During happy events, Hakka people make Hong Ban (red ban), wrapping sweet red bean paste, peanut powder, and red bean filling in ban crusts, and imprinting turtle shell patterns with a "ban stamp" for auspiciousness.

While Chaoshan people have the creative dish fried hemp leaves, Hakka people have Zhu Ye Ban. Made by mashing fresh zhuye (ramie leaves) with japonica glutinous rice and well water in a stone mortar, forming a green ban dough, which is kneaded into small pieces and steamed or fried. It is fragrant, sweet, and moisturizing, satisfying hunger, strengthening the immune system, treating skin diseases, and suitable for all ages.

Fa Ban is a festival ban. After fermentation, the ban surface rises from the bowl, symbolizing wealth (a homophone for "fa", which means wealth in Chinese). It often cracks, hence the name "Xiao Ban" (smiling ban). During the New Year, every Hakka household steams Fa Ban and Tian Ban (sweet ban), with the saying, "No New Year without steaming Tian Ban." Tian Ban must be preserved until the second day of the second lunar month, when it is cut into pieces and fried in oil, called "supporting the waist bones," meaning to straighten up for spring farm work.

There is also Sun Ban, also known as Niang Ban or Bao Ban, with a sweet potato flour skin and filling of fatty pork, bamboo shoots, shrimp, squid shreds, mushrooms, and pepper, similar to Chaoshan sun guo.

Qingming Ban is the most famous, oldest, and distinctive, easily found in Guangzhou restaurants during Qingming. Made from half-japonica, half-glutinous flour mixed with fresh mugwort leaves, ramie leaves, Pulsatilla chinensis, Houttuynia cordata, Paederia scandens, and Quisqualis indica, kneaded into a green ban dough, steamed after repeated kneading. It carries the aroma of spring and has health benefits like dispelling wind and dampness, hence called "medicinal ban."

Huishui Ban is made by filtering rice straw ash or soybean seedling ash water to soak rice, grinding it into a slurry, and steaming it, common in Pingyuan and other places.

Xiandao Ban uses rice straw ash bags not to soak rice but to absorb water from the ground ban slurry, forming a smooth paste. It is spread thinly on the back of a smooth gourd ladle, cut into loach-like strips with ramie thread as a knife, and boiled in soup. Without seasoning, it exudes rice aroma and has a tender texture. Similar to Guangzhou's Shahe Fen, legend has it that Shahe Fen was invented by the Hakka, tracing back to this.

These Hakka ban snacks reflect the essence of the Hakka people and their craftsmanship, shining with spiritual brilliance. Mountains and waters yield clear sounds and delicious food, and the essence of Hakka cuisine lies in this natural bounty.

4.5 Hakka Cuisine Popular Across the Two Banks and Three Regions

The Hakka people originated from various places and have spread far and wide, and so has Hakka cuisine, which once flourished across the two sides of the Taiwan Strait and the three regions (mainland China, Hong Kong, and Taiwan), and still prevails in streets and alleys today. Take Taiwan's "Yonghe Soymilk," a Hakka creation that has become a metropolitan delicacy popular at home and abroad in recent years. In addition to selling soymilk, it offers sesame seed cakes, fried dough sticks, rice balls, pie, scallion pancakes, sesame shortbread, egg pancakes, thousand-layer cakes, and small steamed buns. Founder Qiu Fengcai was invited to the "Presidential Palace" more than ten times during the era of the two Jiangs (Chiang Kai-shek and Chiang Ching-kuo) to make specialty snacks from other provinces. Not only in Taiwan, but "Yonghe Soymilk" can also be found in many major cities on the mainland and Chinatowns in the U.S., Canada, and other countries, perhaps with some connection to this origin. Besides Hakka snack shops, Hakka grand restaurants also became popular. The Taofang Restaurant alone had five to six branches, attracting Taiwanese political giants like Wang Yunwu and Hu Shi to patronize, "(November 23,

1959) Mr. Yunwu invited me to the new Taofang Restaurant on Yuanling Street to enjoy Guangdong's famous dishes (salt-baked chicken, stir-fried □ Guang). I met the owner, Zeng Xiong (a Hakka), who said he had worked in 'party, government, military, police, scholars, farmers, workers, and business' and now focuses on running this restaurant, having opened six branches, all employing ex-servicemen, totaling more than 200 people, 32 of whom have married and started families. Employees earn at least over a thousand yuan monthly, and chefs, also ex-servicemen, can receive a monthly salary of five thousand yuan. We all congratulated him on his success." (*Complete Diaries of Hu Shi*, Anhui Education Press, 2001 edition, Eighth Volume, Page 611)

Before the founding of the People's Republic of China, Guangzhou had a Lingdong Grand Hotel famous for its salt-baked chicken. "In the early morning around 4 o'clock yesterday, a major theft occurred at the Lingdong Grand Hotel in front of the Treasury. The thieves entered through the high wall at the back of the hotel near Hanmin Park by opening the iron net. They stole dozens of pieces of clothing for men and women, a lot of sundries, and cash from the clothes totaling over ten million yuan. Even a remaining 'salt-baked chicken' in the kitchen was stolen. At dawn, shop owner Liang Qiyou reported the case to the police station and detective team for investigation." (*Rat Steals Salt-Baked Chicken: Lingdong Grand Hotel Burglarized Before Dawn with Heavy Losses*, *Star News*, September 3, 1947)

In Hong Kong, due to the influx of immigrants around 1949, Hakka cuisine achieved unprecedented development. Researchers note that although Hakka cuisine appeared in Hong Kong restaurants only in the late 1940s and early 1950s, developed by mainland immigrants, similar restaurants thrived in the 1960s and 1970s, with the number of Hakka restaurants reaching 87 by the mid-1970s. Restaurants like Qichang, Yuanmao, Jiuji, and Yonghe, all run by Hakka people from Xingning who came to Hong Kong, have become highly popular. Later, restaurants such as Qiongyuan, Meijiang, Donghai, Yuedu, Longjiang, Huadu, and Xin Qionglou emerged, with Zui Qionglou and Quanzhangju being the most familiar to Hong Kong people, still promoting themselves as "authentic Dongjiang cuisine" today. Their salt-baked chicken, preserved mustard greens with braised pork, stuffed tofu, Dongjiang tofu casserole, three delicacies with bone marrow, beef balls, and fried pork intestines are still well-known to Hong Kong people. Compared with home-cooked dishes dominated by fresh fish and vegetables, this "authentic Dongjiang cuisine" emphasizes abundant meat and cooking techniques different from Guangdong family cooking, especially methods like (salt) baking, stuffing, (preserved mustard greens) braising, and (red yeast) wine stir-frying, bringing new culinary experiences and consumption patterns to Hong Kong people who enjoy alternatives to daily Cantonese food. (Zhang Zhanhong, *Hong Kong Hakka Restaurants and "Authentic Dongjiang Cuisine", in Hong Kong Hakka* edited by Liu Yizhang, Guangxi Normal University Press, 2007 edition)

Hakkas marinated tofu

Quanzhangju and Zui Qionglou were also frequent destinations for the famous writer Ye Lingfeng, especially for salt-baked chicken: "(November 2, 1951) In the afternoon, at the invitation of Mr. and Mrs. Kaohsiung in Kowloon, I dined at Zhangquanju on salt-baked chicken, which has recently become the most popular Hakka dish in Hong Kong." According to Zhang Yongmei's research, Zhangquanju had its main store and branches between 1949 and 1950, located at Tai Po Road in Sham Shui Po and No. 138 North River Street. In fact, from the diary, it can be seen that he first tasted Hakka cuisine at Dongjiang Restaurant, noting that Hakka food was quite popular in Hong Kong, "(October 7, 1951) Dined with Miao Xiu at Dongjiang Restaurant in the evening. Various Hakka dishes from Dongjiang have recently become popular in Hong Kong. The most common are salt-baked chicken and stuffed tofu. The salt-baked chicken is quite tender, similar to the barrel oil chicken in Jiangsu and Zhejiang, but instead of being cut with a knife, it is torn by hand, resembling wind-dried chicken." "(October 16,

1951) After the meeting, I went to Dongjiang Restaurant with Cao Juren and others for salt-baked chicken and tofu." According to Zhang Yongmei's research, there were several Dongjiang Restaurants at that time, including Jiangji Dongjiang Restaurant at No. 24 Des Voeux Road West and President Dongjiang Restaurant at No. 6 Ningbo Street. Due to the growing popularity of Hakka cuisine, even more than a decade later, dining at Zui Qionglou still required queuing: "January 7, 1968: Crossed the sea back to Hong Kong from Kwun Tong at 6 pm and had dinner at Zui Qionglou. This is Dongjiang cuisine, with extremely good business; we waited a long time for a seat." (*Ye Lingfeng's Diary* annotated by Lu Weiluan and Zhang Yongmei, Joint Publishing (Hong Kong) Co., Ltd., 2020 edition)

The popularity of Hakka cuisine has also attracted the attention of Eugene N. Anderson, a renowned American anthropologist. "Hakka food is simple, easy to prepare, and well-proportioned. The South Chinese emphasis on freshness is more pronounced than usual, typically without imported or expensive ingredients. Hakka people are masters at cooking tripe, liver, kidneys, small intestines, etc., so one of their delicacies is ox marrow, minced and stir-fried with vegetables. It is called 'bone marrow' in Chinese and appears on menus by this name. The most popular Hakka dish is salt-baked chicken, which lives up to its name. Salt seals in the flavor and juices while conducting heat slowly and evenly. Hakkas are also famous for beef balls and fish paste (which makes full use of fish). This fish paste mixed with scallions, ginger, and other ingredients is often stuffed into fresh or fried tofu, as well as into chili peppers, eggplants, bitter gourds, and other vegetables. These stuffed vegetables are usually deep-fried, stir-fried, or steamed. Stuffed foods are not unique to the Hakkas. They are widely popular in the South. But Hakkas have a particular fondness for them." He also noted that "Hakka restaurants are now appearing in the United States and other Western countries," showing a global trend. (Eugene N. Anderson, *Chinese Food*, Jiangsu People's Publishing House, 2003 edition)

Chapter 5 Chinese Cuisine Goes West: Cantonese Cuisine Takes the Lead

Mr. Hu Wenhui said: Before modern times, in the metaphysical realm of ideas, China imported far more from the West than it exported, meaning there was a clear "cultural deficit" in high-end ideological exchanges. Fortunately, in the physical realm, China exported more than it imported. Thanks to silk, ceramics, and tea, we could make up for the "cultural deficit" and regain some pride as the Celestial Empire. In modern times, as Western powers arrived, the cultural exchange tide from West to East became overwhelming, making China an absolute importer. In the metaphysical realm, it was unidirectional "cultural borrowing," and even in the physical realm, silk, ceramics, and tea lost their luster. Over the past century or two, what has China had that can be called "going global"? After some thought, I can only think of three things for now: Chinese cuisine, pandas, and kung fu movies. And the primary credit for Chinese cuisine and kung fu movies taking root overseas goes to the Cantonese people. It might be said that overseas, most of the Chinese history is that of the Cantonese, and most of the Chinese food history is that of Cantonese cuisine.

Dr. Sun Yat-sen, the great pioneer of the revolution, used food as the opening proof for his *The International Development of China* (1919), a modern interpretation of "harmonizing the tripod", "In modern China, civilization has lagged behind in everything, but the progress in food still outshines civilized nations. The foods invented in China are indeed more abundant than in Europe and America, and the sophistication of Chinese cooking is unmatched by Europe and America." His arguments were based on Cantonese cuisine, so most examples cited were of Cantonese dishes. For instance, he mentioned that animal offal, a favorite of Cantonese people, "was not eaten by the British and Americans in the past, but in recent years, they have regarded it as a delicacy." He also said, "When I was in Guangzhou, I once saw Westerners disdain Chinese people for eating pig's blood, considering it crude and barbaric. Now, as studied by medical and health experts, pig's blood is found to be exceptionally rich in iron, making it an unparalleled tonic for the body. In the past, people suffering from post-illness, post-childbirth, and various blood deficiency conditions were often treated with refined iron supplements, but now pig's blood is used instead. The iron in pigs' blood is organic, which is more suitable for the human body than inorganic refined iron supplements. Therefore, pig's blood as food can not only nourish the body for the sick but also benefit the healthy."

Pigs' blood soup

Thus, the history of Cantonese cuisine spreading to the West is not only a glorious page in the history of Chinese food but also a brilliant chapter in the history of Chinese culture.

5.1 Cantonese Servants, Chinese Laborers, and the Rise of Chop Suey

Due to policy reasons, early chefs in the foreign factories and trading complexes of Guangzhou were all Cantonese servants. These Cantonese servant chefs were so skilled in Western cuisine that they were even recommended abroad, "I have sent the following 4 Chinese men introduced by your former compradore to the Sachem. They are: Aluck, the chef, said to be first-class, at 10 yuan per month. Some wages were advanced to your compradore for his travel expenses. Starting from January 25, 1835, the annual salary is 120 yuan." Another individual named Robert Bennet Forbes also brought a Chinese servant with the English name Ashew to Boston to serve his wife's cousin, Copley Greene. Therefore, in their home countries, early Europeans and Americans saw Chinese people but did not taste Chinese food. For those who later vigorously advocated achieving the "Chinese Dream" through the kitchen knife, this was truly a "heart-wrenching regret!"

The Sino-Western food culture exchange led by servants continued, though it was unclear whether it was Chinese or Western cuisine, but at least it could be both. The most famous cases are as follows: First, Ding Long, a "piglet" (indentured laborer) from Taishan, Guangdong, who donated his lifelong savings of $12,000 in 1901 to establish the first Sinology department at a renowned American university—the East Asian Department of Columbia University—moved by whom, his employer, C. P. Huntington, donated as much as $100,000! Second, a Cantonese chef who served from 1871 to 1953 at Mills College in Oakland, the oldest women's college on the West Coast. (Jiang Yi, *Chronicle of Chinese in San Francisco*, *Series of Translations on the History of Sino-Foreign Relations* edited by the Society for the History of Sino-Foreign Relations and the History Department of Fudan University, Translations of Sino-Foreign Relations History (Fourth Volume), Shanghai Translation Publishing House, 1988 edition) In fact, these historical facts to some extent rewrite the history of Western cuisine in China.

The true opening of Chinese cuisine to the West was led by Chinese laborers, especially those from Taishan who went to San Francisco for gold. As we know, early Chinese in the U.S., besides being sold as indentured laborers, mainly made a living with three tools: the kitchen knife (opening restaurants), the barber's knife, and the scissors (tailoring and laundry), with the "kitchen knife" being particularly important as it served both Americans and themselves. However, early Chinese restaurants in Chinatown were not called chop suey houses. According to Liang Qichao's *Travel Notes of the New Continent* (1903), after his visit to the U.S., chop suey houses emerged after Li Hongzhang visited the U.S. in 1896. This was for two reasons: first, Chinese cuisine was inherently excellent, but "previously, Westerners did not set foot in Chinatowns," so few knew about it. Second, Americans had a hero-worshipping complex, and Li Hongzhang was indeed a hero of the era, with enormous positive influence both at home and abroad, far from being as awful as later propaganda. Thus, his visit to the U.S. set off a "Li Hongzhang craze"; when he visited Chinatown, Americans flocked there to snoop around the hometown of this hero.

Liang Qichao also mentioned that Li Hongzhang wanted to eat Chinese food during his U.S. visit and asked Chinatown restaurants to provide it several times. Americans asked what was served, but the Chinese couldn't explain clearly, "collectively calling it chop suey." From then on, chop suey became famous, and the whole country went crazy for it. "Menus of chop suey houses all grandly feature names like 'Li Hongzhang Chop Suey,' 'Li Hongzhang Noodles,' and 'Li Hongzhang Rice. '"

Driven by this demand, chop suey houses flourished, with 300 to 400 in New York alone. Large numbers also emerged in Boston, Washington, Chicago, and other cities in the eastern U.S. Liang Qichao lamented, "Li Hongzhang's greatest merit for Cantonese people lies in this." Since almost all Chinese immigrants in the U.S. were Cantonese, and running restaurants was one of their main occupations, his later personal writing of *Biography of Li Hongzhang* may not be unrelated to this, as noted in Xu Gang's *Biography of Liang Qichao* today.

Influenced by Liang Qichao, Kang Youwei traveled through Europe in

1904 and wrote in *Travelogues of Eleven European Countries*, "Chinese restaurants have thrived in Chicago, USA. Over three years, more than 200 new eateries opened suddenly, and Americans competed to enjoy them." However, these two great figures in modern history from Guangdong, while passionate and pioneering, lacked rigor in academic writing, and their statements became increasingly unreliable. In fact, upon careful reflection, they even found inconsistencies. Thus, Liang Qichao said, "Westerners have profoundly inexplicable traits, such as their love for chop suey," comparable only to "their preference for Chinese medicine." He noted, "Some Westerners favor Chinese medicine, making it a profitable business. There is 'Wang Laoji Herbal Tea,' costing two copper coins per packet in Guangdong, but sold to Westerners for $5 to $10 each; others follow suit. Yet, eight or nine out of ten practitioners hardly understand medicine, and those who do often cannot practice." This left him contradictory: he earlier attributed chop suey's popularity to Chinese cuisine's excellence, but later said, "However, the so-called chop suey is poorly cooked, and no Chinese would eat it."

The crux is that Li Hongzhang never tasted chop suey. Moreover, early Chinese cuisine, primarily served to Chinese people, was quite authentic, unlike Liang's claim of "poor cooking"—later chop suey did acquire such traits. According to A History of Chinese in America by Chen Yifan (from an overseas Chinese family; his father Chen Youren served as Foreign Minister of the National Government, and he lived on the mainland from 1950 to 1970), early Chinese immigrants to America were mostly male laborers, many indentured, unable to cook alone, giving rise to canteen-style Chinese restaurants. Take San Francisco, an early Chinese settlement, as an example, though the population of Chinese was small (three Chinese recorded by U.S. immigration in 1820, seven more in the next decade, and only hundreds by 1850), five restaurants serving Chinese opened around Portsmouth Square in the city center, dubbed “Little Guangzhou.” This formed the prototype of San Francisco’s Chinatown, the oldest and largest in the U.S., and these eateries were the forerunners of chop suey houses.

Report on Li Hongzhang's visit to the U.S.

Research into overseas Chinese history shows that these early gold miners were mainly Taishan people, and we can fairly infer that this early “chop suey” also largely belonged to Taishan cuisine; the American anthropologist Eugene N. Anderson’s *Chinese Food* corroborates this point:

"Chop suey is not (as many would-be connoisseurs believe) an American invention. As Shu-fan Li notes in his delightful autobiography Surgeon in Hong Kong (1964), it is a local Taishan dish. Taishan is a rural area south of Guangzhou, home to most early immigrants from Guangdong to California. The dish is called tsap seui in Cantonese (Mandarin: 'zasi'). It basically stir-fries leftovers or bits and pieces of vegetables, often including noodles. Bean sprouts are almost always present, but other components vary by available ingredients." (Trans. Liu Dong, Jiangsu People's Publishing House, 2003, p. 175)

These early Chinese restaurants quickly won favor with foreigners. Gold miner William Shaw wrote in his 1851 *Golden Dreams and Waking Realities*, "The best restaurants in San Francisco are Chinese, serving mostly spicy dishes like chop suey and stir-fried diced meat, delivered in small plates and extremely delicious. I didn't even care to ask what they were made of." Marked by yellow silk triangles, these Chinese restaurants gained early fame in San Francisco—a city renowned for diverse, tasty cuisines (French, Italian, Spanish, British, American), precisely "because they didn't try to cater to Western tastes." It was also said, "To this day, most Chinese families and the best Chinese restaurants serve food identical to that in China," and "Chinese restaurants have thrived, proving their culinary excellence and San Franciscans' need for them, as the habit of 'eating out' persists—a tradition of early pioneers and bachelors who lacked real homes."

As a dish that later became synonymous with Chinese restaurants, "chow chop suey" is also an authentic Chinese dish with a long history. In 1884, Wang Qingfu, the first Chinese journalist, wrote an article in The Brooklyn Eagle introducing Chinese cuisine, exaggerating that "'Chop suey' may be called China's national dish." Although he had only been in the U.S. for six years, his words were highly credible. In 1888, he further stated in *Chinese in New York*, *Cosmopolitan Magazine* issue 5, "The most common dish among Chinese is chow chop suey, a dish made by stewing chicken livers, gizzards, mushrooms, bamboo shoots, pig stomach, bean sprouts, etc., with spices." Professor Liu Haiming commented that "chow chop suey" follows Cantonese pronunciation. Since most early Chinese immigrants were from Guangdong, and "chop" happens to mean "chop into pieces" in English, to Americans and others unfamiliar with it, "chop suey" might seem like finely chopped chicken, pork, or beef cooked into a dish, which is exactly how Americanized chop suey later developed. However, it's not entirely true that all Chinese love chop suey, though Cantonese have a particular fondness for pig and chicken offal, which remains today. Bamboo shoots in the ingredients also reflect Cantonese characteristics, which are featured in my book *The Flavor of the Republic of China Era*.

"The most delicious harmony comes from the fungi of Yue and Luo," according to Gao You's annotation in the Han Dynasty. This fungus refers to bamboo shoots. The crucial role of bamboo shoots in Cantonese cuisine seasoning was elaborated in my special article in *the Tastes of the Republic of China era.*

After Liang Qichao, another great Cantonese figure, Sun Yat-sen, who traveled overseas for years, indirectly paid high tribute to chop suey. Sun Yat-sen's introduction to chop suey houses focused on the U.S. but extended beyond. He said, "In recent years, wherever overseas Chinese have gone, Chinese food culture has thrived. In New York City alone, there are hundreds of Chinese restaurants. Almost no American city lacks Chinese restaurants. Americans are crazily fond of Chinese flavors, leading local restaurants to grow intensely jealous. They spread rumors that soy sauce used by the Chinese contains toxins harmful to health, even prompting the Detroit city council to propose banning the Chinese from using soy sauce. After rigorous testing by medical and health experts, it was proven that soy sauce not only contains no toxins but is rich in meat extract, similar to beef juice—it not only harms no health but greatly benefits the body, so the ban was lifted. Chinese cooking has spread not only to America but also to major cities in Europe. Since Japan's Meiji Restoration, while adopting many Western customs, it still craves Chinese flavors, so Tokyo is also lined with Chinese restaurants. This shows that people share common tastes." Sun Yat-sen avoided the term "chop suey"; the Chinese food he mentioned, once boycotted by Americans, was certainly different from the so-called "Li Hongzhang chop suey" or "American chop suey".

Report on Chinese food restaurants in the U.S.

Sun Yat-sen's article, written in the early Republic of China, both summarized pre-Republic chop suey houses and inaugurated a new chapter in Republican-era writing.

5.2 From Li Hongzhang Chop Suey to American Chop Suey

The rise of chop suey concerns not only Chinese people or Chinese in America but also Americans. Thus, how Americans view it is also a "Yuanfang-style" question (i.e., a matter of perspective). Li Hongzhang's visit to the U.S. became the focal point of this issue. Research by overseas Chinese historians like Yu Yingqiu and Liu Haiming shows that chop suey gained attention due to Li Hongzhang's visit and gradually became Americanized by removing offal. However, at the popular level, the so-called "Li Hongzhang chop suey" remains a fascinating topic.

There are several versions of "Li Hongzhang chop suey," mostly adapted from Liang Qichao's account—for example, claiming chop suey originated from a banquet hosted by San Francisco Mayor Sutro or a Chaozhou merchant in Chicago, with some even shifting the setting to Tsarist Russia. These tales, especially those spread by ignorant modern rumor-mongers, are hardly worth mentioning. We should instead examine the on-site context of the time to gain real insights.

Historical records show that during his U.S. visit, Li Hongzhang first went to New York, then to Washington, D.C., and Philadelphia, before returning to New York and traveling west to Vancouver, returning home via Yokohama. He neither visited San Francisco nor Chicago, and even in New York, he never ate chop suey. According to *The New York Times*, although the New York Chinese Merchants Association planned to host a banquet for Li Hongzhang in Chinatown on September 1st, 1896, he canceled due to a finger injury from a car door. The claim that "Hefei (Li Hongzhang) craved Chinese food in America" is even more baseless, as he brought three chefs and ample tea, rice, and cooking condiments, ensuring no dietary concerns. Some thus cooking up stories that Li Hongzhang needed to reciprocate an American banquet but lacked ingredients, so he combined leftovers into a dish that unexpectedly gained popularity, leading to "Li Hongzhang Chop Suey." However, Professor Liu Haiming's research shows that *The New York Times* covered Li's speeches and activities in one to two full pages daily, omitting any mention of chop suey, clearly a fabrication by Chinese, mainly

Chinese restaurant staff, to promote Chinese restaurants using Li's visit. As the most important Qing official, Li received high treatment and media attention during his visit, with American journalists and diplomats sailing with him and reporting in detail. Coverage of his diet started on the ship: an August 29th *New York Times* article noted Li's chefs prepared seven meals daily, including shark's fin and bird's nest. Even after arriving, he mostly ate self-prepared food. A September 5th report stated that at a dinner hosted by former Secretary of State J.W. Foster, Li "only drank a little champagne, ate a bit of ice cream, and didn't touch other foods." One reported meal included "diced stewed chicken, a bowl of rice, and a bowl of vegetable soup", the first time Chinese chefs used Chinese utensils to prepare food at the Waldorf Astoria, arousing more curiosity than Li himself. This "curiosity" turned chop suey into a legend, prompting Chinese restaurant owners to seize business opportunities.

When Li Hongzhang, a high-ranking official, arrived from distant China, he naturally disdained chop suey, yet inadvertently became its best spokesperson, elevating it overnight. As Frank Leslie's Illustrated stated, "Americans who taste the magical flavor of chop suey immediately forget disputes about Chinese; an irresistible temptation surges, overriding will and magnetically drawing them to Mott Street." Influenced by media coverage of Li's visit, thousands of New Yorkers flocked to Chinatown for chow chop suey, including Mayor William Strong on August 26th, 1896. Whether Li ate it or not became irrelevant. The Chinese invented stories, and Americans believed them, and an inexplicable fascination with chop suey arose. Demand drove development. By 1898, journalist Louis Beck's *New York's Chinatown* described chop suey houses as upscale, with at least seven fine restaurants on upper floors of "brilliantly decorated buildings," their "restaurants spotless, kitchens rarely dusty." To cater to Americans, Charlie Boston, a Chinese American, moved his Chinatown chop suey house to 3rd Avenue in 1903, sparking a trend. Within months, over 100 chop suey houses opened between 45th and 14th Streets, from Broadway to 8th Avenue, many in Tenderloin, "illuminated by colorful lanterns, decorated with silk and bamboo, luxurious by Eastern standards", competing with elite U.S. restaurants and claiming to "attract the city's most distinguished clientele." A Long Island chop suey house was even called a "recreational resort" by *The New York Times*. As Liang Qichao witnessed, New York had gone "crazy for chop suey" by the time of his visit.

But just as chop suey houses moved out of Chinatown and became Americanized, chop suey itself had already started to Americanize. As Beck noted in his book, chow chop suey was made by "stir-frying pork chunks, celery, onions, bean sprouts, etc.," with celery, onions, and bean sprouts replacing offal as primary ingredients, completely different from its original Chinese preparation. On November 3, 1901, *The New York Times* invited Fairs, a former U.S. vice consul in Xiamen, to write *How to Make Chop Suey*, aiming to help "any smart housewife make chow chop suey at home." Xiamen, in southern Fujian, belongs to the same food culture circle as

Chaozhou in Guangdong, so Fairs were deemed qualified. However, his recipe, whether the ingredients (1 pound tender clean pork, diced; half an ounce green ginger root; two celery stalks) or the cooking method (frying ingredients in a pan over high heat with 4 tablespoons olive oil, 1 tablespoon salt, black and red pepper, scallions, adding a small can of mushrooms, half a cup of bean sprouts or French green peas or string beans, or finely chopped green beans or asparagus tips just before serving), deviated from traditional chop suey and even contemporary Chinatown restaurant practices. Even if one omitted chicken offal, soy sauce was essential! To Americans, chop suey's tastiness "depended on the mushrooms and mysterious black or brown sauce (i.e., soy sauce)" poured into the stew pot. Chinese cooks never revealed chop suey's secrets to "foreign devils," even when employed by American families. "Despite constant attempts to extract the recipe, Chinese chefs never shared their cooking mysteries. When Americans asked about chop suey recipes in books or magazines, they often smiled knowingly and stayed silent."

No chef can cook without (soy) sauce. When Xu Zhongpei, a renowned reporter of the Republic of China era, was stationed in London for *Central Daily News*, she found soy sauce was a hot commodity, "I bought soy sauce there several times; a bottle cost £1 (i.e., $4)." (Xu Zhongpei, *London and I • Chinese Restaurants*, *Central Daily News Weekly*, Issue 5, 1948) Yang Jiang recalled similar experiences studying in Oxford with Qian Zhongshu, "Ginger and soy sauce, Chinese specialties, were rare in Oxford, and the soy sauce was neither fresh nor palatable—salty and bitter." (Yang Jiang, *Collected Works of Yang Jiang*, People's Literature Press, 2004) In France, soy sauce had even more stories. Due to the French love for Chinese food, many Chinese restaurants opened, boosting soy sauce sales. The prestigious Wanhua Restaurant in Paris once sold diluted soy sauce. "Wanhua Restaurant also wholesaled Chinese tea, porcelain, ivory chopsticks, and soy sauce. Soy sauce was shipped from Guangdong in sealed wooden barrels, about 100 jin (500 g) per barrel. In Paris, 60-70 jin of water and 4-5 jin of salt were added (French salt was cheap, about 1 franc per jin; in inland China, salt sometimes cost 1-2 silver dollars per jin. Near the Hunan-Guizhou border, it once surged to 9 strings and hundreds of cash per jin), so the cost wasn't low. After mixing, it was bottled in small glass jars, labeled as original Chinese goods, and sold. Westerners who had never been to China couldn't tell the difference and bought it out of admiration for Chinese fame." (Lu Han, *A Segment of My Work-Study Life in France*, *Revolution Weekly*, Issue 77, 1929)

中國菜館在倫敦

Report on Chinese food restaurants in London

In addition to soy sauce, bean sprouts were also a valuable ingredient in chop suey. In Britain, where food was least emphasized, bean sprouts held a special status and had intriguing stories. Xu Zhongpei noted, "In Chinese restaurants, the most authentic Chinese ingredient is bean sprouts, used in noodle soups, stir-fries, and spring rolls. Sometimes a plate of fried noodles arrives with more bean sprouts than noodles." This gave rise to amusing anecdotes: "A waiter told me, 'Some Westerners pretend to be China experts and pompously order bamboo shoots, but they can't describe what bamboo shoots look like. In such cases, we often serve bean sprouts instead, and the Westerners eat them, exclaiming how delicious they are.'" (Xu Zhongpei, *London and I • Chinese Restaurants*, *Central Daily News Weekly*, Issue 5, 1948) An anonymous article in 147 Pictorial Issue 6 (1946), *Chinese Restaurants in London*, stated that Tanhualou, claiming to be "London's oldest Chinese restaurant," had become so Anglicized that only bean sprouts proved it was still Chinese. "All waiters were British, and almost all diners were British. Except for bean sprouts in the dishes and Chinese characters on the menu, it was indistinguishable from a British restaurant!" Bean sprouts were even pricier in French Chinese restaurants: a whole duck cost 120 francs (equivalent to 17 silver dollars), a whole chicken 150 francs, but a small dish of bamboo shoots cost 12 francs, and a small dish of bean sprouts 8 francs. "Such profitable business was only affordable for American tycoons." Why were bamboo shoots and bean sprouts so expensive? Because France had no mung beans at the time, making these "treasures" rare to Westerners, who, like the Chinese trying Western food, assumed they were Chinese specialties imported from China. Dining at a Chinese restaurant without ordering them was considered uncouth. Their eating manners were even more "remarkable": they would lean over the table, eating and staring, utterly confused about how such ingenious ingredients were made. Cantonese chefs deliberately removed the roots and tips of bean sprouts, leaving only the stems, perplexing Westerners. As rural Chinese joked about foreigners eating steamed buns in China, amazed at how sugar was inserted, Westerners remained clueless about bean sprouts. Some curious Western ladies, after eating China's expensive bean sprouts, would eagerly inquire about their production and transportation from China. The bean sprouts of Wanhualou, Paris's most famous Chinese restaurant, were not only renowned but also highly profitable, with the added profit from wholesaling mung beans. An American hotel in Berlin even hired a Chinese bean sprout technician at a high salary and dispatched special commissioners monthly to Wanhualou in Paris for mung bean wholesale, illustrating the lucrative nature of this business. (Lu Han, *A Segment of My Work-Study Life in France*, *Revolution Weekly*, Issues 76–77, 1928)

Americans often regarded mushrooms as crucial. For example, a plate of chop suey with a cup of tea and a bowl of rice costs 25 cents without mushrooms, but 35–40 cents with them. As Beck put it, mushrooms were like "strawberry jam on turkey." Evidently, under its fame, chop suey had drifted far from its original form and flavor, gradually becoming Americanized Chinese food. Thus, Beck added, "Chop suey enthusiasts claim that to taste the real deal, one must still visit crowded Chinese restaurants in Chinatown."

The issue of naming arose as chop suey Americanized, causing debates over its authenticity. Even the most "authentic" origin story deviated from Cantonese reality. Iris Chang, the renowned Chinese American author, cited a popular folk legend from the Gold Rush era in *Chinese in America*, which went: One night, a group of drunken American miners entered a San Francisco Chinese restaurant about to close and demanded food. The chef, having no prepared dishes, mixed leftover ingredients and stir-fried them into a large plate, which the miners praised highly, thus inventing chow chop suey. This legend completed chop suey's de-Cantonese transformation, severing its connection to Li Hongzhang. Even more extraordinarily, a San Franciscan named Lem Sen claimed to have invented chop suey and sought a patent. In the mid-1980s, when someone sued in a San Francisco court to prove that chop suey originated in California instead of New York Chinatown, the judge, recognizing the case's absurdity, humorously ruled that chop suey was invented in San Francisco.

The greatest evidence of chop suey's Americanization is its adoption as a daily dish in the U.S. military. The 1942 *U.S. Army Cookbook* shows American military chop suey used ketchup and Worcestershire sauce, with General Eisenhower said to be particularly fond of it. A *New York Times* report published on August 2, 1953, stated that even after being elected president, he still occasionally ordered his favorite chicken chop suey for his family. By then, in Americans' eyes, chow chop suey was no longer a Chinese dish but a homely American staple.

The Chinatown in Los Angeles

As chop suey became de-Cantonese and even de-Chinese, on the one hand, chop suey houses became synonymous with Chinese restaurants, with almost all Chinese eateries naming themselves after chop suey, "Chop Suey House," "Chop Suey Bowl," "Chop Suey Cafe," "Chop Suey Palace," "Chop Suey Restaurant," "Chop Suey Noodle Shop", and cand be named with places beyond Guangdong, like "Shanghai Chop Suey" or "Beijing Chop Suey," or even with surnames, such as "Wang's Chop Suey" or "Sun's Chop Suey." On the other hand, chop suey house owners could be Japanese or Korean. In the 1920s, the Crown Chop Suey, one of the largest Chinese restaurants in Los Angeles, was owned by Japanese immigrants, with more Japanese immigrants running chop suey houses in Southern California. Harvey Levenstein, an American food culture historian, noted an intriguing phenomenon: in 1925, a Chinese restaurant owner proudly declared that after retiring, he would introduce chow chop suey business to China, a case of forgetting one's roots. However, in that era, in which the prevailing notion was that China had no chow chop suey, this was understandable. For example, a March 25, 1924, *Los Angeles Times* article titled *China Has Plenty of Chinese Things, but It Doesn't Have Chop Suey There* stated, "The Chinese have played a small joke on the world. Chinese citizens in America have made chop suey a household name, presenting it as a typical Chinese dish. In reality, it is not—this dish is unknown in China."

Another *Los Angeles Times* article about Guangzhou observed, "I have tried almost all Chinese dishes but never seen chow chop suey. The truth is that such a dish seems to have never existed in China, yet in America, it is passed off as authentic Chinese food to meet public demand." In chop suey's hometown, one could not find American-style chop suey, but Cantonese had been stir-frying traditional chop suey. In Shanghai, however, American chop suey made for Americans was indeed visible "because there were Americans there." After Japan's defeat, with Americans holding significant influence in Shanghai, American chop suey flourished, creating a unique scene: "Westerners could easily spot a neon sign on a main road declaring, 'Authentic American Chow Chop Suey Served Here.'" This stemmed from American GIs searching for chop suey in Chongqing, the wartime capital, during World War II, prompting shrewd Sichuanese to advertise "authentic San Francisco-style chow chop suey." After victory, how could they not open American chop suey houses to celebrate? In fact, beyond Chongqing and

Shanghai, a 1928 *New York Times* report mentioned an American-style chop suey house in Beijing, which closed due to small demand, astonishing Americans: How could the Chinese not like chow chop suey?

5.3 Sailor Restaurants and Chop Suey Houses: From Britain to Europe

The spread of Cantonese cuisine to America owed to Cantonese servants and Chinese laborers, while its dissemination to Britain and Europe was due to Chinese sailors, also Cantonese. Owing to the single-port trade policy, the Cantonese had long ventured to Britain. According to Professor Cheng Meibao of Sun Yat-sen University, as early as August 1769, a Guangzhou ceramic craftsman traveled to Britain by ship and was warmly received. Later, a person named Whang Tong visited London in 1775, meeting with British literati and scientists, and likely encountering Sir Joseph Banks, then President of the Royal Society. Of course, unknown individuals also reached Britain. A little later, in 1816, two Cantonese merchants, Feng Yasheng and Feng Yaxue, sailed to Britain out of curiosity because their uncle was a Guangdong customs tax official, then went to Germany, performed the erhu, were received by King William I of Prussia, and assisted Wilhelm Schott, one of the founders of German Sinology, in studying Chinese at Halle University. Previously, some Chinese had been taken to Europe by missionaries for religious reasons, which is a different case.

However, it was the sailors employed by British ships who brought

Chinese cuisine to Britain. As merchant ships traveling between China and Britain relied on monsoon winds, Cantonese sailors often stayed in British ports for over six months after arrival, with some even never returning. Their initial situation in Britain mirrored that in America: mostly single, they had to rely on small restaurants run by fellow Chinese to solve dining problems, so the food in Chinatown remained relatively authentic. London's Chinatown, or the East End, where Chinese inhabited, had no large Chinese restaurants; conversely, those in the relatively upscale West End resembled American-style luxury chop suey houses. As late as the 1930s, Chinese visitors to Britain still observed, "There are three to four large Chinese restaurants in London, while small ones can only be found in Chinatown, where Chinese sailors gather. The area is filthy, with pharmacies and grocery stores selling everything. The restaurant dishes retain more Chinese flavors because these eateries were originally opened for Chinese people." (Yu Ziming, *Fragments of British Study Life*, *Modern Student*, 1933, Issue 6)

Perhaps the earliest small Chinese restaurants were like communal kitchens, unnamed to outsiders. Historians thus confirm, "The first formal Chinese restaurant opened in 1908 in East London's Chinese enclave, with three to five more opening in the same area over the next few years. All catered primarily to Chinese sailors, were very small, simple, and crude. By the 1920s-1930s, London had about a dozen such low-end Chinese restaurants, serving mainly Chinese students studying in Britain and a few lower-class British workers." (Li Minghuan, *History of Overseas Chinese in*

Europe) This reveals the sailor-restaurant nature of early Chinese eateries and shows an obvious developmental trajectory. Zou Taofen's 1933 observation during his UK visit confirms this:

> "A decade ago, there were at least 10,000 overseas Chinese in Britain (said to have reached 15,000 during World War I), but now it has decreased to about 3,000. Most British immigrants worked as sailors or firemen on ships, hard jobs that Britons in prosperous times were reluctant to do, so hardworking 'Chinese' had no trouble securing such opportunities... The largest numbers of overseas Chinese in Britain were in London and Liverpool. In Liverpool, about 380 people, including 180 sailors and firemen, the rest, except a few small merchants (running grocery stores), mostly did laundry... In London, about 450 people constituted the main body of overseas Chinese in Britain, including 200 sailors and firemen, over 150 unemployed; about 100 worked as chefs or waiters in Chinese restaurants (four in London), another 100 in British restaurants, with 40 now unemployed; about 50 ran small stores in East London catering to Chinese customers."

Cartoon: Chinese food restaurants in London

Zou Taofen added that London's Chinese restaurants concentrated in the

"Chinatown" on the edge of East London, which was merely several streets with a high Chinese population, "When visiting East London, I saw that almost all were Cantonese; prominent were Chinese herbal medicine shops and grocery stores selling various Chinese local products." (Zou Taofen, *Letters from Abroad • Overseas Chinese in Britain*, Joint Publishing, 1987 edition) This both shows traces of sailor restaurants and further illustrates the Cantonese characteristics of British Chinese restaurants.

In short, by this time, whether luxurious Chinese restaurants or private Chinese chefs, Chinese cuisine, specifically Cantonese cuisine, had firmly established its position in Britain, gradually entering the era of upscale large restaurants, while sailor restaurants faded into forgotten history.

Not only in Britain but also in the ocean trade ports of other European countries, the Netherlands, along the Europe-China shipping route, had long seen Cantonese sailors. Voltaire (1694-1778), the master of the French Enlightenment, wrote a lesser-known article titled *A Conversation with a Chinese in Amsterdam*, expressing his views on Chinese culture through a dialogue with a Chinese resident of Amsterdam, demonstrating the early arrival of Chinese in the Netherlands. In 1775, a Dutch East India Company clerk even brought his servant, transliterated as Dan Yacai, to Rotterdam. (Chen Guodong, *A Millennium of East Asian Seas: Maritime China and Foreign Trade in History*, Shandong Pictorial Press, 2006 edition)

These sailors resided there, leading to the early establishment of Chinese restaurants with excellent flavors. On February 11, 1916, after visiting a small Chinese restaurant named Longyou on Bantam Street in Amsterdam, a reporter from the Dutch *Algemeen Handelsblad* stated, “If the delicious dishes of the Chinese become widely known, how should we formulate our daily recipes?” (Li Minghuan, *History of Overseas Chinese in Europe*, China Overseas Chinese Publishing House, 2002 edition)

Although it is not explicitly stated whether these were Cantonese restaurants, foreigners could not distinguish and had no need to; most were presumably Cantonese. When Professor Jiang Kanghu, founder of the Chinese Socialist Party, visited Rotterdam (then translated as Luotedamo), another famous port city in the Netherlands, in 1922, he observed, “The harbor is deep and broad, with concentrated masts. Chinese sailors come and go frequently, with an average of 700 to 800 residents, about 60-70% of whom are Cantonese, mostly on Foyenoord Island.” He naturally discovered “chop suey houses and food stores... the largest chop suey house is Huixin Lou”—the owner, Zheng, even used it to launch an overseas Chinese guild! Of course, chop suey houses could not rely solely on local sailors and overseas Chinese; students often formed an important customer base, “In addition to Chinese sailors, there are more than 60 students in the Netherlands.” (Jiang Kanghu, *Five-Day Diary of the Netherlands*, *Eastern Miscellany*, 1922, Issue 3) Originating from this, these students were mostly ethnic Chinese from former Dutch colonies in Southeast Asia, often from relatively well-off families, some even publicly dispatched by local governments, enjoying relatively comfortable lives and playing an important supporting role for Chinese restaurants. As Mei Yiqi said, "Excluding Chinese sailors, there are more than 80 students in the Netherlands, all from Java. Some have wealthy parents and study at their own expense, while others are sent by the Dutch government to study various practical subjects, intended to serve the Dutch government in the future." (Hu Yigu, *European Travel Experience*, Youth Association Press, 1923 edition)

Chinese Restaurant in Lyon Sino-French University

In 1928, Li Hanhun, a famous Cantonese general, visited the Netherlands and several Chinese restaurants. "On September 13, he went to the Overseas Chinese Guild (Luotang Party Headquarters. Note: Luotang is now translated as Rotterdam). Hundreds of overseas Chinese attended the welcoming meeting. After a brief speech, I returned to The Hague with Jianmin by car and stopped by Zhongshan Lou and Yuanhua Lou. Yuan Zixi, a classmate from Sun Yat-sen University, warmly received us... Tonight, I attended a banquet at Zhang Guoshu's Far East Building and visited his home." (Compiled by Kang Puhua, Li Huanxing, etc., *Collected Works of*

General Li Hanhun, China Social Sciences Press, 2015 edition)

When the famous writer Wang Tongzhao visited the Netherlands in 1934, he only went to Cantonese restaurants, then commented, "The restaurant is not large, but it is cleanly furnished, and naturally, there are several Chinese-style calligraphy and paintings as usual. The manager is an old Cantonese merchant who has done business here for more than ten years. Now that he has closed his previous business, he has opened this restaurant." The fewer Chinese there are, the more intimate it feels; later, his experience of being treated to a meal at a Chinese restaurant in Amsterdam by local overseas Chinese left him deeply moved, "The Yantai gentleman I met the day before, accompanied by another Shandong gentleman, along with the host, five of us had Cantonese food costing nearly ten yuan in Chinese currency, which made me quite embarrassed! They earn money through hard labor and usually never spend recklessly on food or clothing, yet they treated their distant fellow townsman like this." Wang Tongzhao continued, in Amsterdam, there were nearly 400 overseas Chinese, half of whom were often sailors on foreign ships, mostly from Zhejiang, Shandong, and Guangdong. Shandong people mostly engaged in peddling, with more than 20 such businesses, carrying bags and boxes daily to cities and villages to solicit business; Cantonese people did not engage in this line, usually only opening restaurants, laundries, etc., proving that running restaurants is indeed a Cantonese specialty. (Wang Tongzhao, *Traces in the Netherlands*, *Middle School Student*s, 1936, Issue 69)

In 1939, someone listed seven Chinese restaurants in the Netherlands at that time, all opened by Cantonese, with store names, personal names, and places of origin, making them valuable materials:

> What China can most proudly showcase to the world is the exquisite variety and richness of its cuisine, with Cantonese chefs standing out as masters. Throughout Chinese restaurants opened by overseas Chinese in Europe and America, only the chef of the oldest restaurant in Paris is from Nanjing, while almost all others are from Bao'an, Guangdong. In the Netherlands, there were seven such restaurants: the oldest was China House run by Yuan Hua [at No. 18 Delistraat, Rotterdam (formerly Luotang)], followed by Guangxing House founded by Wu Fu [in Amsterdam (formerly Hantang Neifandandan)], then Zhongshan House managed by Deng Sheng (Rotterdam), Far East Restaurant by Zhang Guoshu (near the Peace Palace, The Hague), Dadong House by Wu Zixiao (No. 72 Yanbo Street, Amsterdam), Nanyang House by Wen Chouzu (No. 50 Thomsonlaan, The Hague), and the smallest, Hao Restaurant by Feng Sheng [No. 21 Guancong Street, Leiden (formerly Laiding)]. All seven were owned by Bao'an natives. (Anonymous, *Cantonese Restaurants Overseas*, *Healthy Life*, Issue 2, 1939)

However, Chen Lide, author of *History of Chinese Overseas Migration*, claimed that according to his survey, there were 15 Chinese restaurants in the

Netherlands, double the number above, which is hard to believe. This is linked to his obviously inaccurate statement that there were only three Chinese restaurants in Britain, so his claims should be taken with a grain of salt. He also stated there were 16 Chinese restaurants in France, 8 in Germany, 8 in the Soviet Union, 2 in Portugal, 5 in Denmark, and 4 in Belgium. The numbers for Portugal, Denmark, and the Soviet Union, never before mentioned, are appended here for reference. (*Life of Overseas Chinese in Europe*, *Overseas Monthly*, 1933 edition)

In fact, the number of Chinese restaurants in the Netherlands grew over time. A formal statistical report by the Dutch Minister of Justice to the Second Chamber's Judicial Committee in September 1963 stated that there were 2,353 Chinese distributed in cities like The Hague, Amsterdam, Utrecht, Delft, and several other towns, with 1,300 working in 325 restaurants mostly owned by Chinese. (Gu Weijun, *Memoirs of Gu Weijun*, 13th Volume, Zhonghua Book Company, 1994 edition)

To this day, Cantonese dominate the Chinese restaurant scene in the Netherlands. An early 21st-century Chinese tourist's experience dining in Amsterdam confirms this: "The boss told me he's from Guangdong, and most of the staff are too. Non-Cantonese workers have to learn Cantonese. Why? For easier internal communication and trust. According to the waiter, almost all restaurants in this city are owned by the Cantonese. If this is the norm, studying or working abroad here is easiest for Cantonese. Others have to learn both a foreign language and Cantonese—double the hardship!" (Zhou Zimu, *Experiencing Chinese Restaurants in Europe*, *March Wind*, Issue 9, 2002)

5.4 Tanhualou and Wanhualou: From Britain to Continental Europe

The "Chinatown" in London described by Zou Taofen was represented by Chinese restaurants, especially upscale ones. "Among overseas Chinese, those who open restaurants are considered top-tier wealthy! In East London, there is a Zhang Chao who has run a restaurant for thirty years and is now the 'Number One' leader of East London's overseas Chinese." (Zou Taofen, *Letters from Abroad • Overseas Chinese in Britain*) Zhang Chao's establishment was likely Xinghualou Restaurant, said to be London's oldest Chinese restaurant—a plausible claim. Intriguingly, Shanghai's oldest Cantonese restaurant, also named Xinghualou, was founded in 1851 and remains renowned today. Thirty years prior, Xinghualou would have been no different from a sailor's eatery. In fact, both Wanhualou (a benchmark for French Chinese restaurants) and Tanhualou (a benchmark for British Chinese restaurants) originated from such sailor restaurants in Britain:

> The Wanhualou, the largest Chinese restaurant in Paris, enjoys extremely prosperous business. According to those familiar with its history, the restaurant was founded in 1919, after World War I, when

millions of British and American men and women visited France to tour the battlefields each year. Britons and Americans, who already favored Chinese fashion in their home countries, took great pleasure in savoring Oriental flavors during their travels. The French, being particularly curious, flocked to Wanhualou upon hearing of it, spreading its fame throughout Europe and America. Initially established with a capital of only 200,000 francs, it now earns an annual net profit exceeding one million francs, standing as a model of entrepreneurial spirit among overseas Chinese merchants. The manager, Zhang Nan, a native of Bao'an, Guangdong, was employed as a sailor on a British ship 20 years ago. After accumulating modest savings, he began catering to sailors on the ship. A few years later, he and his younger brother Zhang Cai went to London and opened a small Chinese restaurant. Today's Tanhualou in London, all founded by the Zhang brothers just over a decade ago, each has a capital of over one million yuan. (Anonymous, *Wanhualou*, *East Province Economic Monthly*, Issue 3, 1929)

London Xinghua Restaurant

This Tanhualou should actually be Xinghualou, as Tanhualou was another establishment equally famous at the time. Mr. Hua Wu (Guo Zixiong) said, "The most luxurious Xinghualou on Oxford Street was London's first Chinese restaurant, mostly patronized by foreigners—poor students could rarely afford it. In the winter of 1929, the Xinghualou boss was reportedly accused of selling opium and engaging in other improper businesses, and the police forced it to close, resulting in a loss of £18,000 in rent alone. Chinese students at the time lamented the closure of such a large restaurant as a pity. Finally, since few people knew about Xinghualou, how many students passing through Oxford Street today can point out its former location?" (*London Sketch • Chinese Restaurants*, *Cosmic Wind*, Issue 1, 1935) This Xinghualou was the aforementioned Tanhualou; as for the boss being named Zhang Chao, Zhang Cai, or Zhang Nan, these are likely phonetic discrepancies in contemporary records. The closure of Xinghualou not only shocked the British Chinese community but also drew the attention of the Central Overseas Chinese Affairs Commission, which actively consulted with the British side. (*Case of Zhang Cai, a Chinese Merchant in London, Whose Xinghualou Restaurant Was Unreasonably Closed by the British Home Office and Who Was Ordered to Leave the Country: Reply from the Ministry of Foreign Affairs on Handling the Case, for Notification to the Overseas Chinese*, *Central Overseas Chinese Affairs Monthly*, Issues 5–6, 1930)

Roberts stated, "The first Chinese restaurant in London is said to have opened in the city center in 1908, but the Tanhualou (tánhuālóu in Chinese)

Restaurant, which opened on Piccadilly Street, a bustling London thoroughfare, in 1923, claims to be not only the first Chinese restaurant in London but also in Europe." (*Eastern Cuisine Spreading West: Chinese Food Culture in the Eyes of Westerners*) There must be an issue here—how could 1923 be the earliest? This is likely a translation error; if "Tanhualou (tánhuālóu in Chinese)" refers to "Tanhualou (tànhuālóu in Chinese)", the timeline becomes plausible.

Tanhualou was highly successful. Hua Wu noted, "Tanhualou on Piccadilly had grand space, beyond the means of poor students." Due to its success, it opened a new Tanhualou on nearby Wardour Street with even greater pomp: "The lower floor allows dancing and is more expensive, while the upper floor meets students' needs." "Diners at the new Tanhualou included not only Chinese but also Siamese, creating an endless Oriental atmosphere." (Huawu, *London Sketch • Chinese Restaurants*) Following the closure of Xinghualou, Tanhualou rose to prominence, becoming a center of attention and social interaction. When Hu Die, the famous Chinese film actress, visited Europe and arrived in Britain in 1935, she dined at Tanhualou and met Anna May Wong, the first Chinese American movie star from Hollywood and a fellow Cantonese, "At the (embassy) tea party that day, Ms. Anna May Wong was also present, introduced to us by Mrs. Ma. Ms. Wong was tall, with yellow face powder, bright red lips, wearing a colorful dress with wide sleeves and a black straw hat (shaped like those worn by Qing dynasty soldiers). After we met, I greeted her in Cantonese, but when I spoke further, she seemed not to understand much Cantonese, only the Taishan dialect, so we didn't converse in depth. The next day, at lunch in Tanhualou, I met Mr. Li and his wife and relatives, whom I had also encountered in Paris. Mr. Li was not only a Cantonese but also from Heshan County, the same county as me." (Hu Die, *Miscellaneous Notes on European Travel*, Shanghai Liangyou Book Company, 1935 edition)

Paris Wanghua Restaurant

Tanhualou also frequently served as a venue for diplomatic banquets. According to Jing Qing's *On Eating*, "For formal banquets or when male and female foreign guests were present, they would go to Tanhualou. The restaurant's luxurious facilities, along with the dignified waiters in formal attire, opening champagne to music, enjoying shark's fin and bird's nest soup—though somewhat incongruous, made for an impressive spectacle." Zheng Tianxi, the last Chinese ambassador to Britain in the Republic of China era, likely frequented Tanhualou, as he had used his legal knowledge to assist the restaurant significantly during his early studies in Britain.

Located in the busiest downtown area of London's West End, many shops rented billboard space on the street-facing walls, driving up competition and rental prices. Tanhualou followed this practice, but the landlord objected. At the restaurant's request, Zheng Tianxi invoked British law and the lease contract to negotiate with the landlord, ultimately prevailing.

Regarding the old and new Tanhualou, the general view was that the new one was superior, as Cang Sheng also believed. However, he attributed its excellence not to newness or luxury but to its more down-to-earth service and unexpectedly affordable prices. "In London, I often dined at the new Tanhualou on Wardour Street in Piccadilly. There were many Chinese diners, and they treated compatriots with great hospitality. The set meal, costing about one shilling and ninepence, included a soup, two stir-fries, unlimited white rice, and a pot of fine Yuqian tea—more substantial than a five-shilling Western meal. When I first arrived in London, I mistakenly went to another Tanhualou on Piccadilly, owned by the same proprietor. It had no set meals; a bowl of sliced meat soup cost at least five shillings. After several visits, I discovered the new Tanhualou, which became my go-to affordable and delicious dining spot in pricey London." (Cang Sheng, *Miscellaneous Notes on European Travel XXI*, *London Life*, *Renyan Weekly*, Issue 26, 1935) This indeed represents one of the highest compliments from the Chinese for London's Chinese restaurants.

Thanks to favorable timing and advantageous geographical position, or perhaps due to early hardships, most early overseas Chinese laborers or indentured workers were Cantonese, so overseas Chinese restaurants, especially upscale ones serving Westerners, were mostly opened by Cantonese. This held true not only in America but also in Europe, not only in Britain but also in France. Although non-Cantonese first established Chinese restaurants in Paris, major ones later came under Cantonese management, primarily because "Eating in Guangzhou" was renowned globally, and Cantonese migrated overseas earlier than others, familiarizing themselves with local customs and markets. Early Chinese travelogues offer glimpses of this trend.

Of course, Cantonese did not pioneer the first Chinese restaurants. The earliest Chinese food establishment in France was likely the teahouse opened by Zhejiang native Xie Daming at the 1900 Paris Exposition, using fortunes amassed from selling antiques. To capitalize on Western curiosity, he recruited over a dozen Chinese youths from Shanghai, dressed in blue gowns, to serve visitors. Later, Zhang Jingjiang and Li Shizeng, as embassy attaches accompanying Sun Baoqi's study tour to France in 1902, followed Xie's model with Zhang's family wealth, "First, opening an antique shop in front of Paris's grand Madeleine Church, then a teahouse on the bustling Boulevard des Italiens," with help from Xie's former tea servant Luo Qinzhai, who remained in France. (Wu Yun, *The Struggle of Chinese in France over the Past Fifty Years*, *Eastern Miscellany*, Issue 8, 1928)

If Zhang Jingjiang only opened teahouses, Li Shizeng went further by opening a restaurant that truly competed with French establishments. Li Shizeng's food business in Paris not only profoundly influenced the expansion of Chinese cuisine in France but also made significant contributions to spreading Chinese food culture. In 1914, he opened the Zhonghua Restaurant at 163 Rue de Montparnasse in the 6th arrondissement of Paris, becoming one of the earliest and most famous Chinese restaurants in France. Managed by Qi Zhushan, son of his mentor Qi Qiting, and with head chef Gao Er'an, a family cook from a prestigious background, the restaurant boasted exquisite culinary skills. With over 50 seats, it featured classical elegance and imitated Western restaurants by setting up a hotel salon. Renowned French sinologists like Edouard Herriot and Georges Mandel, along with politicians and artists, frequented the restaurant, enjoying its popularity. However, it was unfortunately timed with the outbreak of World War I and closed two years later. (Li Minghuan, *History of Overseas Chinese in Europe*)

Running restaurants has always been a Cantonese strength. In the winter of 1919, a Cantonese partnered with a Belgian to reopen a "Zhonghua Restaurant" at Rue Des Ecoles in the 5th arrondissement, which became a hub for work-study students and appeared in many related documents. Chen Chunsui (Dengke) described various activities at the Zhonghua Restaurant in *A History of Chinese Students in the West*, such as a student association welcome party where "so many people arrived that the restaurant was almost packed, and latecomers had no chairs to sit on." (New Moon Bookstore, 1928 edition) On February 6, 1928, Fu Lei's first meal in Paris was at the Zhonghua Restaurant, "(Arrived in Paris in the morning) Waited at Mr. Zheng's residence because going to 'Zhonghua Restaurant' too early, they said meals weren't ready. So, we waited until 12 o'clock to eat. Of course, Zhonghua Restaurant serves Chinese food to Chinese! A fried egg, shredded pork, and a soup cost 16 francs total, very expensive! But I was extremely satisfied, as I hadn't tasted Chinese food for over 30 days." (Fu Lei, *Letters from France*, *Contribution*, Issue 9, 1928)

The opening of Wanhualou marked the climax of Paris's Chinese restaurant industry and a new model for Cantonese cuisine's westward spread. In *Young Liang Zongdai*, researchers Liu Zhixia and Lu Lan wrote that Liang "studied in Europe for seven years, receiving regular, ample remittances, always living in comfortable private hotels and dining daily at the best Chinese restaurant"—this best restaurant was Wanhualou.

Wanhualou thus gained widespread fame, almost becoming essential knowledge for those traveling to France. The 350th issue of *Pictorial Times* in 1927 published a photo of its manager, Zhang Nan, on the first page with the caption, "Mr. Zhang Nan, manager of Wanhualou in Paris, the largest Chinese restaurant in Paris." Chen Zhaifu's *A Brief History and Mission of Chinese in France* introduced, "Chinese restaurants are like a proud sign for Chinese people. Chinatowns exist everywhere in Britain and America, while

Cantonese and Ningbo restaurants can be found across Japan. In Paris, France, there is the large-scale Wanhua Restaurant (owned by a Cantonese, with a branch in London)." In 1925, Weng Zhixi, great-grandnephew of Weng Tonghe, accompanied the legendary general Xu Shuzheng on a European investigation as a secretary and frequented Wanhualou in Paris, "(March 12) I went to Wanhualou, set up by Cantonese, with Bo Yizhong, Wang Peiyi, Song Rendong, and Li Yousong. Chinese dishes served Western-style; we ordered 'wonton soup,' which was wonton, costing 12 francs (1 yuan) per small square bowl; a plate of fried noodles cost 10 francs—quite expensive. Waiters were all French, business was good, and the accountant was a French woman. I heard it started with a capital of only 600 yuan, but now has accumulated profits of 60,000 yuan." (*Into Mongolia and Travels in Europe*, Zhongxi Bookstore, 2013 edition)

Hu shi

Cheng Wanfu, founder of Renjian Bookstore and *Renjian* magazine, recalled his 1931 study tour to France, "I ate dry bread for ten days straight on the Siberian train. So I thought that upon arriving in Paris, I should feast at Wanhualou, even if I had to pawn my clothes, even if it made me diarrhea. I'd heard so much about Wanhualou." (Cheng Wanfu, *Miscellaneous Memories of European Travel: Several Chinese Restaurants*, *Hua An*, Issue 1, 1935)

"Wanhua's blooms dazzle the eye." While Liang Zongdai dined at Wanhualou daily, other celebrities residing in or passing through Paris also frequented it, making Wanhualou a gathering place for literati. On June 26, 1927, upon arriving in Paris, Zheng Zhenduo rested briefly before heading to Wanhualou for a meal, noting, "This is a Chinese restaurant opened by a Cantonese. Having not eaten Chinese food for over a month, seeing stir-fried string beans with shredded pork and egg drop soup, though the taste might not be perfect, was still delightful." After lunch, "dinner was also at Wanhualou." (*Diary of European Journey*, Phoenix Publishing House, 2009 edition) Xu Xiacun from Peking University, traveling with him, remembered in more detail, "Wanhua Restaurant wasn't far from the hotel—just across a main street to see its large signboard. Although the building was Western-style, the interior exuded Chinese charm, with vermilion colors and Oriental patterns filling the hall. Groups of Chinese students gathered at tables, occasionally mixed with a Western man or woman. When a Chinese waiter speaking northern dialect approached, Mr. Gao (Yuan) told him the dish numbers, and soon the food arrived. Each of us had a plate; all dishes were first spooned onto the plate before being eaten with chopsticks." (Xu Xiacun,

Travel Notes of Paris, Guangming Bookstore, 1931 edition)

During his stay in France, Zheng Zhenduo dined at Wanhualou countless times. For example, Yuan Changying, who also “ate at Wanhualou daily,” self-financed her studies at the University of Edinburgh in 1916, earning a master’s degree in English literature. She returned to China for a short teaching stint in 1926, married economist Yang Duanliu, and then entered the Sorbonne for further studies. As director of the Economic Research Institute and researcher at the Institute of Social Sciences of the Central Research Institute, Yang had sufficient means to support her “daily Wanhualou” habit. On the evening of July 2, 1927, she treated Zheng Zhenduo, Zhu Guangqian, Wu Songgao, and others to a high-end meal at Wanhualou, “the dishes were especially good, as they were pre-ordered,” which Zheng specifically noted in his diary. Liang Zongdai also invited Zheng Zhenduo and others to Wanhualou multiple times; Zheng recorded on July 16, 1927, “Zongdai invited me and Guangqian to dinner again at Wanhualou,” and on August 19, “Zongdai came, woke me up... Doctor Cai from Yuanhe also came, and we went to Wanhualou for dinner together.”

From August to December 1926, while traveling in Europe to handle British Boxer Indemnity matters, Hu Shi’s diary, especially during his time in France, frequently mentions visits to Chinese restaurants, with Wanhualou featuring most often and memorably. Arriving in Paris on August 23, “in the evening, went to the embassy... dined at Wanhualou with Xianzhang and (Lin)

Xiaosong (deputy ambassador)." He also met many "distinguished figures," "Encountered Yao Xixian and his wife, who invited us to join their table. Met Secretary Shen Yangji and his wife. Yao was sent by Zhang Xueliang and is very close to him." The next evening, he met Zhao Songnan at a meal, "In the evening, Xianzhang invited me to dinner and introduced Consul General Zhao Songnan of Paris... Studied in France in 1897, most acquainted with Wu Zhihui and Li Shizeng. This gentleman is an eccentric, nearly a second Wu Zhihui in his views." On August 29, he noted, "Had lunch at Wanhualou, meeting Li Xianzhang and his wife, Chen Tianyi, and his fiancée Ms. Ye."

Lu Han, who once worked as a chef at Wanhualou, observed many Chinese "celebrities" in the dining hall through a small hole in the partition while serving dishes. Besides secretaries from the consulate, these regular patrons were primarily "students (naturally not work-study students)"—truly notable figures. "Most arrived with a beautiful French lady; occasionally with a Chinese lady, though rarely. There were two Chinese ladies, whose names I didn't know, who dined there every evening, always on the arm of one or two Chinese gentlemen. After the meal, the accompanying man would invariably pay the bill, with the escorts changing every two or three days—rotating by some schedule, perhaps? Or were those ladies social stars?" Of course, he also encountered and served a genuine celebrity: Mr. Jiang Menglin, Chinese delegate to the Washington Naval Conference and former acting president of Peking University, who dined at Wanhualou during a stopover in Paris.

Zhang Nan: Manager of Paris Wanghua Restaurant

Jiang Menglin arrived at 4–5 p.m., when few guests were present. Sitting alone in a corner, he was ignored. When someone finally approached, he ordered only a few inexpensive dishes, costing just 29 francs total, leading waiters to deem him "unworthy of special attention." After finishing, he lingered. A manager, perhaps wanting him to leave, struck up a conversation and learned he had just arrived from America and was unfamiliar with the streets, hence visiting a Chinese restaurant first. Discovering his identity as the renowned Jiang Menglin, the staff immediately showed respect. As Jiang wanted to read Chinese newspapers—only Lu Han subscribed to *Current Affairs Newspaper*—this lowly chef got a chance to attend to the celebrity.

By dinnertime, panic spread not just among staff but also among

Chinese students arriving arm-in-arm with French women, "Mr. Jiang, having witnessed the opening act of this 'romantic comedy,' set aside his newspaper to watch the unsold 'performance.' None of the 'actors' recognized him, so he was ignored. Before the tables grew disorderly, Mr. Zhang quietly revealed Jiang's identity to one 'actor,' and in an instant, the news spread, causing panic and embarrassment. The 'performance' ended abruptly in disarray." Just then, Consul Li of the embassy arrived with a Belgian woman and several French ladies for dinner, deepening the awkwardness. "In just three hours, Mr. Jiang experienced first contempt, then flattery; first loneliness, then hubbub, ending again in solitude—like traversing several worlds." As amends, Consul Li invited Jiang to dine at Wanhualou the next day, and henceforth, Jiang ate there daily for lunch and dinner. This so intimidated regular student patrons that they avoided Wanhualou for a week until Jiang left Paris—a most intriguing Wanhualou anecdote. (Lu Han, *A Segment of My Work-Study Life in France*, *Revolution Weekly*, Issues 78–79, 1929)

Hu Shi's diary records two other banquets hosted by Zhang Nan (also spelled Zhang Nan), owner of Wanhualou, revealing its role not just as a literary gathering place but also as a political platform for Kuomintang and Communist activities. The first occurred on August 30, 1926, "Zhang Nan, owner of Wanhualou, invited me to dinner. A Kuomintang member, he is highly patriotic and despises European-based Chinese ministers. I can't blame him." It wasn't until December 30, 1940, that he supplemented his diary with a note about a flyer received at this meal:

> This "flyer" was distributed at Wanhualou in Paris. One evening, I had made an appointment with Fu Sinian and others for dinner at Wanhualou, but I was delayed and arrived late. At the door, I met Zhang Nan, the owner of Wanhualou, who whispered, "Someone upstairs is distributing flyers scolding you. I specifically waited at the door for you—better not go in!" I laughed and said, "It doesn't matter. I need to eat and also want to see the flyer." When I went upstairs, Fu Sinian, Liang Zongdai, and others were all waiting for me to dine.

In fact, overseas Chinese restaurants involving themselves in politics have a tradition. After all, the overseas Chinese food industry is one of the main businesses of the Chinese community and was also an important source of funding for Sun Yat-sen's early revolutionary activities. Those who have lived in humble positions or are relatively vulnerable overseas often have stronger nationalism and revolutionary spirit, which still holds true today. The revolutionary tradition of Chinese restaurants overseas can be said to have a long history, and Parisian Chinese restaurants have been at the center of historical events, almost each restaurant representing a political party, each with its own political stance or tendency, which is amazing. At that time, someone said, "The strangest thing is that each restaurant represents a political party: Wanhua represents the Zhang Nan (manager of Wanhualou) faction, the Oriental Three Principles Society or the Xishan faction, No. 41

Beijing represents the Tianjin Reorganization faction, and Shanghai represents the Nationalist faction; Mengri and Zhonghua have no factions. Publications of each faction are sold in their respective restaurants, and members of each faction dine in their respective restaurants. Otherwise, everyone would call it an outflow of rights and interests." (Ding Zuoshao, *Chinese Restaurants in Paris Like Crucian Carp*, *Current Affairs Monthly*, 1930, Issue 1) In particular, since Zhang Nan was a Kuomintang member and Wanhualou was a gathering center for Chinese celebrities, it naturally became an important overseas political platform for the Kuomintang. Who would have known that it would soon become a political platform for the Communist Party?

Young Liang Zongdai states that in 1927, Zhang Nan sold his business to Jiang Junhuan from Hunan. Among Jiang's management staff, there was a bookkeeper named Zhou Zhu'an, who was one of the responsible persons of the Communist Party of China in France. After returning to China in 1939, he continued his underground work. Zhou Zhu'an entered the Ministry of Foreign Affairs in 1949 and was appointed as the Ambassador to Bulgaria in 1954. Wanhua Restaurant closed in 1939 when he left. In fact, what many do not know is that the political aura was not only on this bookkeeper, Zhou Zhu'an. The owner, Jiang Junhuan, was even more remarkable. It is true that Jiang worked in France and ran a small factory, and may have had some connection with World War I, but he was by no means an ordinary poor Chinese laborer from World War I. His elder brother, Jiang Jihuan, styled

Yonghong, was from Changsha, Hunan. After the 1911 Revolution, he served as the first magistrate of Changsha, obviously a big shot in the Kuomintang from a distinguished family. He successively served as a member of the Hunan Branch of the Kuomintang, a member of the Hunan Provincial Assembly, the Director of the Hunan Provincial Finance Department, and the Secretary-General of the General Headquarters of the Hunan Army. During the Northern Expedition, Jiang Jihuan entered Jiangxi with the army, initially serving as the Director of the Jiangxi Provincial Finance Department, Deputy Director, and Acting Director of the Jiangxi Provincial Government Affairs Committee. While acting as the Chairman of the Jiangxi Provincial Government, he participated in the Nanchang Uprising and made great contributions, becoming the first Chairman of the Jiangxi Provincial Revolutionary Committee after the uprising.

Regarding the origin of Wanhualou and the Communist Party, Zhou Zhu'an, the person involved, later recounted it, and it is also related to the famous educator Tao Xingzhi. After the victory of the Anti-Japanese War, when Mr. Wang Min, a famous editor, was editing *Xingzhi Poetry Collection*, he found a long narrative poem written on October 10, 1936, *Chinese and French Friends Celebrate Double Ten Day at Wanhualou in Paris*, among which one of the friends was exactly Zhou Zhu'an, who co-edited Xingzhi Poetry Collection with him. It turned out that in July 1936, Tao Xingzhi was dispatched by the National Salvation Federation of All Circles (Tao was an executive committee member and standing committee member) as a national diplomatic envoy to visit 28 countries in Europe, America, Asia, Africa, etc., to publicize anti-Japanese national salvation and introduce China's mass education movement. When passing through Paris, he got to know Zhou Zhu'an. Zhou Zhu'an said to Wang Min, "When I was keeping accounts at Wanhualou in Paris, I got to know Tao Xingzhi there." But he did not make further introductions. Until 1954, when Wang Min was transferred to Sanlian Bookstore in Beijing and Zhou Zhu'an was about to be dispatched as an ambassador to Bulgaria, he finally told the whole story. Zhou said that he was engaged in underground work in Paris at that time and served as one of the persons in charge of the Paris Branch of the Communist Party of China. Because he had the friendship of fellow townsmen with Jiang Jihuan, the manager of Wanhualou, he was hired as the accountant of the restaurant. His true identity was naturally inconvenient to tell Wang Min at that time. Wu Kejian, Zhou Zhu'an's superior and the person in charge of the European Branch of the Communist Party of China, also came to Paris in 1936 and served as the general manager of *Salvation Times* in Paris. Therefore, Wanhualou became a stronghold of revolutionary activities and was eyed by the Kuomintang spies in Paris. It should be known that Tao Xingzhi can also be described as a famous democratic personage close to our party. Therefore, as soon as he arrived in Paris in August 1936, he got in touch with Wu Kejian, Zhou Zhu'an, and others. Since then, he has frequently entered and left Wanhualou, jointly initiated and contacted celebrities from all walks of life in Paris, such as Chen Mingshu and Wang Lixi, to form the "All-Europe

Overseas Chinese Anti-Japanese Salvation Federation". On September 20, a grand founding conference was held, at which he delivered a speech titled *Re-Explanation of the Basic Conditions and Minimum Requirements for Unity and Resistance to Aggression*, and improvised the poem *Great Unity of the Chinese Nation*, etc. He was so impassioned that he could not help himself. Therefore, on the Double Ten Day of the National Government, he wrote another poem to record its grand occasion. (Wang Min, *Tao Xingzhi, and Wanhualou in Paris*, Shanghai *Century Magazine*, 2007, Issue 2)

5.5 Return to the Authenticity of Cantonese Cuisine

Immigrants in the new era, especially new immigrants from Guangdong and Hong Kong after the reform and opening up, have much higher requirements for diet and can no longer be satisfied with the previous "chop suey". At the same time, the current global trade environment also enables overseas Chinese restaurants to easily obtain authentic ingredients from their hometowns, and some local seafood is even better than that in their hometowns. All this has created superior conditions for chop suey to return to its authenticity. In this regard, chefs from Shunde have made great contributions. For example, "Feng Biji", a century-old brand in Shunde, has bloomed in Houston, the United States. The Chinese restaurant run by Feng Hai, the descendant of "Feng Biji", lives up to the reputation of "the first cooking family in Shunde" (as said by Luo Funan), and its authentic and excellent products have attracted Presidents George H.W. Bush and George

W. Bush to visit frequently. How can this be compared with the era of Li Hongzhang! Another example is that Shi Chunqi, a chef from Shunde, resigned from the Miramar Hotel in Hong Kong in 1969 and went to work in a chain of Chinese restaurants in Leeds, the UK. Although there were no Hong Kong grocery stores there, he could make do with the local conditions to cook Shunde dishes, such as Daliang fried milk and so on. He then settled in Fulin Restaurant in London's Chinatown. There are Chinese food stores such as "Heng Sheng Hang" in London, so the "Daliang fried milk", "Daliang pheasant rolls", "fish soup", "fish skin dumplings", and other dishes he cooked are authentic and famous throughout Britain.

Driven by the pursuit of authenticity, Mr. Luo Funan, the leading chef of Shunde and President of the Shunde Chefs Association, has been frequently invited to Houston and San Francisco in the U.S., London in the UK, Paris in France, and other places in recent years to teach cooking skills. Some restaurant owners even offered a million-yuan annual salary to retain Mr. Luo for on-site guidance. In October 2010, under the promotion and arrangement of Mr. Ho Fuk Kei, the Asian Affairs Commissioner of French President Sarkozy and a native of Shunde, the "Shunde Gourmet Week" was successfully held in Paris and even entered the headquarters of UNESCO. Shunde chefs represented by Mr. Luo Funan live-demonstrated seven classic Shunde dishes such as "Golden Medal Four-Cup Chicken" and "Eight-Treasure Stuffed Dace," as well as famous snacks like "Double-Skin Milk" and "Ginger Juice Coagulated Milk." Mr. Luo said it was a great challenge to cook without an open fire or white liquor! The deeper background of this event was that since 1975, Mr. Ho Fuk Kei had achieved great success by opening two Shunde restaurants, Fuli and Fu'an, in Paris, becoming a renowned overseas Chinese leader. He has successively received the Paris Gold Citizen Award, the French National Order of Merit (Knight, Officer, and Commander), and served as the Vice President of the French International Gastronomy Association and the French International Tourism Federation. Remembering his roots, Mr. Ho believed it was necessary to further enhance the authenticity of Shunde cuisine in France. During this event, Mr. Ho indeed achieved much: he presented the most authentic Shunde dish to President Sarkozy and his family, having formed a long-standing friendship with Sarkozy since 1975, when the latter, then a city councilor, visited his Fuli Restaurant for "Sweet and Sour Pork" and "Blanched Prawns." The friendship deepened over time, and in April 2010, Mr. Ho attended a Chinese state banquet during Sarkozy's visit to China. All this relied on Shunde cuisine as an important medium; authentic Shunde cuisine will surely further promote economic and cultural exchanges between China and France.

Chinese restaurants in Japan in the Republic of China era

As a close neighbor, Japan has seen relatively authentic Cantonese cuisine, especially Shunde dishes. In the early years, Zhou Jingwen (1880–1957), a Shunde-born overseas Chinese leader in Yokohama, founded Wanxin Restaurant, while his nephew Zhou Chaozong (1898–1980) opened Tongfa Chinese Cuisine, gradually developing it into a large catering chain with five branches in Yokohama and two in Tokyo. Today, Cantonese cuisine accounts for 80% of Japan's Chinese restaurant market, with Shunde chefs still exerting the greatest influence. In 1949, Tan Hui, a disciple of Ou Cai (one of the "Three Masters of Fengcheng"), went to Japan and single-handedly supported Liang Shuneng's Chinese restaurant, helping it grow into Japan's largest Chinese food enterprise, with Liang Shuneng later elected President of the Japan Chinese Cuisine Association. According to President Liang, the largest seafood and catering logistics distribution enterprise in Japan is Guangji Trading, founded by a Shunde native nicknamed "Abalone Chu."

The development of Cantonese cuisine (especially Shunde dishes) in Japan has provided a grand stage for chefs. In 1966, Tan Hui returned to Hong Kong to bring his son Tan Guojing and nephew Feng Chongquan (son of Feng Man) to Japan. Tan Guojing first worked as a head chef at Honglou Chinese Cuisine in Ginza, Tokyo, for four years, then became the head chef at the five-star Shinagawa Prince Hotel, causing a sensation with his performance on Fuji TV. In 1979, Tan Guojing returned to Hong Kong at Feng Man's request to manage Fengcheng Restaurants in North Point and

Mong Kok, maintaining Fengcheng's status as the hub of Shunde cuisine in Hong Kong. Cai Lan, the "Gourmet God," wrote in the preface to True Legacy of Shunde, "Every time I visit Fengcheng, I leave satisfied—a rare experience in Hong Kong."

Leveraging these connections, when Japan hosted the World Chinese Cuisine Competition in 1988, they invited Kang Hui, a national treasure-level chef from Shunde, to serve as a judge and perform on-site, hailed by the media as the "Number One Chinese Chef." To further enhance the authenticity of Japanese Chinese cuisine, from late August to early September 2010, the Japan Chinese Cuisine Association invited three Shunde culinary elites—He Jinbiao (Executive Director of Nanguo Garden Hotel), Lin Chaodai (Executive Chef of Country Garden), and Ma Chenggen (Executive Chef of Beijing Jiuzhaohui)—to Japan for cooking demonstrations and training. "Look, milk can be stir-fried, and it's so delicious! Incredible!" Shunde chefs held special cooking shows and training sessions in four cities—Tokyo, Osaka, Okayama, and Yamaguchi—becoming legends in Japan's catering industry. This prompted the Japan Chinese Cuisine Association to send key members to Shunde for training in October of the same year.

Starting from the end of the 20th century, due to the need for overseas Chinese cuisine to return to its authenticity, Cantonese chefs, especially those from Shunde, have gone abroad in batches to cook. On January 27, 2015,

Zeng Yi from the *Guangzhou Daily* reported on Chef Li from Shunde, who was the subject of the story *"The Qualification for Dividends of a Chef Working Abroad was Cancelled, and After 13 Years of Pursuit, His Wish was Finally Granted"*. In 1999, Chef Li crossed the ocean to work as a chef in a Cantonese restaurant in Peru, South America. In that same year, 30 other chefs also went to various countries to take charge of cooking. And this was just the initial stage. Later, even more and more advanced chefs went abroad. Mr. Luo Funan, the president of the Shunde Chef Association, has been continuously recruited by overseas catering enterprises with salaries much higher than those of pilots in recent years.

The most authentic move is that Shunfengzhuang, a top-tier Cantonese restaurant in China, directly opened a branch in Perth, Australia. Of course, this is based on the fact that Cantonese cuisine has become quite popular in Australia. In the major cities of Australia, there are hardly any white people who don't know how to use chopsticks. With the increasing popularity of Cantonese cuisine and Chinese cuisine overseas, it is believed that more large-scale catering enterprises in Guangdong will open branches overseas or directly open authentic Cantonese restaurants, thus completely subverting the existing concept of "chop suey". Having developed to this point, the long-cherished wish of Dr. Sun Yat-sen may be realized; the taste of Guangdong will eventually tempt the whole world.

The latest notable case is that during Premier Li Keqiang's visit to the UK in June 2014, the Chinese-style lunch held at 10 Downing Street on the

17th was cooked by the sisters from the Sweet-Sweet Chinese Restaurant in Manchester, whose ancestral home is Guangzhou. The main dish was casserole - braised chicken, with the iconic Cantonese sausage in the ingredients, and the staple food was five-treasure fried rice. All of these were quite typical and authentic Cantonese dishes, which brought honor to “Food in Guangzhou”. After the meal, Premier Li Keqiang also told Lisa, the elder sister who did the cooking, that he hoped all Chinese people would have the opportunity to taste the dishes they cooked.

www.ingramcontent.com/pod-product-compliance
Lightning Source LLC
LaVergne TN
LVHW010604100826
845148LV00014B/2837

* 9 7 9 8 9 0 1 8 6 0 1 4 4 *